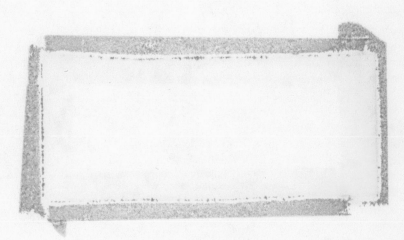

Dynamic Interpersonalism for Ministry

Dynamic Interpersonalism for Ministry

Essays in honor
of Paul E. Johnson

Edited by
Orlo Strunk, Jr.

Abingdon Press
Nashville   New York

DYNAMIC INTERPERSONALISM FOR MINISTRY

Copyright © 1973 by Abingdon Press

Library of Congress Cataloging in Publication Data

Dynamic interpersonalism for ministry.
Includes bibliographical references.
CONTENTS: Strunk, O., Jr. Introduction.—
Bertocci, P. A. Dynamic interpersonalism and
personalistic philosophy.—Schilling, S. P.
Dynamic interpersonalism and contemporary
theology.—[etc.]
1. Pastoral psychology—Addresses, essays,
lectures. 2. Pastoral theology—Addresses, essays, lectures. 3. Johnson, Paul Emanuel,
1898- I. Johnson, Paul Emanuel, 1898-
II. Strunk, Orlo, ed.
BV4012.D96   253   73-7813

ISBN 0-687-11280-X

MANUFACTURED BY THE PARTHENON PRESS AT
NASHVILLE, TENNESSEE, UNITED STATES OF AMERICA

Foreword

This book honors Paul E. Johnson and salutes his contributions to the field of pastoral care and counseling. His
contributions consist in a significant development of interpersonal psychological theory, in clinical participation, in
theological and philosophical interpretation, and in institutional administration. During twenty years of this activity he
and I were closely associated colleagues in Boston University
School of Theology and the Division of Theological Studies of
the Graduate School. A phenomenal growth in pastoral
counseling as a professional discipline and a dimension of
theological education took place in those years. Nowhere in
the profession did this development proceed more solidly and
constructively than at Boston University between 1945 and
1964, when he retired. His publications add to an illustrious
bibliography of writings which have established him firmly
in the theoretical and practical traditions of pastoral care and
counseling.

Continuity and discontinuity have characterized Johnson's
relationships to counseling as a mode of ministry in the church
and to personality theory as well as to psychology of religion.
He began his career as a missionary to China, and this vocation involved him in a study of world religions and cultures
outside Christianity. When I became his dean in 1945, he
was dividing his teaching duties primarily between psychology
of religion and world religions. He was also active in the
Institute of Pastoral Care and the then slowly growing move-

50416

5

ment in clinical training of theological students. I advised Professor Johnson to devote himself fully to psychology of religion and pastoral counseling, and it was possible for him to unite research, writing, teaching, and administrative skills into a remarkable career.

Paul Johnson's openness to multidisciplinary approaches in pastoral counseling and psychology of religion gave his program a certain eclectic character. This was inevitable because of the plurality of schools of thought in theology, philosophy, and dynamic psychology. Each of these fields has been undergoing rapid change and development during the past three decades. In its eclectic and cross-disciplinary approach the rapid growth of Johnson's department at Boston University paralleled that of Christian social ethics. Here, too, the insights and claims of theology, the principles and concepts of philosophy, and the methods and findings of the social sciences merged into a major ethical constellation. If in social ethics the overarching middle axiom became the "responsible society," in psychology of religion and pastoral care Johnson's dynamic interpersonalism may be said to have focused on the quality of "responsiveness" between pastor and parishioner and among the laity. In both cases the extent of interdisciplinary openness in the psychological areas and in social ethics served to influence the whole spirit of the School of Theology and to reinforce its sense of vocation to church and society.

The essays in Part I stress, in part, Johnson's breaking through the individualistic tendencies of the personalistic tradition in philosophy in which he had been reared. These tendencies had been strongest in Bowne and Knudson and can be ascribed to the influences of Leibniz, Kant, and Lotze. Scholars can either be prisoners or creators of tradition; and one of the imprisoning tendencies is the acceptance of key concepts and methods as limiting ideas. Brightman, Bertocci, and Johnson have been creators in the personalistic tradition by their radical attention to empirical actualities respecting selves and persons and by their wholistic methods. Without

6

denying the creative activity of thought which Kant contributed, they have broken through the formal prison house of the Kantian logic and have created new personalistic traditions. Both of Johnson's first books exhibited continuity with the traditions of psychology of religion but indicated at the same time the seminal idea that shaped what he called dynamic interpersonalism. This *Festschrift* stresses this concept, its perspective, and implications of its method.

To some it may seem strange that the history of world religions and psychology of religion were yoked together at Boston University. They had been so yoked when Francis L. Strickland taught at the School of Theology. These fields mutually enriched each other. Traces of the wide-range record of data of religious experience in the great world religions informed Johnson's writings on psychology and gave them a rich ecumenical quality. Students and successors of Johnson have quite naturally studied the great crises of life in pluralistic settings and in cross-cultural contexts. Likewise they have become concerned for the role of symbolization in the interpretation of meaning, drawing on non-Christian as well as on Christian sources.

The ecumenical spirit of pastoral counseling under Johnson's leadership attracted highly qualified doctoral candidates from many denominational backgrounds into his program. Students from Jewish, Roman Catholic, Orthodox, and numerous Protestant denominations sought the clinical training and the advanced theory that he made possible. Additional faculty entered the department; contacts through the Institute of Pastoral Care and the Council on Clinical Training expanded; hospital programs developed and standards improved; cooperation with other seminaries grew; and collaboration with clinical psychologists and psychiatrists became increasingly significant. Deep and distressing human quandaries are no respecters of class, religion, and race; hence, a ministry devoted to the dynamics of caring rapidly becomes ecumenical in appeal as it becomes interdisciplinary in method and design.

Brightman and Johnson, at crucial stages in their development, gave special attention to Royce and his notion of community. In Johnson's case the *inter*personal aspects of personality theory go considerably beyond Brightman's theory. Bertocci's caution on the need to preserve an ontic view of person in a dynamic interpersonalism has special interest here, both inherently and in view of the personalistic tradition in which Johnson belongs. The reader will note this in Bertocci's essay.

Creators of tradition have an advantage if their work can be institutionalized by relation to a university, by having foundation support, by growth in numbers of student assistants, by publication, by doctoral candidates, and the like. Professor Johnson had the good fortune of being related to an institution like the church, which was ready for the added professional competences of counseling and special ministries as by chaplains in many settings. He also had the good fortune of being a teacher in a school of theology and in a graduate school of a major university. But he had the insight and leadership of bringing the concerns of the Danielsen Fund into the above setting and of skillfully designing the Pastoral Counseling Center as an agency of service, teaching, and research. He put his own interpersonalism to work in developing the advisory board and using professional resources from many contributing fields in a mutually supporting and coherent way. In due course the Danielsens gave a substantial endowment to assure the Center, and Paul Johnson naturally became the first Albert V. Danielsen Professor. His own interpersonal skills and capacity to make others responsive to vital human needs, his depth of religious commitment, his philosophical and theological grounding, his openness to empirical social science, and his persistent institutional leadership have challenged others not to be prisoners but creators of academic and professional tradition. This book contributes both praise and creativity.

WALTER G. MUELDER

Acknowledgments

Most books are the result of the labors of large numbers of persons beyond the author or editor. This is especially true of the *Festschrift*, which has its being in the contributors and in their willingness to write as a labor of love. To them I express my sincere appreciation.

I should also like to acknowledge the contributions of the following individuals: James Hagadorn, my faculty assistant during the 1972-73 school year, for reading and offering comments on Part I of the volume; Father Kevin G. Culligan, O.C.D., Chairman of the Institute of Carmelite Studies and the holder of the Paul and Evelyn Johnson Teaching Fellowship during the 1972-73 school year, for his observations on Part I; Dr. Walter G. Muelder, Dean of the Boston University School of Theology at the time the project was started, for his encouragement and willingness to write the Foreword; Dr. J. Robert Nelson, present Dean of the Boston University School of Theology, for his support in providing clerical assistance; Miss Doris M. Poisson, office manager of the Ecumenical Counseling Service, Inc., of Melrose, Massachusetts, for typing Part II of the manuscript; and Mary Louise Strunk, my wife, for typing Part III of the volume and for assisting in the preparation of the index and the biographical section.

ORLO STRUNK, JR.

Contents

Introduction

Orlo Strunk, Jr.

Undoubtedly the factors leading to a *Festschrift* are many and complex. In the case of this one, however, I believe it is possible to identify the major motive in a simple and declarative way: *A Festschrift honoring Paul E. Johnson seemed a natural way of recognizing his contributions to theological education generally and to pastoral care and counseling particularly.* Although Paul has been honored in many ways, it did seem strange that no one had utilized the *Festschrift* mode of recognition and appreciation—especially when one considers the obvious importance Paul has placed on written expression.[1] Thus the *Festschrift* idea was born!

But once the notion was established, many other questions surfaced. Should the contributors be limited to Paul's students or extend far beyond the immediate community of his students and colleagues? Should the chapters range wide with little attempt at establishing any kind of symphonic theme, or should they be tightly assigned in a concerted effort to demonstrate and develop dynamic *inter*personalism as a cogent system? Should the emphasis on praxis be illustrated by exhaustive yet necessarily brief accounts, or should sampling be utilized to demonstrate the wide range of ministries being expressed by Paul's former students? And so it goes.

Of course, the readers of this volume will need to be the

1. Paul Johnson is himself a prolific writer. A partial bibliography of his works may be found in the January 1969 issue of *Pastoral Psychology*.

ones to judge just how these and other questions were finally answered. Still, the editor's confession may give some hints as to how some decisions were made.

For instance, although the letter of invitation to contributors indicated that the volume itself was to be an expression of appreciation to Paul and no attempt to witness to the position of dynamic interpersonalism would be required, a surprisingly large number of the chapters demonstrate a direct acknowledgment of the theoretical framework developed by Paul. Thus the contributors, quite independently, answered the question of whether or not the volume should attempt a systematic look at dynamic interpersonalism.

Another example centers on the question of praxis, its scope and depth. As I examined and considered this issue, I was struck by the wide range of activities in which Paul's former students were participating. Even when the decision was made to invite only those persons who had done advanced work under Paul—usually at the doctoral level and at Boston University—the breadth of ministries was quite impressive. Thus it was that because of the hard fact of space limitations, the decision to use a sampling approach was adopted. For me this proved to be an especially painful limitation, for it seems to me that one of the major strengths of Paul's theoretical project is its viability in an almost boundless expression of ministries. In more specific terms, there are many, many more of Paul's students who ought to be represented in this volume, just as there are many more forms of ministry being expressed by Paul's former graduate students.

In this introduction my purpose is not to provide the reader with a great deal of biographical data on Paul (such data are embedded in some chapters). Nor do I wish to strain after any coherent theme not really present in the chapters themselves. Instead, I should like to offer some general comments on the three sections and perhaps in the process make some interpretative notations which might help the reader as he makes his way through the volume.

Introduction

I

The construction of theoretical models in the areas of pastoral care and counseling has been an interesting phenomenon in many respects. Anyone coming to the literature for the first time cannot help but be impressed by the propensity to borrow from the sciences, especially the behavioral and social sciences. At times the tendency has been anything but sophisticated, and in many instances the procedure has been downright and unforgivably naïve. This propensity has been one of the central problems in the attempt to formulate a good theoretical project to assist in the practice of ministry. And not only has the propensity itself at times been a crippling factor (it has also been rewarding, it must be noted), it too often has been carried out clumsily and with little appreciation for the complexity of the task. How often have we got "hung up" on the latest concept or the most recent "therapeutic modality"? Perhaps even more important has been our tendency to do our borrowing from narrow and exceedingly restrictive disciplines. When one considers, for instance, one of the primary root meanings of the term "religion"—to bind together all of reality—it does appear strange that religious counselors frequently seem content to settle for a theoretical stance embracing a precious little area of human real estate! More than one visitor to the literature has been perplexed by the religious counselor's paucity of imagination and his conspicuous willingness to be preoccupied by a pimple on his nose when cancer is eating away his innards.

Although it is certainly true that dynamic interpersonalism does not entirely escape these somewhat scathing observations, the project comes about via a process far more dynamic than "borrowing" and from a root system of considerable scope and complexity. It seems to me that someone coming to dynamic interpersonalism for the first time can pick up this mood by reading Part I of this *Festschrift*. In this section it is easy to see that the theoretical project has been continuously dynamic and forever questioning. Although the conspicuous contributions may be classed as philosophical, theological, and psychological, these are only the broad outlines of the main rootage system. A careful reading reveals a much more subtle system, one containing many historical, anthropological, sociological, and literary roots.

Some who have known Paul E. Johnson will not be surprised to discover these varied sources. They remember that Paul himself did not come up through a single-root system. As a missionary in China, he had come to know a great deal about mind-sets of a non-Western sort, a rare sensitivity hardly discoverable in contemporary psychology. And as a college administrator he came up close to those hard realities associated with the decision-making process in a very real world of harsh complexities. His many years at Boston University conditioned him to the scholarly life, at the same time providing him with a stimulating atmosphere in which to participate in dialoguing a system. The establishment of the Albert V. Danielsen Pastoral Counseling Service in the Boston University School of Theology is a tribute to Paul's ability to interpret his theological project to a wide range of persons, including Albert and Jessie Danielsen, whose interests have persisted up to the present time. Indeed, at the time when I write these words the Danielsen Institute is becoming a reality, partly a residue of Paul's interpretive genius. Following his retirement from Boston University in 1963, he came to apply some of his model to practice outside the Boston area, especially in establishing the Indianapolis Pastoral Counseling Center and in his teaching at the Christian Theological Seminary of that same city. These, along with many other biographical aspects, can perhaps help account for the fact that dynamic interpersonalism has been forged out of a wide variety and range of systems, personal as well as academic.

How well this difficult task of synthesis has been accomplished remains for the reader to judge. That the process itself, however, has been continuous and dynamic is clearly manifested in these first chapters.

Equally important, it seems to me, are the tone and spirit of these theoretical chapters—for it is quite obvious that whatever dynamic interpersonalism is, it gets its identity from process and search.

But it must be noted that the continuous searching, probing, and synthesizing is not the easiest way to go about ministry today. As theological students in pastoral psychology too often discover, it is much easier to lock oneself into a relatively narrow system and ride it out with like-minded cohorts. That kind of decision, however, usually has much more to do with one's personal humanness than with one's familiarity with the total human condition.

Finally, it seems to me worth noting that the theoretical section dramatizes not only Paul Johnson's tendency to draw larger and larger circles but do so in process with the act, in this instance the act of ministry. Af..r all, it does not take much genius to devise utopian schemes or to weave comprehensive theoretical projects. The trick is to do this while grasping firmly to the stuff of life, to the raw realities that daily confront the practitioner. To have one foot in theory building and another in practice is not any easy assignment. Yet it seems to me that dynamic interpersonalism is the product of just such a stance.

Some years ago when Paul Johnson was making a plea for a clinical approach to religion, he illustrated my point while dealing with the subject of pastoral counseling:

> If we ask what is the goal of pastoral counseling, we must recognize that the pastor pursues his vocation in a religious context. Consequently, pastoral counseling is concerned to find the ultimate meaning of life, and to help each person to see his own responsibility in reference to that larger purpose. The presenting problems may vary as widely as the whole range of human perplexities. There will be conflicts in marriage and family to resolve; there will be health problems and limitations to face; problems of doubt and faith or anxiety and guilt; problems of aspiration and growth, of vocation and destiny. But the goal of pastoral counseling will always press beyond the local

distress to the ultimate meaning of life for the one who is asking how to decide.[2]

The scope of the project—the circumference of the circle, if you will—is implicit in the term "ultimate meaning of life," yet the commonality dimension is firmly acknowledged in the problems mentioned. It has always seemed a bit strange to me to see how easily many pastoral counselors lose, or fail to discover, this dimension of their counseling project, often settling for a smaller circle. Dynamic interpersonalism tends against this premature closure by being generated out of the full scope of ministry where versatility, mystery, and complexity are always found. If Christian ministry is a problem-solving activity having its *raison d'être* in the unmanifest, mediated, or expressed through personhood and community, then it seems part of its project be that that search take place in a dynamic interaction between theory and act.

II

Ministry is what is manifest. Here it is where the religious as well as the nonreligious communities can make some kind of empirical evaluations, even enlightened judgments. It is here where theories, including theologies and psychotheological systems, are put on the spot, tested, and interrogated, and, if the practitioner is committed to search, fed back into the theoretical framework. This cyclic dynamic is what generates new hypotheses and corrective interpretations—or so it ought to be. Far too often, however, under the impact of the need for closure or out of the wish for an illusion of control, the practitioner permits himself to become prematurely encapsulated—encapsulated in the sense in which Joseph R. Royce uses the term to mean "claiming to have all of the truth when one only has part of it, looking at life partially, but

2. "The Clinical Approach to Religion," *The Journal of Pastoral Care*, 15 (1961), 11.

issuing statements concerning the wholeness of living, . . . projecting a knowledge of ultimate reality from the perceptual framework of limited reality image." [3] When this happens prematurely, we come under the chains of what the late Gordon W. Allport used to call "simple and sovereign theories," a condition, I maintain, hardly suitable for a ministerial project, which by its very nature contains all levels and modes of being.

As indicated earlier in this introduction, Part II represents a sampling of ministries being expressed by Paul's former students. The illustrations are, it seems to me, impressive and mark an important characteristic of both Paul himself and the psychotheological theory he developed. That characteristic is best seen in the term "versatile comprehensiveness." I venture to say that there is not a single expression of ministry in which Paul's students are not participating.

Although the laymen may not think of this as an extraordinary accomplishment—after all, why shouldn't the world be the minister's parish—for those of us caught up in the day-by-day professional concerns of educating and training, the phenomenon is quite startling. For the tendency in professionalism is to draw smaller and smaller circles, ruling out more and more, restricting with each new spurt of movement. In recent years, especially with the development of pastoral counseling as a specialization, the propensity to narrow in has come to be seen as a downright virtue. At times it has seemed almost certain that pastoral counseling would move outside the project of ministry, lose its rootage in the religious community, and exist as just another form of psychotherapy alongside the dozens of others making messianic claims. Certainly this possibility is a live one even as I write these words. [4]

But in the development of dynamic interpersonalism this

3. *The Encapsulated Man: An Interdisciplinary Essay on the Search for Meaning* (New York: Van Nostrand Co., 1964), p. 30.
4. See, for example, the special issue on "Pastoral Counseling at a Crossroad," *The Journal of Pastoral Care*, 26 (1972), No. 4.

propensity has served only as a tension point, a catalytic factor, never as a viable alternative. This is partly due to Paul's commitment to the essential qualities of religious community and especially to the church. For Paul the essential *raison d'être* for the development of an authentic psychotheology was the beingness of the faith itself. The faith commitment is first, not the theoretical structure. And since the faith commitment is made in the crucible of a community, theoretical work is done as a service to that community.

If one accepts this sort of stance, he cannot afford the comfort or luxury of centering in on a single expression of ministry—whether parish work, counseling, chaplaincy work, or whatever. He is geared into the community's total project of ministry. It is true that most of us need to emphasize some kinds of ministries over others due to our finite limitations and interests, but if we are committed to the task of building a comprehensive theoretical system, we open ourselves to a risk of no little magnitude.

The ministries described in Part II of this *Festschrift* illustrate the fruits of each ambitious project, as well as the limitations. The point is that Paul's former students are deeply involved in a wide variety of ministries and are still able, either explicitly or implicitly, to utilize the conceptual fruits of dynamic interpersonalism. And this, it seems to me, is a tribute to both the men and the process which attempts to work continuously at the project of meaning-building.

III

At this point in the life of religious communities and in the development of professional careers within religious and theological contexts, we simply do not know what will be the future of Christian ministry. The present situation is confused and not a little depressing. Still, there are some significant signs that ministry as a viable mode of being is not only possible but that new expressions are being explored and evaluated, the Report on the Ministry in the 70s Project representing a fine example of this development.[5]

In one sense, however, no one really knows exactly what the future holds for ministry. Some educated guesses, however, are better than others. And this was why William E. Hulme was asked to author Part III—for not only has he been deeply involved in a wide range of ministry projects, but he is one of the most prolific of Paul's former students. His observations and comments represent at least one set of possibilities, a set worth the consideration of those interested in expressions of ministry, especially as related to a theoretical framework like dynamic interpersonalism.

As I write these final words of this introduction, I learn that Paul E. Johnson is in the midst of a serious illness. He has returned from the hospital and is recuperating at his home on Cape Cod. Although weak and weary, he still writes and is reflecting on his most recent experience. Undoubtedly, if he is given the strength and time, this most recent crisis will find its way into his project of existence, shape it a bit, and be shared with others. It is this spirit which we who have prepared this *Festschrift* hope will come through in these pages and will stimulate and encourage those involved in a similar commitment to life.

5. G. Douglass Lewis, *Explorations in Ministry* (New York: IDOC, North America, 1971).

Part I

Dynamic Interpersonalism and Personalistic Philosophy

Peter A. Bertocci

Paul Johnson is one American psychologist whose personal experience, as well as philosophical and theological education, riveted attention on dimensions of personality that threaten a myopic conception of science. William James in his day had labored to remove arbitrary rationalistic and scientific restrictions to the study of every aspect of human experience. In the same spirit Paul Johnson gave himself to the re-examination of both methodological and philosophical presuppositions which blocked the way to the study of man as a whole. He acclaimed the fact that James "opens more doors than he closes"; he agreed that in religious experience there is a kind of evidence that must forever challenge a humanistic and naturalistic view of man; and he himself was challenged by James's view that the conscious self is "continuous with" a wider self through which saving experiences come.[1]

The nature of the relation of conscious persons to their unconscious, to each other, and to God, was a persistent problem for Johnson. His doctoral dissertation, "Josiah Royce's Philosophy of Religion" (completed in 1928 under Edgar S. Brightman at Boston University), focused on the relation of persons to God.[2] As Johnson's vocation as teacher, pastoral psychologist, and scholar developed, he became increasingly

---

1. See Paul Johnson, "William James: Psychologist of Religion," *The Journal of Pastoral Care*, 7 (1953), 137-41.
2. See Josiah Royce "Theist or Pantheist?" *The Harvard Theological Review*, 21 (1928), 197-205; "The Religious Philosophy of Josiah Royce," *Theological Review, Hibbert Journal*, 33 (1935), 575-84.

convinced that the conception of the person developed not only by Mary W. Calkins,[3] William James, and Josiah Royce, but also by his teachers at Boston University, needed to be revised in accordance with fertile trends in the psychology of personality.

What I hope to do in this essay, accordingly, is to draw attention to a tension in Johnson's conception of the person in his relation to other persons and to God. And I shall come to this by focusing on major trends in the personalistic idealism and theism that formed the background of Johnson's movement from the "received" personalism to new-personalism, as he called his interpersonalism. The underlying issue, as I hope to show, is not an interfamilial one among personalists such as Edgar S. Brightman, Albert C. Knudson, Francis McConnell, or Ralph Tyler Flewelling (who had been immediate pupils of the founder of American pesonalistic idealism, Borden P. Bowne [1847-1910]), or among Paul Johnson's personalistic colleagues in Boston University, including Walter G. Mueller, Harold DeWolf, and the present writer. Instead, the problem has to do with an issue that faces contemporary theory in philosophy and psychology regarding the presuppositions of change in reality and in personality.

The Person in Personalistic Idealism and Theism

What is real? Is it the natural world—described as spatio-temporal systems of nonmental energies and process—that is the last word about what we see, smell, hear, touch, taste, measure, and reason? The personalist as a metaphysician says no, and not because he is a personalist first and a metaphysician later. He thinks that a nonpersonal account of nature does not explain adequately the fact that persons who sense, measure, and reason about reality can do so. As Bowne said,

3. See Orlo Strunk, Jr., "The Self-Psychology of Mary Whiton Calkins," *Journal of the History of the Behavioral Sciences*, 9 (1972), 196-203.

it is the arrival of persons and not their survival alone that must count. The world of persons, of which nature forms a part, is a world in which persons love truth and appreciate the harmonies and tragedies of existence, in which persons condemn themselves by the norms of justice and mercy, in which they are inspired by a sense of what James, in minimal terms, called the *More*. The metaphysical personalist never ceases urging that persons—who seek truth in a realm they at once appreciate and understand, who join together as members of a community dedicated to truth, justice, and love, who respond to each other's appreciation of the aesthetic and the holy—provide the most revealing clues to what is real.

Again, the personalist as a metaphysician gladly accepts any fact carefully established by any science. But he is all the more puzzled by the failure of both scientists and philosophers to realize that these facts could hardly be discovered if the values by which they guide their minds had no kinship with the universe. In pursuing such a line of argument many philosophers have become personalistic theists and have insisted that a Personal Mind creates, sustains, and guides the nonmental world of nature. But the personalistic idealist takes a further step in which traditional personalistic theists do not join him. Indeed, he receives the label "idealist" from the fact that he thinks that the realm of (nonmental) nature is more reasonably interpreted as part of the activity of the mind of God and his norms.

The personalistic idealist, accordingly, holds that nature is God but not that God is nature alone. The fullness of God's being, including the so-called nonmental beings and events in nature, are activities of a God at work in that dimension of his being. This view has not been philosophically popular in the last fifty years in the West, but much of its fabric can be found in Plato and Plotinus, Berkeley, Spinoza, Schopenhauer, Hegel, Lotze, F. H. Bradley, and Josiah Royce, and in recent panpsychistic or panentheistic philosophers like A. N. Whitehead and Charles Hartshorne, who developed themes suggested in Fechner, James, and Henri Bergson. Without attempting to articulate specific arguments, I must mention a basic theoretical refrain common to both personalistic idealism and to panpsychistic views of nature.

To rephrase, the personalistic idealist concludes that the realm of nature that seems so impersonal—so orderly that the individual everywhere seems to be just a part of a vast care-less system—is in fact the *omnipersonal* activity of a caring Person. Why? Because he sees that this supposedly natural, nonmental system is a predictable realm in which finite minds appear and develop. There is no fact of physics or chemistry requiring that this system be nonmental.

Traditional theistic personalism (as represented, say, by Aquinas) insists that God is immanent in the created nonmental beings in nature. But it seems unreasonable to suppose that God creates nonmental beings as the basis for the creation of both living and personal beings. God "lives" in this orderly and predictable world, and this orderly system, expressing his providential activity, hardly needs to be nonmental. In any case, God for the personalistic idealist is no abstract or distant God; he is the continuous creator and sustainer, at work within that aspect of his being we call nature and its laws. (Can it be that much of human abuse of nature ecologically is encouraged by the view that nature after all is no more than an insensate, mindless, impervious set of events, a neutral stage on which both man and God act?)

I have been saying that for the personalistic idealist all reality is of the nature of mind. But the idealism of personalists (such as Bowne, Brightman, Flewelling, and their followers) differs from the absolutistic or monistic idealism of Hegel, Bradley, or Royce, who hold that finite persons are also part of, ultimately one with, God. Here traditional personalistic theists and personalistic idealists join in stressing that man has delegated autonomy as a created being. Man in his created being is not a mode of God; he is no drop in the ocean of pure consciousness, as some idealists, East and West, have contended (sometimes in the name of religious experience). Here, as Johnson early protested against Royce, theory must build especially upon the immediate experience of freewill—a will, to be sure, related to and limited by the rest of an individual's makeup and by the environment, but not to the point that personal responsibility for thought and behavior is neglected. The individual person is created as a co-creator in God's world; he is free to be parasitic upon, or destroy, what is God's, in himself, the world, and in others.

In a word, once we learn to think of physical nature as the direct activity of a dependable, intelligent, and caring Person-Creator, once we learn to think of the person as a caring, reasoning, and willing being who is able, within limits, to choose sequences in a world whose consequences are ultimately determined by God, then we have the foundation for the realization that persons cannot develop their constituted nature apart from their interaction with each other, with God's world, and with God directly.

I suggest that anyone who spends years of his life trying to understand and appreciate what it means to say that reality in its many dimensions is an intersupportive, interaction of persons and Person will come to psychological studies more receptive of explorations in every area. Whatever their mistakes, idealistic philosophers have been committed to the ideal so well epitomized by Hegel: the truth is the whole. The catholicity of Paul Johnson's spirit, his sensitivity to the ways of mind in its varied dimensions, his commitment to the ranges of value that strengthen the quality of human lives, his own experience of the Thou which keeps things as well as persons from becoming senseless and aimless—all these were nurtured by the personalist idealism of the teachers he knew best. I turn now more specifically to the personalistic doctrine of the person.

The Personalistic View of the Person

Already I have suggested that personalists postulate creation by God to stress that the person is never one with God.

If the finite person is not a mode of Infinite Being, if he is not a center of the Absolute, how is he to be conceived? I limit myself to Brightman's emphasis (since he epitomized in most respects the views of Bowne, Knudson, Flewelling, and other personalists). Each person is—whatever else—created as an indissoluble unity; he is no collection of parts of anything! A person is distinguished by self-consciousness as we find it in reasoning, willing, wanting, and feeling, and in ethical and aesthetic response, as well as religious activity.

As Johnson himself paraphrases Brightman: "No little confusion has arisen in the history of thought by identifying . . . the person with the causes that affect him. Because consciousness is dependent on the brain or the social environment of God." [4] Again, as Johnson himself summarizes Brightman's view, the person is immediately and indubitably aware of his conscious activities, but he cannot be undeniably aware of his total being since he must depend upon "backward-looking memories and forward-looking purposes." Thus a person believes in his unconsciousness by the same process as he believes in bodily processes, namely, by reasonable inference from what he experiences in consciousness. But within any conscious moment a person can distinguish spatial and temporal self-transcendence as well as his reasoning and evaluating capacities and norms. [5]

I must stress that this view of the person is a metaphysical or ontic psychological one (personality). The personalist does not deny interaction between persons and between persons and God. But unless the person is a unified being in and for himself, he has no way of understanding the more or less systematic unity and continuity as a person develops in his personality.

I emphasize this distinction between the ontic person and personality because this ontic conception of the person was to be lost from sight, or denied, as many psychologists grad-

4. "Brightman's Contribution to Personalism," *The Personalist,* 35 (1954), 64.
5. *Ibid.,* pp. 65-66.

ually decided, especially in the middle decades of the twentieth century, to free themselves from the "speculative" foundations of philosophies, and from the "dogmatic" revelations upon which theologies depend. In their studies of man they tended to accept the criterion of truth that had been successful especially in physics and chemistry and to assume that theories of biological evolution required them to regard man as essentially a higher animal. They also tended to maintain that even what is most distinctive in man is governed by the same goal of survival that controls physiological cells. Thus while they still use the term "the person," they identify the unity and the activities of personal being with brain events, or with behavior, or with functions of either or both. Success in studies of the behavior of animals, where appeal to conscious reporting is impossible, encouraged the thesis that the really important factors in human living did not depend upon any observation or appreciation of what is consciously experienced. Accordingly, for soul, for mind, for person, read a characteristic way of the behavior of living organisms and proceed to observe, predict, and plan, if possible, the way in which different kinds of organisms dependably respond to each other and to the physical world. Even when the reader has not been warned, in much psychological literature "human organism" is used interchangeably with "person" and "personality," the tacit assumption being that, after all, the "real" action takes place in the body.

It might seem that, during the middle decades of the twentieth century, Freud's hypothesis that there is an unconscious, nonphysiological psyche to which we must look to explain much in the orientation, normal and deviant, in human experience reintroduced psychic or mental agency in psychological science. But (granting that more than one reading of Freud is possible), his own final faith seemed to rest on physiological explanation. In any case, central tendencies in his thought hardly favored the view that the conscious person is free, that his thinking can be more than rationalization, that his morality has any roots independent of his own basically unconscious wishes, or that his religious sensitivity is more than an obstinate illusion.

Over against such tendencies to physicalistic and evolutional reductionism, the personalism with which Johnson came to psychology of personality stressed the counter-evidence, especially as found in human beings. As Whitehead graphically summarizes it:

> The struggle for existence (survivalist evolution) gives no hint why there should be cities. Again the crowding of houses is no explanation why houses should be beautiful. . . . The appetition towards esthetic satisfaction by some enjoyment of beauty is equally outside the mere physical order. . . . Mere blind appetition would be the product of chance and could lead nowhere. In our experience, we find Reason and speculative imagination. There is a discrimination of appetitions according to a rule of fitness. This reign of Reason is vacillating, vague, and dim. But it is there.[6]

The Person and Personality
in Johnson's Interpersonalism

This metaphysical personalistic orientation was to keep Johnson a constant critic of behavioristic and psychoanalytic reductionism and to orient him favorably to much in such psychologists as Jung, Adler, Gordon W. Allport, Carl Rogers, Abraham Maslow, Erich Fromm and Erik Erikson, Viktor Frankl and Harry S. Sullivan, and to phenomenological and existential psychology. But in these varied perspectives, generally speaking, a different shift had also been taking place surreptitiously. This shift was from a philosophical-theological-ethical conception of *person* to *personality*. For the unity of the (ontic) person we are now to substitute the healthy, mature, productive, or self-actualizing personality. Thus psychology of personality and psychotherapy were also moving into the domain of values despite protestations that they were, as science, to be neutral to considerations of value. Thus, when

6. *The Function of Reason* (Boston: Beacon Press, 1959 [1929]), pp. 89, 90.

person was conflated with *personality* the structure and
dimensions of the person were absorbed into a psychology of
personality, and physiological and social conditions were
deemed crucial both to the very existence and the value of a
person.

The remainder of this essay concerns itself with the viability
of this conflation, both theoretically and practically, as it is
expressed in response of Paul Johnson to the "received" personalism. Paul Johnson became increasingly convinced that
personalism received via Bowne, Knudson, and Brightman
could not account for what he called the dynamics of interpersonal relations—between mother and child, between members of a family, between persons in their encounters with
each other in social contexts, between counselor and patient,
and between man and God.

I have been suggesting that a theistic personalist stresses
that the ontic person does interact with nature and with God,
that the personalist also stresses that the quality of a person's
existence depends largely on his interaction especially with
other persons. But this view of the person still seems inadequate to Johnson, who was reaching for a new and more adequate synthesis of philosophical, theological, ethical, and
scientific data. This dissatisfaction becomes evident in several
passages which I shall quote in my own order so that we
can have before us some of the flavor as well as the intent
of Johnson's concerns and of his counter-thesis. I shall italicize
telling phrases that will enter into my later discussion:

> The basic issue here is whether to view the person as a
> *closed system* . . . or to see the person as an *open system* whose
> life is *engaged* with other persons in a *community of mutual
> interests* and responsive relationships with other persons. If we
> go apart to formalize our *individuality*, we take with us what
> we have learned with other persons. And when we achieve a
> *unique individuality*, we bring our findings to other persons
> to see how they respond, and what value they will place upon
> our contributions.[7]

7. "The Trend Toward Dynamic Interpersonalism," *Religion in Life*,
35 (1966), 752.

Dynamic Interpersonalism for Ministry

My own position is dynamic interpersonalism, holding that no person is *truly a person in himself alone,* but only as he enters into mutual relationship with other persons. . . . We can agree with the personalist that the individual is unique, significant and representative of reality. But the unique person, as I see him, attains *significance* and *reality through* his *participation* with other persons in the interactive relationships of our world.[8]

The aim is to keep the person central in interpersonalism. But never *one person alone,* for his *unique individuality* is always *intertwined with* and responsive to the uniqueness of other persons. Whatever *a person has become* is causally related to other persons who *enter* into his personal life. And whatever he *intends to beco ıe* will be purposely related to the persons who share with him the adventure of living.[9]

If the person is seen as a closed system, self-contained and confined to his own conscious experienc?, we can only talk about (in Martin Buber's terminology) a remote person as *IT,* rather than address him directly as Thou. The intentional thrust of new-personalism, as I have called my interpersonal approach, is to move out from the isolate person as a closed self-consciousness to an open, *inter-relating person,* who finds *direct encounter* with Thou.[10]

I am not a *self-sufficient* or self-contained monad *sealed within myself.* I seek among the vast and varied resources of this interdependent world for someone to respond to me. . . . We cannot know what Thou would be in *complete separation* as an *isolated* Being.[11]

The philosophy of interpersonalism is an organic pluralism of persons united by a Cosmic Person. This has been called personalism but to accent the social relations of our universe we call it *interpersonalism.*[12]

These passages, if taken at face value, would and should spell the death knell of "classical personalism"—if they repre-

8. *Ibid.,* p. 753.
9. *Ibid.,* p. 775.
10. *Ibid.,* p. 758.
11. *Ibid.,* p. 759.
12. "The Theology of Interpersonalism," *Sociometry,* 12 (1949), 225.

34

sent the whole story. It would be easy for me to reply—and in part I must—that they do not construe accurately the basic thesis of Bowne, Knudson, Brightman, and other personalists. But I wish to do more than this and show that interpersonalism as a psychology of personality and its development requires the kind of ontic person that philosophical personalism stresses.[13]

I must first demur at Johnson's view that personalistic idealism adheres to the concept of a "closed person." That each person is ontically no other person, is not reducible to brain and body, does not overlap with either nature or God, is basic personalistic doctrine. But does this justify the label "closed system"? Surely not. With Plato, the personalist contends that to be is to act and to be acted upon. In the context of much in Judeo-Christian biblical tradition, this means that God creates the person as an actor and interactor, a co-creator with God and with his fellowmen.

The ontic person is "closed," if this means that man is responsible for his own free acts. He is closed also in the sense that what affects him must, in the crucible of his own finite being, have some bearing on what he will be in the future. He is closed in the sense that his activities—be they sensing, remembering, perceiving, thinking, feeling, emoting, and willing, moral, aesthetic, and religious activities—are his own.

But the ontic person is not closed in any other way. Every

13. I have argued elswhere, also, that personality must not be conflated with the ontic person, as it is, for example, in Freud, Jung, Erikson, Sullivan, Maslow, Fromm, and Gordon W. Allport. ("Foundations of a Personalistic Psychology," in *Scientific Psychology*, ed. by Benjamin B. Wolman and Ernest Nagel [New York: Basic Books, 1965; reprinted in P. A. Bertocci, *The Person God Is*, New York: Humanities Press, 1971, chapter III.]) I am not taking adequate account in this essay of Johnson's uneasiness with the view that *person* as such is to be restricted to a conscious and self-conscious unity of experience, as Brightman stressed. I am not satisfied with Brightman's solution to the problem of the relation of the conscious person to the body and to the unconscious. Yet in Brightman's view the conscious person is not sealed off from interaction with matter or with God. The problem was, and is: How should the relationship be articulated in any theory that takes adequate account of the differences between these?

person, from conception onward, is a unity-continuity, interacting with his total environment as far as his limited capacities allow. Even as relatively passive, a person is act-or: the unique unity of the caring-willing-knowing activities just mentioned. However, the quality which this agent-person can develop as he matures is the joint by-product of his own nature as influenced by his immediately effective environment.

To illustrate: at the ontic level John Doe as a person—whether born in China or the United States—is the unity of his activities and their potential as inherited. But this agent-person became John Doe with his pattern of learned responses because he organized his responses to his environment—and especially to those persons upon whom he depends. This *quality* of the agent-person (John Doe) is the personality we know as John Doe. We understand the personality as the result in good part of the interaction between the person and the environment. The personalistic doctrine of the agent-person, rejecting the closed person, opens his windows to interaction that results in the person's development of personality. In short, Johnson's interpersonalism is hardly new-personalism at the philosophical level; personalism is inter-personalism at the level of the development of a person's personality.

But as I have already hinted, we are confronted in the psychology of personality with a persistent source of confusion if we conflate or confuse the individual unity-continuity of the agent-person with the uniqueness of the acquired personality and its pattern of organization. The ambiguities I am suggesting in Johnson's thought are rife in contemporary psychology of personality and psychotherapy, and they persist in similar forms.

As in the texts quoted above, the words *person, personhood, personality,* are used in more than one sense, in large part because of the conflation of *person* and *personality.* For example, there is no denying in Johnson's terms that a person is "engaged with other persons in a community of mutual interests and responsiveness." But when Johnson goes on to say,

"It is my experience that we grow into personhood through vital relationships," ambiguity appears. Does one become a person ontically? Could a nonperson develop personhood? Clarity is achieved once we note that personhood refers here to a certain valued norm of personality, the product of persons open to persons. Personhood means in this context a quality of living deemed worthy of an ontic person's interaction with other persons.

This shift from person to (acquired) quality of personality is also clear when Johnson says, "No person is truly a person in himself alone, but only as he enters into mutual relationships with other persons." The dog is a dog (truly a dog). To speak of becoming truly a person is reasonable only if Johnson has in mind some quality of personality which persons achieve only as they enter into mutual relationship with other persons. (And "mutual" implies a norm also.)

The same distinction between person and personality must be drawn if other previously quoted passages are to become clear. Every person is unique as an ontic agent, and the personality he develops (ideal or not) will have its own individuality because the unique agent-person interacts with his environment in discriminating ways. His life is indeed intertwined with and responsive to the uniqueness of other persons-personalities. Again: "whatever a person has become" and "intends to become" can hardly refer to person. These passages become clear if we recall that personality is a product of the interaction of a person with other persons-personalities. If I am correct, Johnson's own view is clearer if we keep in mind that it is the agent-person who develops his personality and continues to alter that personality as he acts selectively in his environment. The personality, as Gordon Allport has stressed, is the more or less systematic mode of response an individual acquires as he learns to respond, in thought and in action, to his environment. If this is so, the personality that senses, remembers, perceives, thinks, wants, feels, wills, and experiences obligation, responds aesthetically and religiously.

To be sure, as Johnson would no doubt insist, the personal-

37

ity, as the by-product of the person's interaction, in turn helps to shape the further responsiveness of the person. One does not take off a personality as he does a coat. Still, each person is unique because his constitutive activity-potentials are unique; each personality is unique both because the person is unique and because he acquires his personality as he interacts selectively with complex environments to which he is especially responsive. *It is the person with his personality, as developed at a given point, that interacts with the effective environment.*

Again it is the person who can develop more than one personality in his lifetime. For example, a person born a Jew in a Greek town, Tarsus, develops the personality we know as Saul. "Saul" is the personality with a certain pattern, which, let us say, did not survive such experiences as the stoning of Stephen and the confrontation with God on the road to Damascus. "Paul" is the personality that results from this person's identification with Jesus as Savior. We might say that the personality, Paul, at once fulfilled and challenged the person as Saul never did.

If this reasoning is correct, we cannot say that either the person or the personality is a self-sufficient or self-contained monad sealed within himself. On the personalistic view, any personality represents the pattern or quality of being that a person as agent has selectively become. Accordingly, the interpersonalism that Johnson suggests is welcomed by personalistic philosophy as a psychology of personality but not as a theory of person.

The theory of the agent-person provides a needed foundation for psychologies of personality in which the formation of the ego, self-concept, self-image, and ego-identification play an important part. In such psychologies there is an inadmissible confusion between the agent involved in identifying itself, or expressing itself, as personality is formed. In them we find the ego as organizer and the ego as organized—as if agent could be both cause and effect!

For example, this confusion persists in the writings of Erik

Erickson, the neo-Freudian, whose name is immediately associated with the concept of ego identity. Usually for him the ego is both the synthesizer of experiences and the product of the synthesis. For instance, he says: "For man's need for a psychosocial identity is anchored in nothing less than his sociogenetic evolution." [14] Here psychosocial identity is a product of "man's" need. But we are left in the dark, here as elsewhere, as to the nature of the agent in need. The ego seems at once to be the "individual center of organized experience and reasonable planning" and the organizer.[15] Again, the ego is said to be "capable of integrating effective steps toward a tangible collective future . . . and developing into a well-organized ego within a social reality." [16] Can ego identity be both agent and by-product?

In a little-noted passage Erikson seems to make but never develops the distinction which the personalist welcomes. In this same context he writes:

> But here it is necessary to differentiate between personal identity and ego identity, the conscious feeling of having a personal identity is based on two simultaneous observations: the perception of the self-sameness and continuity of one's existence in time and space and the perception of the fact that others recognize one's sameness. . . . Ego identity, then, in its subjective form, is the awareness of the fact that there is a self-sameness and continuity to the ego's synthesizing (agency) methods, the style of one's individuality, and that this style coincides with the sameness and continuity of one's *meaning* (product) for significant others in the immediate community.[17]

As the parentheses indicate, the distinction should be made explicit between the sameness and continuity of the agent-person, who persists as synthesizer and evaluator, and the sameness and continuity of the personality whose unique, learned style or quality identifies an agent-person in his

14. *Identity: Youth and Crisis* (New York: Norton, 1968), p. 41.
15. Cf. *ibid.*, p. 46.
16. *Ibid.*, p. 45.
17. *Ibid.*, p. 50.

interactive response to the social environment in particular. Most ego psychology, as a form of interpersonalism, remains systematically ambiguous unless something like a personalistic view of the ontic agent-person is introduced.

The Person and Personality in Pastoral Psychology

It remains for me to indicate that the theoretical clarification provided by a personalistic view of the person and personality is not without consequences for pastoral psychology. I limit myself to three comments.

First, it is the person with his personality who counsels with another person and his personality. The counselor assumes that the present personality (say, in distress) does not express the organization, the quality of identity, which the person requires, and of which he is still capable. The counseled person is in distress presumably because some present pattern in the personality acquired thus far is not allowing him as a person to realize what is still open to him.

Second, if the personality is the person finding what he can become but never exhausting what he can become, the pastoral counselor ultimately must see through, and help the counselee see through, the problems created by present formations in personality. The personality can be changed because it is not identical with but rather a very important function of the agent-person. The person's potential may be confined but not destroyed by his present pattern of personality.

On this view, accordingly, being "a woman" or "a man" is a style of becoming. Persons are real. Persons, as male or female, as colored or not, as saints or sinners, are real. It is persons who are the bearers of value; it is persons who are the creators of value (and disvalue). Their personalities distinguish in large measure the quality of achievement in a given society. This means that the focus in pastoral psychology must be both on the person and on his present personality—for it is the person who becomes Saul and then Paul. The person does not exist without a personality in some stage of formation. But there could be no personality worthy of the name if there were no person.

Finally, the counselor never confronts the person without his personality pattern. Both the counselor's and the counselee's personalities may restrict fresh and desirable perception of possible meanings. We need to break through present formations not merely to the "real person" but to the person who so far has expressed himself inadequately in his personality.

There is a sense in which the counselor must not respect the counselee's present personality too much. The important fact is that it belongs to a person; it is his, his to improve, hopefully as a result of the counseling relationship. But there can be no creative respect for personality which is not also respect for the person.

Dynamic Interpersonalism and Contemporary Theology

S. Paul Schilling

In Paul Johnson's view of personality the complex connectedness implied by the prefix in the term *inter*personalism is not limited to relations among persons. It applies equally to the varied dimensions of human life and the different disciplines which investigate human activities. Each person is a creature of many deeply intersecting relationships. He or she can be understood, therefore, only when seen from multiple perspectives. A sound psychology is concerned with all the interests of persons as individuals and in their group relationships. Ultimately it involves a world view.

In *Personality and Religion* Johnson calls special attention to four dimensions of personality, portraying them in a chart in which a Greek cross is superimposed on the circular face of a compass. In the center is the individual I. The horizontal bar represents on the west the I-It relation to the environment, investigated by field psychology and the physical sciences; and on the east the I-We relation of group life which is the concern of interpersonal psychology and the social sciences. The vertical bar portrays in the south the I-Me relation of mind and body examined by psychoanalysis and the biological sciences, and in the north the I-Thou relation to God the ultimate creative Being, considered by personalistic psychology and the "ideal sciences," philosophy and theology. Both the inseparability of center and circumference in the circle and the intersection of the four arms make plain that the relationships are to be seen not as discrete, but as intermeshing aspects of an integrated whole.[1]

The present chapter in this *Festschrift* will necessarily focus attention on the theological dimension, but always in the context of the other relations. We shall begin with a brief sketch of the main features of dynamic interpersonalism, go on to examine its theological and philosophical roots and affinities as these are identified by Johnson himself, and finally investigate the relation of interpersonalistic psychology to several representative movements in present-day theology.

Dynamic Interpersonalism

In 1943 Paul Johnson added to his professional identification with psychology of religion a deepening interest in clinical pastoral education, which became the subject of a course which he taught with Rollin J. Fairbanks at Massachusetts General Hospital in 1943-44. In this connection he first came across the term "interpersonal relations" in Stanley Cobb's *Foundations of Neuropsychiatry,* where the author lists among four types of diseases classified by etiology the psychogenic disorders which arise from disturbed interpersonal relations.[2] The term had already been used in 1912 by Robert MacDougall in his article, "The Social Basis of Individuality." [3] Jacob Levy Moreno advanced the basic concept in his poetic writing entitled *Einladung zu einer Begegnung (Invitation to an Encounter).* Here he portrays two persons who exchange eyes and thereby attain true understanding of each other. About the same time Harry Stack Sullivan began developing

1. *Personality and Religion* (Nashville: Abingdon Press, 1957), p. 233. Johnson's own interpretation of the chart comprises chapter 13, "Dimensions of Personality," pp. 232-58.

2. (Baltimore: Williams and Wilkins Co., 1941).

3. *American Journal of Sociology,* 18 (1912), 1-20. For Johnson's references to Cobb and MacDougall see his *Psychology of Religion* (rev. ed.; Nashville: Abingdon Press, 1959), pp. 43, 232, n. 3, and 274, n. 2.

his interpersonal psychology along somewhat similar lines. In 1918 Moreno wrote of "interpersonal communication" in an article in the literary magazine *Daimon* which he edited. The phrase "interpersonal relations" came to prominence in his book *Who Shall Survive?* (1934) and in *Sociometry: A Journal of Interpersonal Relations,* which he founded in 1937. Johnson himself first used this term in print in the preface to the first edition of his *Psychology of Religion* (1945) and made the idea central in the revised edition of this work (1959). The index to this volume contains eighteen references to interpersonal relations and six to interpersonal theory.[4]

From these sources Johnson derived the terms used in formulating the position which he calls dynamic interpersonalism. The meaning of this conception will emerge most clearly if we interpret successively the noun and the adjective. Interpersonalism finds the essential nature of persons in their encounters with each other. Johnson is critical, for example, of the early concentration of William James on the individual mind with scant attention to its relations with other minds, and he notes with favor that the "radical empiricism" of the mature James overcomes the disjunction between subject and object in experience by recognizing the dynamic continuity of the individual consciousness with events beyond it. It is true that each person is unique, with his own distinctive identity, and we can learn from James the need to look within the stream of consciousness if psychological understanding is to be attained. The individual needs distance enough to breathe and sufficient freedom from other persons to discover who he is. Yet no individual can exist in self-sufficient isolation. With Freud we must see each human being as "a system open to other persons in significant relationships." He grows as a real person only through his interaction with other persons in a network of shared interests and mutual responses.

4. For Johnson's references to these backgrounds in Moreno and Sullivan see *Psychology of Religion* (1959), pp. 31, 42-43, 106, 272.

Dynamic Interpersonalism for Ministry

He finds meaning and fulfillment "in the community of his constellating interpersonal relationships." [5] These connections include, and indeed are grounded in, the relationship between finite persons and the Cosmic Person, God. "A real community is an organic pluralism of interrelated persons who are seeking to understand and respond to one another in the context of cosmic reality." [6]

Defining interpersonal psychology as "the scientific study of persons interacting with other persons," Johnson summarizes his view in seven propositions: (1) Persons understood wholistically are central. (2) Every person confronts other persons in interactive relationships. (3) Persons are motivated in response to other persons who are significant to them. (4) Persons seek goals which they regard as valuable. (5) Values multiply in sharing. (6) Creative living requires spontaneity. (7) Healthy persons grow through love.[7]

Although interpersonalism so interpreted can hardly fail to be dynamic, the specific meaning of the adjective needs to be examined. For Johnson the term means three things. First and most obviously, it refers to the active, moving, energetic quality of the "relations within and among outreaching, outgoing, and interacting persons." [8] Persons do not exist in static detachment; they are marked by spontaneity, the erupting and overflowing life energy that moves forth and calls out a response from other persons. They are seekers of ends whose purposive striving influences and is in turn influenced by the activities of others whose lives are intertwined with theirs. Secondly, interpersonalism is dynamic because, in indebted-

5. *Person and Counselor* (Nashville: Abingdon Press, 1967), pp. 45-49, 51, 55-56; "The Trend Toward Dynamic Interpersonalism," *Religion in Life*, 35 (1966), 752; *Psychology of Religion*, p. 47; *Psychology of Pastoral Care* (Nashville: Abingdon Press, 1953), p. 320; *Personality and Religion*, p. 270.

6. "The Theology of Interpersonalism," *Sociometry*, 12 (1949), 234; *Psychology of Pastoral Care*, pp. 320-21.

7. *Psychology of Pastoral Care*, pp. 27-30.

8. *Person and Counselor*, pp. 52, 69; "The Trend Toward Dynamic Interpersonalism," p. 755.

ness to Freud, it recognizes the intimate relation, in both supportive and conflicting ways, between the conscious ego and the unconscious life of the individual. It asserts the centrality of the conscious person, but does not restrict the data or the causes of his action to his conscious experience. Consciousness is constantly subject to powerful influences from the unconscious. Human motives "spring from all levels and dimensions of conscious-unconscious transactions in the whole personality." [9] Thirdly, to characterize interpersonalism as dynamic calls attention to the belief that the community of interacting persons is sustained by the creative power and love of God.

The fact that both "interpersonal" and "dynamic" have theistic implications makes desirable some further consideration of this basic aspect of Johnson's thought. In his view the manifold capacities and resources of persons, as well as the interdependence and organic wholeness which are manifest in human social relations, are cosmically upheld by a Creative Source which religion knows as God. Reality is ultimately "an organic pluralism of persons united by a Cosmic Person." God is the "Person-in-Relationships at the creative center of this dynamic cosmic community." In their religious lives men and women seek to bear witness to and enhance "the relatedness of each person to God and to every other person in a universal community of reverence and love." [10]

In this perspective interpersonal psychology may be aptly described as psychotheology. It is inseparable from a theology of relationship in which the I of psychology meets the Thou of theology. Ultimately the context in which the individual person carries on his life extends beyond human society to the life of God himself.[11]

9. *Person and Counselor,* pp. 47-48, 52-53; "The Trend Toward Dynamic Interpersonalism," p. 752.
10. *Psychology of Pastoral Care,* pp. 321, 303; "The Theology of Interpersonalism," p. 234.
11. "Pastoral Psychology in the Christian Community," *Pastoral Psychology,* 20 (1969), 63-64; *Person and Counselor,* pp. 68-69, 63.

Theological Influences

In formulating the theological dimensions of his thought, Johnson has found especially congenial the work of two psychiatrists, Jacob L. Moreno and Fritz Kunkel, who have developed their interpersonal views of man in theological terms, and the I-Thou theology of Martin Buber. A brief examination of some of the major emphases of these interpreters of human existence is therefore pertinent.

Moreno is most widely known as a pioneer in sociometry (the psychological and experimental measurement of interpersonal relations), psychodrama, and group psychotherapy. Not always recognized is the basically religious motivation of his work. "My work," he writes, "is of a religious nature from early youth on. The theory of interpersonal relations is born of religion." [12] In his early life Moreno found himself confronted by the pressing question, "Who is this me? . . . Am I nothing or am I God? Am I, this perishable thing, a hopeless existence, or am I at the center of all creation, of the entire cosmos?"

The answer slowly took form in Moreno's conviction that God communicates himself to men not from outside but from within our own persons, "through the I itself, through me, through you, through every me, the millions of me's." Basically the universe is not a bundle of directionless forces, but infinite creativity which binds us all together in a responsibility for all things, which makes us also creators of the world:

> I began to feel that I am, and . . . that I am the father and that I am responsible, I am responsible for everything which happens. . . . Everything belongs to me and I belong to everybody. And so I saw the cosmos as an enormous enterprise, billions of partners, invisible hands, arms stretched out, one to touch the other, all being able, through responsibility, to be Gods.[13]

12. "The Religion of God-Father," *Healer of the Mind*, ed. Paul E. Johnson (Nashville: Abingdon Press, 1972), p. 212; *Who Shall Survive?* (rev. ed.; New York: Beacon House, 1953), p. xxxi.
13. "The Religion of God-Father," pp. 198-201.

These thoughts came overwhelmingly to a focus in a profoundly vivid mystical experience when Moreno was about twenty-seven. The words rushed into his consciousness so rapidly that he did not have the patience to sit down to write them; instead he went into the top room of his house near Vienna and wrote on the walls the words which he found himself speaking aloud: "I am the Father"—of his relatives, the sky and the earth, the birds and the beasts, the mountains and the flowers, human tongues and eyes, the dust from which they come, and the silence into which they sink. He testifies that as the subject of all these and other affirmations he heard "I," not "he" or "thou." In this fact he finds deep meaning: "It's 'I.' It's *my* responsibility." However, he did not feel that the words were his. He felt rather that they passed through him, and that with some modifications they might as well pass through other persons, since all are parts of one reality. [14]

This event, later recorded in *Das Testament des Vaters* (*The Words of the Father*, 1920), brought to a climax what had been the central impulse of his life from his earliest years —"to be God, the Father himself." In 1972 Moreno could still write, "How to embody God, to give him a tangible reality, was my question and still is." His own effort to formulate the divine activity he regards as humble rather than arrogant and as "just a natural expression of the highest form of reality." "The people needed a living father, encounterable, present, not manufactured or canonized." However, he admits a certain absurdity in his own intervention in this process. "Who am I to incarnate and portray him? *That* is absurd and insane. May I be forgiven for this crime." Moreover, he admits that he has failed to concretize effectively the image of the God-Father. "I have remained amorphous as a living God. . . . My megalomania is shattered." [15]

Nevertheless, he believes it to be imperative that human

14. *Ibid.*, pp. 201-3.
15. *Ibid.*, pp. 205-14.

fragmentations be overcome through the concrete establishment of the Father-God as the uniting bond between all people. God has "an irresistible drive to include everything into one," and this requires the cooperation of every element of existence. Especially urgent in this connection is the need for persons to enter sensitively into relations of spontaneous encounter with others. When they really meet eye to eye and face to face, each can say as it were to the other:

> . . . I will tear your eyes out
> and place them instead of mine,
> and you will tear my eyes out
> and will place them instead of yours;
> then I will look at you with your eyes,
> and you will look at me with thine.[16]

When persons respond to each other with openness and spontaneity, they become channels of the creative activity of God, hence co-creators. This is the basis for such experimental procedures as group therapy and psychodrama. In the latter, initiated in the Theater of Spontaneity in Vienna in 1921, Moreno placed the stage in the center and invited both actors and audience to portray dramatically their own situations, responding to each other by impromptu expression of their feelings and ideas. Through such practices men and women often experience the healing of inner and group conflicts and learn with God the meaning of spontaneous creativity. [17]

> In interpersonal relations, therefore, we are called on to develop the capacity to hear everything which happens all over the world, to see everything, to feel everything, to share with everybody pain and joy, hope and the excitement of living, to become more and more all-sharing, all-creating, all-involving. Then they will see you everywhere and recognize you, that you are not only one man or another man, but the God-Father himself.[18]

16. *Ibid.*, p. 209.
17. *Psychology of Religion*, p. 43.
18. "The Religion of God-Father," p. 215.

In the interpersonal psychology of Fritz Kunkel the pantheistic mysticism of Moreno is absent. Nevertheless, Kunkel regards psychology as a philosophical rather than a natural science, and he is willing to call his psychology "theocentric." Acknowledging indebtedness to Freud, Adler, and especially the collective unconscious of Jung, he finds in every person a primitive longing describable as collective unconscious power, involving urges like hunger, love, or the desire for self-preservation or adventure. This power must be lived out in relation to an external world, and to be creative it must be consciously developed. It moves us not as a push from behind but through the attraction of values ahead, goals which elicit our creative efforts. These goals are attained in we-experiences, and ultimately they depend on the creative action of God, who works in and through the person. Thus the religious and the unconscious aspects of human experience tend to merge, and both come to a focus in we-experience. "There is no experience of God without the experience of the human We-relationship." [19]

Truly understood, the self is not I, but We, and the individual's relation to the group should not be seen as I-You, but I-We. The person grows to maturity by moving from I to We, and then to He.

> Our creative center, the Self, is our positive relationship to God. Our Selfhood is the experience of our dependence on and our support by the Creator whom we know only partially. We realize creative power if we live from our real center. Then we are channels of creation. [20]

Such fulfillment is defeated when we make the ego central. Misunderstanding and misusing the creative powers entrusted to us, we idolatrously seek to live for our own sake. The result is the opposite of creativity—anxiety, with its accompaniments

19. Fritz Kunkle, *In Search of Maturity* (New York: Charles Scribner's Sons, 1943), p. viii.
20. *Ibid.*, pp. 42, 90.

of tensions, frustration, and fear. True selfhood can be restored or attained only as we seek the fulfillment of our highest aspirations in the positive relationships of human community, through which are released the creative and redemptive powers of God. [21]

In Martin Buber's writings, Johnson has found theological support for his dynamic interpersonalism, which in key respects is comparable to that derived from Moreno and Kunkel. In Buber's thought the individual is equally incomplete whether he isolates himself from the community or submerges himself in the crowd. The person finds his real life in meeting, in a dialogue in which each participant addresses and responds to the other, endeavoring to take his point of view and so to perceive what life means to him. In this relationship the whole being of each communicates something of himself to the other.

Moreover, in a genuinely dialogical situation the two persons are not simply objects of each other's experience; instead, they encounter and address each other as subjects. We quite properly make things our objects, separating ourselves from them as we do in scientific investigation where the relation can be described as I-It and where things can be classified according to their past. In contrast, persons confront each other in the living present: I meets Thou in a mutual relation in which the whole being of each contributes significantly to the whole being of the other, and both grow in personhood. We become whole selves neither alone nor in reference to objects but only in relation to other selves whom we learn to address as Thou.

This duality is inherent in personal existence. There is an over-againstness in human life—Buber calls it the inborn Thou —which gives rise to tension and conflict; yet the self attains wholeness by unifying opposition. Willingness to enter into I-Thou relations is thus a mark of our acceptance of

21. *Personality and Religion,* pp. 246, 278-79; "The Theology of Interpersonalism," pp. 232-34.

duality with its inevitable tension as essential to our being. Thus interpersonal relations are a clue to and grounded in the ultimate character of reality. Every such relation discloses the eternal Thou. "In each Thou we address the eternal Thou." God is not to be inferred, as one object is from another, by a line of reasoning. Rather he is "the being that is directly, most nearly, and lastingly over against us, that may properly be only addressed not expressed." He is not the conclusion of an argument, but the Thou whom we meet in firsthand encounter, and who makes himself known whenever we enter into the living dialogue of interpersonal relationships. [22]

Johnson finds further theological reinforcement in the thought of Paul Tillich. Personal life, declares Tillich, "emerges in the encounter of person with person and in no other way." Here the individual "experiences the limit which stops him in his unstructured running from one 'here and now' to the next and throws him back on himself." For Tillich, too, this situation reflects the finite person's relation to God, the ulti-mate ground of our being. Confronting the mystery of exis-tence in its multiple dimensions, we are led in religious devo-tion to the God beyond the god of traditional theism. In "the dynamic encounter of inner meeting" we know him as Spirit. As our spirits respond to him who is our ultimate concern, we are brought into closer relations with other human beings and empowered to transcend our estrangement and realize the New Being.[23]

If the theologians surveyed were examined in any detail they would exhibit many significant differences, but in the present context they agree in two all-important respects. First, they affirm that human beings become real persons only as they sensitively encounter each other in an I-Thou relation, which enables each to adopt in some real measure the point

22. Martin Buber, *I and Thou*, tr. R. G. Smith (New York: Charles Scribner's Sons, 1937), pp. 6, 79-81; *Psychology of Religion*, pp. 44-46.
23. Tillich, *Systematic Theology*, III (Chicago: University of Chicago Press, 1963), 40, 58, 156; *Person and Counselor*, pp. 44, 60; *Personality and Religion*, p. 279.

of view of the other. Secondly, they find this relationship grounded in and thus revelatory of something in the ultimate character of reality itself—in the Thou who is himself Subject-in-relations, and who thus provides the living context in which persons-in-community find fulfillment in lives of shared values. These are the major theological bases of Johnson's dynamic interpersonalism.

Building on them, he outlines a theology of relationship which parallels his interpersonal psychology. Indeed, so thoroughly is he imbued with relational imagery that he offers a diagram in which the I of psychology meets the Thou of theology! They can be no more complete in isolation than the human lives with which they deal. Interpersonal psychology may be summarized in five propositions: (1) person meets person; (2) person resists person; (3) both suffer aniexty; (4) person accepts person; (5) persons grow in love, in dialogue, as it were. With this psychology are the five points of the theology of relationship: (1) God creates man; (2) man rebels against God; (3) both suffer conflict; (4) God forgives man; (5) community of love. The dynamic principle of this theology is creative Spirit, which in reconciling love answers the spontaneity of the overflowing life energy manifest in human interpersonal relations.[24]

This account of the theological affinities of Johnson's position as he conceives them would hardly be complete without some reference to his understanding of the relation between his neo-personalism and the personalism with which he has always been to some degree identified.[25] He is concerned not to reject personalism but to modify or revise it by removing difficulties and correcting oversights which he finds in its traditional expressions. He offers three main criticisms.

(1) He quotes with approval the judgment of Gordon W. Allport that personalism tends "to sidestep the countless

24. *Person and Counselor,* pp. 67-70.
25. This discussion will be kept brief in order to avoid undesirable overlapping on the opening chapter of this volume.

intersections that occur between the personality system." Instead, the intentional thrust of Johnson's interpersonal approach "is to move out from the isolated person of a closed self-consciousness to an open, interrelating person, who finds direct encounter with Thou." [26]

(2) Johnson is unwilling to follow Borden Parker Bowne and Edgar S. Brightman in regarding personality as equivalent to conscious experience. Brightman recognized the influence of the unconscious but persisted in treating it as part of the environment of the self. In contrast, Johnson emphasizes the openness of the conscious ego to the dynamic motivations of the unconscious, which he sees as "essential and integral in the dynamic wholeness of personality." [27]

(3) Johnson is critical of the personalistic interpretation of religious experience for its failure to recognize with sufficient clarity the unmediated directness of the I-Thou encounter. For Bowne, Brightman, and Albert C. Knudson "any view of God arises, not from immediate encounter, but a mediated inference from the rational structure of conscious experience." Though they practice communion with God in prayer in upholding a "dualistic closure of persons from all else" and stressing rationalistic proofs of God they have tended "to infer that God is over there at the end of a long line of reasoning, instead of immediately here in revelatory encounter." [28]

I find myself in basic agreement with the positive intention of all three of Johnson's concerns. His inclusion of the unconscious in the self rather than in its environment is a coherent interpretation of the experienced data. However, his first and third criticisms are based in part on questionable assessments of the views which he finds wanting and are inclined to exaggerate the differences.

26. Allport, *Personality and Social Encounter* (Boston: Beacon Press, 1960), p. 23; *Person and Counselor*, pp. 53, 66.
27. *Personality and Religion*, pp. 234-35; *Person and Counselor*, p. 52; "The Trend Toward Dynamic Interpersonalism," p. 752.
28. *Person and Counselor*, pp. 65-66.

In Bowne, as in James, there is little recognition of the intimate interconnections between the individual person and other persons, and this is true in lesser measure of Knudson and the early Brightman. However, the Brightman of the mid-thirties and later cannot be soundly charged with a dualistic closing off of the individual from his relations. The difference between him and Johnson on this point seems to be mainly one of emphasis. On the one side, Brightman declares that the world of persons is "a social world." Johnson himself quotes a passage in which Brightman, portraying the person as "a remembering identity, binding a multiplicity of experience into personal unity," adds that "each person in the world of persons interacts with many other persons in social relations." On the other side, Johnson clearly asserts the unique individuality of each person who is involved with others in responsive and fulfilling interrelationships. "We aim," he writes, "to keep the person central," and each person is "unique in his own identity." Moreover, the religious quest is "essentially personal from the center of my being." [29]

I am also unable to find in the writings of the personalists cited warrant for the judgment that for them faith in God springs from rational argument rather than from direct encounter. Brightman clearly supports mystical awareness as a pathway to the knowledge of God, and his teaching and scholarly writing manifest a positive appreciation of mysticism, as did his personal life. He does insist that the truth content of the mystical experience must be tested by its relation to other beliefs and experiences seen as a whole.[30]

There are passages in Knudson which seem to regard knowledge of God, like that of the physical world, as knowl-

29. E. S. Brightman, *Nature and Values* (New York and Nashville: Abingdon-Cokesbury Press, 1945), pp. 64-65; *Person and Counselor,* pp. 52-53; "Religion and Psychotherapy," in *Progress in Psychotherapy,* V, ed. Jules Masserman and J. L. Moreno (New York: Grune and Stratton, 1960), 205.

30. E. S. Brightman, *Person and Reality,* ed. Peter A. Bertocci (New York: Ronald Press, 1958), pp. 301-9, 312-13, 318-21.

edge of an external object apprehended in an I-It relation. However, in the central thrust of his thought he strongly affirms the reality of the direct experience of God in which both God and man are subjects interpersonally related. He points out that the immediacy is psychological rather than metaphysical, since no immediate relation between man and God "excludes the possibility of error." Indeed, there is no "pure" or absolutely "immediate" experience of any kind. "All experience is mediated or interpreted," since it is always colored by the attitudes, memories, and relationships of those who have it. Nevertheless Knudson stresses repeatedly the reality in religious experience of human "consciousness of the Divine Presence." Christian experience involves "a direct personal relation to a living Christ," and "to experience Christ is to experience God." "There is in religious experience an 'immediate certitude of God,' and this certitude justifies itself." Indeed, Knudson goes so far in championing the self-verification of religious faith that he might be faulted for overemphasis on uncriticized religious experience and insufficient recognition of the need for coherent evaluation of the beliefs which arise from it.[31]

The above remarks suggest that at some points the differences between personalistic theology and Johnson's interpersonalism are less marked than he recognizes. However, his concerns are sound, his emphases are needed, and his critique provides constructive guidelines for a better understanding of the relationships of human persons with each other and with God.

---

31. Knudson, *The Validity of Religious Experience* (New York: Abingdon Press, 1937), pp. 97, 98, 231, 220-21, 261. Following Schleiermacher and Rudolf Otto, Knudson affirms the reality of a religious a priori, a native capacity of the mind which is as constitutive of human nature as the theoretical, aesthetic, and moral prioris. "Religion is rooted deep in human nature," and represents an original, unique, and independent capacity of the human spirit. It is therefore as trustworthy as any of our other fundamental interests. Like them, it has autonomous validity. "It stands on its own feet. It verifies itself." (*Ibid.*, pp. 161-67, 186, 232-33.)

Dynamic Interpersonalism in Present-day Theologies

In addition to the influences identified by Johnson himself, contemporary theology exhibits a variety of ideas which parallel or overlap those of dynamic interpersonalism and which might significantly reinforce and enrich it. Three types of theology seem particularly pertinent: some forms of Christian existentialism, Barthian incarnational theology, and process thought.

Christian Existentialism. As we have seen, Johnson makes extensive use of the sights of Martin Buber, and he also utilizes some of the concepts of Paul Tillich. He relates the question-and-answer procedure of Tillich's method of correlation to the finite person's quest for a response from the reality beyond him; it is worth noting that the method also implies dialogue between persons representing different perspectives and positions, hence the willingness of each participant to really listen empathetically to the dialogue partner. Among the aspects of Tillich's thought which Johnson omits, the following are especially relevant for interpersonalism. (1) The individual's acceptance of God's acceptance of him, in spite of his unacceptability, implies also his acceptance of other finite persons. (2) The overcoming of the estrangement of existence through the New Being of Jesus as the Christ relates the individual to his fellows, whose being, like his, is grounded in the being-itself of God. (3) The essentialization involved in the coming of the kingdom of God, which restores men to their true essence by reuniting them with the divine ground of being and meaning, advances their communion with each other as well as with God. It should be pointed out, however, that some elements in Tillich do not lend themselves readily to interpersonalistic interpretation. God as being-itself is not readily construed as the God who addresses us in I-Thou encounter. Likewise, Tillich's ultimate pantheism, with its corollary of man's oneness with all forms of being— man is a microcosm in which all levels of reality are present—

hardly preserves the distinctness of persons which is necessary if relations between them are to be truly interpersonal.

The existentialist theology of John Macquarrie also conceives God primarily as being, or as holy being; and like Tillich he makes little use of the imagery of address or encounter. However, his elucidation of being takes directions which are quite congenial to interpersonalism. He defines being as the *is-hood* in virtue of which one can say that anything is. Its essence is "the dynamic 'letting-be' . . . of the beings." It lets things be; it enables to be, empowers to be, or brings into being. Thus "being 'is' present-and-manifest in every being." This provides the context for Macquarrie's interpretation of love between persons. Ontologically, love is equivalent to the "letting-be" which defines being. To be means to enjoy the maximum range of being which is possible for a particular being. Hence loving (letting-be) another means helping him to realize his fullest potentialities—a concern which recalls Moreno's image of the exchange of eyes. The love of God denotes his "self-giving and letting-be"; his very essence "as Being is to let-be, to confer, sustain, and perfect the being of the creatures." [32]

The interpersonalism implicit in Macquarrie emerges more clearly when his view of being as love is joined with his assertion that the holy being which he identifies with God is best represented as personal being:

> Personal being is the most appropriate symbol for Being itself; for personal being stands highest in the hierarchy of beings which all seek to be like God, and personal being, as showing the richest diversity in unity and the highest possibilities for creativity and love, gives to our minds the fullest disclosure of the mystery of Being that we can receive. [33]

In this connection attention should be called also to the existentially oriented hermeneutical theology of Gerhard Ebe-

---

32. Macquarrie, *Principles of Christian Theology* (New York: Charles Scribner's Sons, 1966), pp. 99-100, 103, 105, 109, 310-11, 452.
33. *Ibid.*, p. 250.

ling. He emphatically rejects the subject-object antithesis in theology. God must not be viewed as an object at man's disposal; likewise the attempt to isolate man in terms of externally ascertainable facts obscures and falsifies the distinctively human. " 'God and man' are not two themes, but one." They are known only in their mutual relation. Indeed, all of man's relations are a part of him. "They are not additional to his life, but they constitute it." In faith, God, world, and man must be spoken of as a single interconnected reality. A corollary of this is that we cannot know God as he is in himself; such knowledge, which would keep God at a distance, is self-contradictory. "True knowledge of God is of God who is for us and with us." God is known only by what he does in relation to man. Conversely, true knowledge of man has to do not with what man is in himself, but as he is in relation to God, the reality which concerns him.[34] Clearly Ebeling champions a theology of relationship which offers a harmonious counterpart to interpersonal psychology.

Incarnational Theology. At two points Johnson cites Karl Barth to illustrate his views,[35] but without developing the connection. However, the Christocentric, incarnational theology represented by Barth, Josef L. Hromádka, Helmut Gollwitzer, and others has implications for interpersonal psychology which deserve to be made explicit. With a revelational stance which completely rejects natural theology, these thinkers differ radically with Tillich and Macquarrie, yet offer positive and distinctive support for dynamic interpersonalism. During the years 1928-38, writes Barth, he came to the view that Christian doctrine must be in all its aspects "doctrine of Jesus Christ as the living Word of God spoken to us." He is the "ground, content, and object of Christian faith." But a theology centering in the Word made flesh could no longer affirm, with Kierkegaard and Barth's own earlier dia-

---

34. Ebeling, *Word and Faith*, tr. James W. Leitch (Philadelphia: Fortress Press, 1963), p. 200; *The Nature of Faith*, tr. R. G. Smith (Philadelphia: Muhlenberg Press, 1961), pp. 123, 108.
35. *Person and Counselor*, pp. 65, 67.

lectical theology, an eternal qualitative distinction between God and man, eternity and time. The incarnation makes the idea that God is wholly other "untenable, and corrupt and pagan." The world is different from God, but he affirms it; in all his absoluteness he is free love, entering into fellowship with his own, and making himself solidaristic with men. Man is created by God to be God's covenant partner, and even his sin cannot negate his covenant relationship.

As God in Christ calls man to himself as his covenant partner, he directs him also to his fellowman. He who is himself trinitarian, God in relationship, wills that man should find fulfillment in relationship with both God and his fellows. At the very center of his being he is related to the being of the Thou, "under his claim and . . . constituting a claim upon him." Thus human being is being in encounter with the Thou. "Humanity, the characteristic and essential mode of man's being, is in its root fellow-humanity. Humanity which is not fellow-humanity is inhumanity." This has profound implications for the responsibility of the Christian and the church in society. Christians must recognize in thought and practice the solidarity with all men and women, Christian or non-Christian, which God himself has manifested in Christ. All who exist in bondage are our brothers as men who like ourselves are reconciled to God. The fact that Jesus Christ is every man's brother and God is every man's Father impels Christians to deep concern for human worth and rights. The church likewise dares not be neutral in the face of injustice, since it is a community commissioned to embody in speech and action God's love for men.[36]

The same Christocentric emphases appear in the thought of Hromádka, though with a distinctive flavor reflecting the

36. Barth, "Parergon," *Evangelische Theologie*, 8 (1948), 272; (*The Humanity of God*, tr. John Newton Thomas and Thomas Wieser (Richmond: John Knox Press, 1960), pp. 30, 53; *Church Dogmatics*, III/2, 247, 274-75; III/4, 116-17, 340; IV/1, 186-88; IV/3, 340, 346-47, 780, 816, 818-19, 892-93. *Christ and Adam*, tr. T. A. Smail (New York: Harper & Brothers, 1956), p. 86.

theological heritage of the Czech reformation and the impact of revolutionary social events. According to Hromádka we can rightly understand the nature and destiny of man only in the light of Jesus of Nazareth. The incarnation is God's coming to man; when God speaks he speaks to man. Therefore when we speak of the Word of God, we are talking simultaneously of man. Though Pilate's ironic words *"Ecce homo"* were spoken of Jesus, they also express effectively the apostolic understanding of man.

Moreover, every aspect of human life is related to the God who became man. The Word made flesh is the point of intersection "where the Lord of glory broke (and continually breaks) through the horizontal line of human life." Hence no believer in Jesus Christ may pursue the spiritual life in separation from the world. Earthly society is the sphere of the creative and redemptive activity of God himself. To come to God is therefore to find ourselves instantly in the presence of men, and we cannot rightly love him unless we love those to whom he has given himself in infinite love. "Every man is our concern, and every man, believer and unbeliever, decent or living in degradation, healthy or leper, righteous or unrighteous, churchgoer or prodigal is to us equally dear." Such love leads inevitably to concrete action for a better social order. Every aspect of human life is related to the purpose of the God who in Christ became man and who purposes to establish in this world his kingdom centering on an enduring fellowship between God and man.

Here obviously is a profoundly interpersonal theology— and one which has far-reaching practical implications. It calls on Christians to listen to atheistic communists and recognize that some of their ends may be closer to the righteous purposes of God than are the reactionary social attitudes and the self-righteous indifference to justice which typify many traditional churches. It requires the church in its witness to transcend the divisions between East and West and minister to people on both sides, refusing to allow its attitudes to be determined by political, economic, and ideological antagonisms.[37] Such convictions have led Hromádka and others, in a period of widespread anti-communism among professing Christians, to courageous and persistent efforts to promote between Marxists and Christians understanding, dialogue, and cooperation for humanitarian goals shared by both. They constitute a valuable reminder that consistent interpersonalism must concern itself responsibly not only with the direct contacts of individuals with each other but also with the dynamic complexities of the relations of groups in society.

Process Theology. When Johnson writes that God "is to be found in the nexus of relationships to his creation," [38] he gives voice to a prominent emphasis in contemporary process theology. Similarly, all four of the propositions on man which provide the theological basis for his most recent book—man as a future-oriented, related, creative, and self-transcending being—are affirmed by process thinkers.[39] However, he does not so identify them, and his writings as a whole contain only a few passing references to representatives of process thought. Both dynamic interpersonalism and process theology might benefit from closer contact. We therefore close this essay with consideration of some of the motifs in process thought which demonstrate the affinity.

As portrayed by Daniel Day Williams, process theologians seek to relate biblical faith to the scientific understanding of existence as the scene of dynamic self-unfolding processes, in which God as immanent Cause and transcendent Subject is working to move the world toward a future which is real for God as well as the creatures. The metaphysical basis for

37. For detailed references to these ideas in Hromádka's writings, as well as a fuller account of his theology, see S. Paul Schilling, *Contemporary Continental Theologians* (Nashville: Abingdon Press, 1966), pp. 69-70, 75-76, and the whole of chapter 3.

38. *Person and Counselor*, p. 64.

39. Lowell G. Colston and Paul E. Johnson, *Personality and Christian Faith* (Nashville: Abingdon Press, 1972), pp. 35-50. The four themes are connected respectively with Pierre Teilhard de Chardin, Martin Buber, Paul Tillich, and Reinhold Niebuhr.

these conceptions is the philosophy of Alfred North White-head, who regards the universe as a society constituted by the creative processes of becoming of actual entities or occasions. This society is possible because of the supreme reality, God, who contributes to all individuals their ultimate structure and is capable in fullest measure of receptivity and objectivity in relation to them. Being is dynamic movement in significant mutual relations. God acts creatively in and on the world but is also enriched by its becoming. In this way Whitehead seeks to preserve both free individuality and organic social relation in reality.[40]

With this background, the dipolar theism espoused by theologians like Charles Hartshorne, W. Norman Pittenger, Schubert M. Ogden, John B. Cobb, Jr., and Williams recognizes both the absoluteness of God in his primordial nature and the relativity of God in his consequent nature. The latter is of primary importance in the present context. God for Ogden is "the eminently relative One." His absoluteness is "simply the abstact structure or identifying principle of his eminent relativity." His reality is thoroughly social and temporal so that he is the recipient of and intimately affected by the achievements of finite beings.[41] This view affirms both the dynamic creativity of reality and the mutual relatedness of God and the world—the two major concerns of dynamic interpersonalism.

For Pittenger, God is no changeless essence but rather

a living, constantly creative, infinitely related, ceaselessly operative reality; the universe at its core is movement, dynamism, activity, and not sheer and unrelated abstraction. Whitehead's view that the cosmos is "alive," is basic to the whole enterprise of process-thought; and this carries with it a conviction that the

40. D. D. Williams, "Prozess-Theologie: Eine neue Möglichkeit für die Kirche," *Evangelische Theologie*, 30 (1970), 571-82.

41. *The Reality of God* (New York: Harper & Row, [1963] 1966), pp. 65, 141; Hartshorne, *The Divine Relativity* (New Haven: Yale University Press, 1948), pp. 11, 76, 88-89, 129, 143.

only reasonable explanation of the living cosmos is in fact "the living God." [42]

This dynamism extends to all aspects of reality. In Hartshorne's view God's own unending creative becoming or self-creation is constantly bringing forth new realizations of value. "Life is process, divinity itself is process, nothing matters but the kinds of processes which occur or can be made to occur. . . . And all process brings new values into existence." [43]

The relational nature of the process appears at many points, including Hartshorne's interpretation of divine love. To speak of God as love focuses attention on his social character. To love is to share deeply in the joys and sorrows of others, hence to be influenced by those loved; it means to give oneself rather than to receive. Love asks above all else for an opportunity to contribute to the being of others. However, in men this relationship is limited, partial, mixed with indifference and self-centeredness, while the divine love which excels all others is, as Charles Wesley saw, "pure and unbounded." Love is essentially social awareness; taken without qualification, and literally rather than merely metaphorically, love so conceived is God. The highest kind of love is the ideal form of social interdependence, and both are ultimate. Deity, then, can be described as "the unsurpassably interacting, loving, presiding genius and companion of all existence." [44]

Moreover, the God in and through whom all things interact is personal consciousness. "The first (and last!) thing to be said about God is that He is the supreme Self or Thou, whose absolute relativity or all-embracing love is the beginning and end of man and, indeed, of the whole creation." [45] "What

42. "A Contemporary Trend in North American Theology: Process-Thought and Christian Faith," *Religion in Life,* 34 (1965), 502.

43. Perry Le Fevre, ed., *Philosophical Resources for Christian Thought* (Nashville: Abingdon Press, 1968), pp. 65-66.

44. Hartshorne, *The Divine Relativity,* pp. 26, 36, 65-66; *A Natural Theology for Our Time* (LaSalle, Ill.: Open Court, 1967), pp. 45, 75, 137.

45. Ogden, *The Reality of God,* p. 66.

is a person," asks Hartshorne, "if not a being qualified and conditioned by social relations, relations to other persons? . . . Either God really does love all beings, that is, is related to them by a sympathetic union surpassing any human sympathy, or religion seems a vast fraud." [46]

In effect, therefore, these theologians equate personal and social in their conception of God, and thus ground dynamic interpersonalism in their interpretation of ultimate reality.

46. *The Divine Relativity*, p. 25.

Dynamic Interpersonalism and Contemporary Psychology

Orlo Strunk, Jr.

Although there is little doubt that modern psychology has played an important role in theological education in the United States in the past five decades, the specific nature and the precise historical data of that role remain ambiguous at least, mysterious at most. On an impressionistic level, it would be easy to conclude that the broad and pervasive impact has come from psychoanalytic psychology. An uncritical look at such volumes as Peter Homans' *Theology After Freud* can easily give the impression that a single psychological system has in some strange and powerful way made a profound and substantive impact on theology proper. But this is simply not true, at least not in the sense in which the impressionistic view would have it.

It is of course true that psychoanalysis has fingered its way into theological education. But the influx has been partial and minimal, generated mostly out of a context of response; that is, certain proper theologians—e.g., Reinhold Niebuhr and Paul Tillich—have given cognitive attention to the psychoanalytic literature. These explorations are frequently seen as the way in which psychology relates or gets involved in the theological enterprise. And most assuredly it is one way, but this cognitive response-like project is far more academic, political, and journalistic than it is existential. My argument is that the psychological impact on theology must be seen in terms far more subtle and far more complex than the impressionistic stance allows. Indeed, the influx is often personal and existential and even highly secret and, perhaps most important of all, takes place in the matrix of personhood.

This seems especially true in that domain of theological education which has come to be known as the pastoral care and counseling movement and in the clinical pastoral education project. It has often been within these activities that psychology has found its sluice into the larger theological endeavor. And despite the tyrannical propensities of theology proper—a propensity, I venture to say, of far greater strength than we in our passive tendencies are ever able to recognize or admit—psychology has been able to find a footing in the theological matrix.

I believe the nature of this interaction is important to understand if we are to have a full appreciation of the peculiar impact psychology has had in the development of theological education, particularly in the areas of pastoral care and counseling and specifically in the formulation of the kind of dynamic interpersonalism forged by Paul E. Johnson. Indeed, Paul Johnson's understanding of the interaction is itself instructive. His own analysis is worth contemplating:

The conflict of theology with psychology intensified during the years when psychology was enjoying a crescendo of influence in the modern world. Earlier in the 20th century, theology was accommodating its perspectives to a modernism influenced by the natural sciences and secular culture. This seemed to endanger the supernatural revelation and unique authority of the Christian position. The conflict came to a dramatic crisis in Germany when Hitler was reaching out to engulf the church in Nazi statism and genocide. Then Karl Barth gave a ringing challenge to be faithful to the Word of God, with undivided allegiance to the biblical revelation of Christ. Theologians of that generation rallied with Barth to proclaim a faith in the transcendent unapproachable God revealed in the Pauline Christ.

So there developed a cult of supernaturalism, in which theology recoiled from engagement with a scientific culture and retreated into other worldliness. This was a productive awakening of biblical studies and historical theology. There was in fact a renaissance of classical theology in its prescientific grandeur. Charismatic leaders brought a glowing enthusiasm to this other-worldly supernaturalism which attained high authority over theological education. Esoteric vocabularies were debated endlessly like the medieval chanting of plain song.

By some slight of hand or black magic, psychology has become invisible in the halls of theology. Psychology of religion was displaced by existentialism and ontology. Pastoral psychology yielded to pastoral theology and pastoral care. Psychological studies were disguised as personality and religion or personality and theology (when religion also was discredited as the enemy of Christianity). There must be no lingering doubt that theology is the queen of the sciences.

Like the parable of the purist who swept his house clean of worldly dirt, this was not the end of the story. More devils moved in lustier than ever, including the other sciences and arts of man, such as sociology, anthropology, communications, field engagement in the community, and the theater, once out of bounds to puritans and evangelicals. Psychology has returned in our psychological testing, counseling, psychotherapy, psychiatry, personality and culture, human development and pastoral care.

The theologians are by this time vying with each other to employ psychology as an auxiliary science, to understand the nature of man, Christian education, pastoral theology, and Christian ethics. There is scarcely a theological doctrine that has escaped this searching and mounting dialogue with psychology.[1]

My own conviction is that this is an essentially accurate depiction of the process activated in the psychology-theology encounter. Several years have passed since this analysis was written, but I venture to claim that the general tableau remains accurate. The extension may be seen in the growing use of such a term as "empiric theology" and the resistance of such a term as "psychotheology."

This general dynamic of theological tyranny has conditioned the ways in which psychology has found its way into theological education. Lapsley's recent evaluations of Carroll A. Wise and Paul E. Johnson are illustrative. He writes, "We must conclude that as great as the contributions of Johnson and Wise have been to the pastoral field generally, their contribu-

1. "Pastoral Psychology in the Christian Community," *Spiritual Life,* 15 (1969), 58-64.

tions to pastoral theology have been indirect, through the stimulation they have given students and readers, rather than direct." [2] It seems to me that such a statement must be made in the full recognition of the theological tyranny already noted. What this means is that psychology has had to find its way into the theological schema in sundry and at times subtle ways. Frequently this has meant that psychological facts and theories have had to come via personhood, through the professors and clinical instructors who were convinced of the importance of psychology, at the same time remaining in the theological community. It has also meant that one must come to tolerate the fact that the impact will be more on ministry and on persons than on the formal theological superstructure with its visible and prestigious media.

Of course, this type of invasion is fraught with all kinds of dangers, and most of these dangers have been felt within theological education: the tendency to distort both projects, the inclination to polarize the disciplines, the desire to cannibalize one another, etc. Like it or not, this sort of process puts a great deal of pressure and responsibility on the agency or the carrier of the new discipline. If the full homogenization is to be creative and positive, trust in the agent on the part of the communal—in this instance theological faculties—must be considerable.

All this leads me to the main purpose of this chapter—to identify the major psychologies which have found their way into the dynamic interpersonalism of Paul E. Johnson. In one sense, dynamic interpersonalism is a fine example of the complex way in which psychology can finger its way into the theological project via the open stance of a person holding firmly yet tentatively to a variety of behavioral science modes. For it must be noted here, as it is clearly demonstrated in the first section of this *Festschrift*, the streams that fed into dynamic interpersonal theory are not exclusively psychologi-

2. James N. Lapsley, "Pastoral Theology Past and Present," in *The New Shape of Pastoral Theology*, ed. by William B. Oglesby, Jr. (Nashville: Abingdon Press, 1969), p. 38.

cal; they are philosophical and theological as well. To me this is an essential and crucial fact to keep in mind in evaluating dynamic interpersonalism as a viable theory for ministry in all its forms. My task, however, is to concentrate on the psychological contributions which have made an impact on the formation of dynamic interpersonalism.

History and Theory

Perhaps it is important to note that the general stance of dynamic interpersonalism was generated out of a matrix of praxis and inquiry. In fact, many of its emphases may be found in the first edition of *Psychology of Religion,* a book not primarily concerned with pastoral care and counseling. Indeed, that book is often listed as one of a line which imitated the early pioneers of classical psychology of religion. But, as Hiltner observed, even in 1945 Johnson had introduced a new note:

> In its general outline, list of subjects considered, and in several other features, it must be classed as an imitator of the pioneers. In certain other respects, notably Johnson's belief that dynamic or therapeutic psychology has created new bases for the psychological understanding of religion, it belongs in a different group.[3]

Although the "dynamic or therapeutic" element is important to note, it is equally significant that it is within a field of inquiry that the recognition occurs. As I have tried to point out in another place,[4] it was really the hope of some of the early pioneers in clinical pastoral education and pastoral care and counseling that these developments would never lose sight of the inquiry dimension of the project. Thornton rightly observes that

3. Seward Hiltner, "The Psychological Understanding of Religion," in *The Psychology of Religion: Historical and Interpretative Readings,* ed. by Orlo Strunk, Jr. (Nashville: Abingdon Press, 1971), p. 75.
4. "Relationships of Psychology of Religion and Clinical Pastoral Education," *Pastoral Psychology,* 22 (1971), 29-35.

the training program that Boisen conceived for the summer of 1925 was not designed to develop competence in pastoral ministries. It was a program in "cooperative inquiry" into the psychology of religious experience. . . . Boisen was intent upon the construction of a clinical theology by the use of empirical methods. . . . He lamented the demise of the psychology of religion as an academic discipline and repeatedly, in the journals, complained that workers in clinical pastoral education were neglecting the task of under-girding their efforts with a program of "inquiry." [5]

This general stance—certainly not characteristic of all aspects and phases of the movement—was present from the beginnings of the evolution of dynamic interpersonalism. For a very long time the *Bulletin of the Boston University School of Theology* has stated that one of its objectives is to relate meaningfully the behavioral and social sciences to the theological project, an intention which has been taken far more seriously than is customary in educational institutions. Surely Johnson's own personal propensities as a psychologist of religion were congruent with this institutional objective.

At the same time, professional education was a historical reality so that the kind of psychology of religion explored by Johnson even in the early 1940s was much closer to being within the "body of divinity," as outlined by Hiltner,[6] than it was to Tillich's[7] assumption that it is one of the "empirical disciplines" providing the philosophy of religion with data for interpretation. It was in this continuous tension between praxis and inquiry that dynamic interpersonalism was formed, and continues to evolve. And it is my thesis that this tension helped to establish the criteria for the selection of psychologies to be incorporated into dynamic interpersonalism, as well as one of its specific expressions, responsive counseling. This can be seen most conspicuously in the fact that most of the

5. Edward E. Thornton, *Professional Education for Ministry: A History of Clinical Pastoral Education* (Nashville: Abingdon Press, 1970), p. 58.
6. *Preface to Pastoral Theology* (Nashville: Abingdon Press, 1958), p. 28.
7. *What Is Religion?* (New York: Harper & Row, 1969), pp. 31-32.

psychologies playing significant roles in Johnson's writings have been primarily clinical, not experimental. Even the theoretical psychology of Gordon W. Allport, certainly influential in Johnson's writings, must be counted as a "soft" approach, far more humanistic than experimental.

But perhaps this point will become even clearer as I identify the kinds of psychologies which have made their contributions to the development of dynamic interpersonalism.

The Psychological Input

The neophyte coming to pastoral psychology may find it difficult to understand why psychoanalysis appears to have played such an important role in the development of the pastoral psychology project. I recently taught an introductory course in personality theory to a class of fifty first-year theology students. Toward the end of the course, as part of an examination, I asked these students to pick one theory of personality which they considered to be most relevant and helpful in the practice of ministry. Not one student chose Freudian psychoanalysis as a viable theory! Instead, most elected to go with the Third Force theories. Yet if these same students should decide to continue their studies in pastoral psychology, they would soon learn from both the literature and their professors and supervisors (especially those over thirty!) that the psychoanalytic bias is deeply embedded in the field.

Why is this?

The usual explanation is that psychoanalytic psychology offers the most comprehensive personality theory. It has also been argued that given the kind of background and education of the typical ministerial student, he needs the corrective of the biological-medical approach indigenous to the psychoanalytic stance. Undoubtedly these two factors were at work in the complex process of accepting psychoanalysis as one important theoretical base in the development of pastoral psychology as well as clinical pastoral education. However,

I would suggest that there were other far more political reasons for this acceptance. After all, as a psychological theory psychoanalysis in the early 1900s did not present the sort of sober and sound project ordinarily expected from the theological community. As one psychiatrist has put it: "The generous use of psychoanalytic terms . . . within theology bespeaks premature and overenthusiastic commitment to a sectarian psychology that has not been able to win for itself a comparable acceptance within science." [8]

Of course, the assumption here is that the theological community would draw into its project only those behavorial science data thoroughly documented via careful research. This is simply not true, then or now. It would seem far closer to the truth to recognize the political reality at the time when pastoral psychology and clinical pastoral education were making their bid for a place in the sun.

Generally speaking, it was not with psychology proper that pastoral psychology was making its overtures. It was with psychiatry, and then as now psychiatry was committed to a psychoanalytic framework, to a medical model. The practical implications of this historic fact were many, and they were intense. To secure inroads into clinical areas, leaders had to deal with psychiatrists. Mental hospitals were run by psychiatrists. At the time, even the psychotherapeutic endeavor was believed to be the peculiar province of the psychiatrist. Little wonder that in the early days of pastoral psychology and clinical pastoral education the situation was similar. Although the first edition of Johnson's *Psychology of Religion* had a strong affinity with academic psychology, what made it somewhat different—as Hiltner noted in his survey[9]—was its *therapeutic* orientation. Therapeutic in this context meant dynamic and clinical, and, at least for the psychology of religion, a stress on the concept of the unconscious.

In this regard, it is interesting to note that the scientific

8. Orville S. Walters, "Theology and Changing Concepts of the Unconscious," *Religion in Life*, 37 (1968), 125.
9. "The Psychological Understanding of Religion," p. 75.

psychology contained in the 1945 edition of *Psychology of Religion* is mostly of the academic kind characteristic of the late Gordon W. Allport, a scholar whose major theoretical project was to provide a corrective to the stress on the unconscious. This, I believe, is symbolic of the tension characterizing the evolution of dynamic interpersonalism.

If we remember that the kind of psychology generated out of the philosophic inquiry called personalism tended to be one in which *conscious* selves became the primary data, we can sense the intellectual dynamic with some ease. For example, Mary Whiton Calkins' self-psychology was in many respects a paradigmatic project out to discover a single datum for the young science of psychology. For her this datum was the *self*, but it was the conscious self. Although, as I have tried to show elsewhere,[10] Miss Calkins was able to assimilate several schools of psychology into her self-psychology, psychoanalysis was not one of them since she judged the concept of the unconscious to be "illogical and untenable."

But Calkins was a prototype of the sort of academic psychology which is manifested in the 1945 edition of *Psychology of Religion*. It is in the Jamesian tradition. And it was Gordon W. Allport who thrust this tradition into the heart of the psychoanalytic bias not by denying the unconscious, but by putting it in its place as an important, but not the only, crucible of motivation.

Given these factors, it was natural that the psychology of Allport and the psychology of Freud should be brought together in Johnson's early attempts to formulate a religious psychology. In one sense, the vital balance between these two theoretical projects constitutes a central force in the evolution of Johnson's dynamic interpersonalism. They are not, however, to be seen as academic vs. clinical, since for Johnson even James's *Varieties* is a clinical approach to religion.[11]

10. "The Self-Psychology of Mary Whiton Calkins," *Journal of the History of the Behavioral Sciences*, 8 (1972), 196-203.
11. Johnson, "The Clinical Approach to Religion," *The Journal of Pastoral Care*, 15 (1961), 7-12.

Rather, the tension is between the reality of unconscious motivation and the fact of conscious intentions. In *Psychology of
Religion* and in most of his later work, Johnson set about trying to give full recognition to both of these motivational problems.

It must be noted here that the influences of Carl Rogers,
especially his phenomenological emphasis, and the later
impact of Viktor Frankl, especially in his doctrine of the will
to meaning, were significant in the development of dynamic
interpersonalism. But when Johnson responded to Rogers, it
was at a time when Rogers had not as yet developed a full
personality theory. Indeed, the response was more in terms
of psychotherapeutic modes, as William Hulme points out
in the last chapter of this volume. And in the case of Frankl,
the appeal was based mostly on the psychiatrist's stress on
intentions and the potential power of the cognitive in motivation. In this sense, Rogers and Frankl contributed illustrations
to what was implicit in Allport's more systematic personality
theory. Said another way, Rogers and Frankl dramatically
showed a humanistic-personalistic thrust which was quite
compatible with Allport's theoretical psychology.

But the contributions coming from personalistic psychology
and psychoanalytic psychology do not exhaust the historical
aspects of dynamic interpersonalism. For if Johnson found it
necessary to synthesize the conscious-unconscious issue, he
found it equally essential to recognize the individual-social
problem. In this project, he turned to the theories and practices of Harry Stack Sullivan and Jacob L. Moreno.

In Allport and in Freud we find an emphasis on the individual. Society, the group, and the community are not ignored,
but they do not play central roles in the theories of the
personologists. And for Johnson, given especially his theological propensities and his growing interest in pastoral care
and counseling, this individual thrust needed the conditioning
and balancing of psychologies which placed greater stress on
the social.

In this regard and in keeping with Johnson's own writings,

it is necessary to note a stimulus from a nonpsychological source. I refer here to the contributions of the Jewish theologian Martin Buber, especially to his little book *I and Thou.*

If one were to do a reference analysis of Johnson's writings, undoubtedly Martin Buber would be in the top five referents. But it was not to the technical scholarship of Buber which Johnson turned, but rather to a relational modality able to encompass certain developments of interpersonal psychiatry and psychology, at the same time enriching naturalistic theories with a spiritual thrust. It is interesting to note in this regard that Buber's *Ich und Du* entered the English language as *I and Thou,* not as *I and You,* as some critics would have it.[12] For Johnson, the Thou apparently was a needed designation in that its numinous quality appeared greater than is caught in the word *You.* His general appreciation of Buber's designations is characterized in the following typical passage:

> To be religious is a person-to-person experience. The response of one person to another is radically different than his behaviour toward a thing. I will use a thing as a tool for some purpose, such as a chisel to shape a piece of wood to fit into a fireside bench. When the bench is finished it may have a number of practical uses, and also a rugged beauty which I may admire as the product of handcarft art. And yet whatever its use and however admired, it is still an inert thing to serve as an instrument for some person who uses it for his own sake. My relation to a thing has been called the I-It relationship. A thing may be manipulated according to the desire of the owner because it is a thing.
>
> But a person is not rightly to be manipulated or exploited, because he is a unique and creative center of experience and value. . . . A person is to be treated with respect for his feelings, because he is capable of joy and sorrow in the sensitivities and appraisals of self-consciousness. If I truly comprehend from my own experience what it means to be a person, and realize that another person is conscious of himself in equivalent though distinctive ways, will I not take him seriously enough to con-

12. See Walter Kaufmann's prologue and notes to his new translation of Martin Buber's *I and Thou* (New York: Charles Scribner's Sons, 1970).

sider what life means to him? For he is likewise a center of reference in sensing the meaning of our relatedness. In relation to another person I may experience an *I-Thou* relationship.[13]

It was this general theoretical and ethical framework of a relational sort which provided a psychotheological context for Johnson to place the psychiatric theories of Harry Stack Sullivan and much of the praxis of Jacob L. Moreno, primarily the psychological or social-psychological contributions which served the interpersonal aspect of dynamic interpersonalism.

In Sullivan dynamic interpersonalism found a friend with the prestige of the psychiatric community but without the strictly Freudian doctrines. Although Sullivan was influenced by Freud, he was also greatly inspired by the works of cultural anthropologists and philosophers. Even in his psychiatric orientation, Sullivan had been influenced by William Alanson White, a man whose theories already had an appreciation of the social built into them. We must remember that Sullivan's mature theory centered in the concept dynamisms, relatively stable configurations of energy which manifest themselves in interpersonal relations.[14] At the time, this sort of theoretical and clinical thrust ran counter to the individualistic bias implicit in much of orthodox psychoanalysis. But its general movement, as well as some of its specific theories, meshed well with Johnson's desire to find ways—authentic ways—of appreciating the role of social forces and conditions in the development of the individual without going the way of the sociologist.

Moreno provided Johnson with a similar interpersonal emphasis but with the added aspect of a social science *and* a therapy. It was Moreno's thesis that when persons respond to each other with open spontaneity, healing takes place. For Moreno these instances can take place especially well in group psychotherapy and in psychodrama, two expressions of healing

13. *Personality and Religion*, pp. 150-51.
14. Sullivan, *The Interpersonal Theory of Psychiatry* (New York: W. W. Norton & Co., 1953).

which recognize the social and interpersonal dimension of personhood.

As early as 1950 Johnson was writing about group therapy. His work with Joseph H. Pratt had sensitized him to the group approach,[15] and there is no doubt that the commitment to this form is deeply embedded in dynamic interpersonalism. But in more than technique and therapy, Johnson found Moreno's approach compatible with his total psychological-theological-philosophical project. "Moreno," wrote Johnson in 1957, "portrays God as the Father of all, who freely gives his creative energy to all creatures in every event and experience of spontaneous relationships. Spontaneity everywhere arises from the creative activity of God moving through interpersonal relations." [16] Again we see how a psychological theory generates a religious mode, a criterion essential if a psychological mode is to be assimilated into the total theory of dynamic interpersonalism.

If personalistic psychology and psychoanalytic psychology provided a dynamic in the area of conscious-unconscious, and interpersonal psychology added the necessary social corrective, it was left to systems psychology to round out the full appreciation of the whole person in relationship. Undoubtedly this attempt had its beginnings in the work of Kurt Lewin and its culmination in contemporary systems psychology and environmental psychology, the latter not fully assimilated into the design even today.

It seems to me that contemporary ministerial students who read Johnson often fail to grasp this particular dimension of dynamic interpersonalism. Again, it is necessary to appreciate the historical situation at the time when Lewin's writings came to the attention of American psychologists. There were, of course, the psychoanalytic and the behavioristic biases, and although markedly different in most respects, they both tended to center in on molecular units—psychoanalysis on the indi-

15. Pratt and Johnson, *A Twenty Year Experiment in Group Therapy* (Boston: The New England Medical Center, 1950).

16. *Personality and Religion*, p. 278.

vidual and his intrapsychic conflicts, behaviorism on the S-R bond and avoidance of intervening variables. Neither seemed to take interactional dynamics or the individual-environmental transaction seriously. Lewin attempted to do this without going to an existentialism which would rule out the approach for the scientific community. The task was to include the *whole* person in the attempt to understand behavior. Lewin turned to the concept of topology, a nonquantitative discipline concerned with the various kinds of connections and relationships between "spaces" and their parts. The topological psychologist saw behavior as a function of the momentary whole situation which includes the momentary structure and state of the person and of the psychological environment. The dynamic structures of person and environment may be represented by means of mathematical concepts. The language in this system was one of psychological regions, boundaries, field forces, vectors, valence, and locomotion.[17]

For Johnson, it was Lewin's emphasis on the dynamic and incessant intercourse of person and world which most attracted him. In Lewin's scientific attempt, however, impersonal forces are stressed—the person appearing somewhat incidental and temporary. It was there that some of Lewin's concepts must be seen as contributing to dynamic interpersonalism but girded and interpreted by a religious dynamic rather than a strictly scientific one.

Much of contemporary systems theory and research can be traced to Lewinian beginnings, and it is not surprising to discover in Colston and Johnson's recent volume the following definition of personality: "Personality is the dynamic mutual interaction of all systems which comprise and effect the organism."[18] Although in elaborating on these systems the authors include "physical, social, economic, political, ecological, etc.," it seems to me that dynamic interpersonalism has

17. Kurt Lewin, Ronald Lippitt, and Sibylle Escalona, *Studies in Topological and Vector Psychology* (Iowa City: University of Iowa, 1940).

18. *Personality and Christian Faith*, p. 22.

not considered seriously many of these nonpersonal forces. Nevertheless, a systems approach intends to take seriously the totality of man and his world, as in the case of dynamic interpersonalism, with the focus still being on personal consciousness.

Certainly a systems approach attempts to find ways of including modes of the personalistic, the intrapsychic, and the interpersonal, but the project of doing this in a balanced and authentic way is an exceedingly difficult one. In the case of dynamic interpersonalism, that project achieves its direction not alone from within the psychological theories themselves but from a crucible of philosophical and theological meanings.

The Selection and Interpretation Process

Although the above overview does ¬ot exhaust the identification of contemporary psychology's contributions to dynamic interpersonalism, I believe it does illustrate part of the process involved in the attempt to take seriously the developments in nontheological disciplines in the building of a form of psychotheology suited to the ministerial project. But such a major project does not happen—or ought not to happen —in a haphazard or frenzied way. Any reader coming to any pastoral psychology for the first time will note the presence of the "borrowing" propensity. But if he is at all familiar with the psychological world, he will note too the selectivity principle at work. In the case of dynamic interpersonalism, for example, he cannot help but observe the absence of the "hard" aspect of contemporary psychological science. Crass behaviorism or a pure experimentalism are not significantly represented. Nor is there in dynamic interpersonalism a hard line of theory construction, and very little in the way of experimentally based research. By the general standards of the scientific psychologist, the psychological contributions I have noted would be counted as "soft," far more clinical and existential than experimental and quantitative.

Why is this so?

Undoubtedly, there are many forces at work, empirical as well as speculative, in the working out of theoretical systems. Although space does not permit a full account of those apparent in the development of dynamic interpersonalism, I would like to note three which seem to me to be important in the formation of this particular pastoral psychology or psychotheology.

First, there is present in the selection and interpretation of particular psychological theories a broader theme than the strictly psychological. The theological and philosophical dimensions, for instance, are continuously present in the dynamics of selection and synthesis. This simply is not true in some other attempts at building a truly pastoral psychology where the psychiatric or the psychological cannibalizes the rich theological and philosophical traditions. In dynamic interpersonalism, the philosophical and the theological are ever present, providing a critical crucible of meaning with far greater diameter and circumference than a single behavioral science. This factor alone, I am convinced, discourages the premature closure which always appears at the throat of the young minister in search of a theoretical position. As it protects against premature closure and a reduction to a single behavioral science or medical model, it also guarantees a searchful stance open to the developments in the nontheological sciences. For those capable of tolerating this never ending search and able to stand a high level of ambiguity, this sort of guiding principle will be appealing. But appealing or not, the theological-philosophical circles continuously have encircled the psychological theories identified in this chapter.

Secondly, the empirical realities of ministry have played an important part in the formation of dynamic interpersonalism. In the years in which Paul Johnson hammered out his position, there was not a time when he was uninvolved himself in some form of ministry—teaching, counseling, psychotherapy, group work, supervision. The constant input from these experiential forces greatly conditioned the evaluation of psychological contributions. It is one thing to speculate about personality and religion, but it is another thing to have such speculations buffeted, gnawed, and smoothed out by the raw realities of the "clinic."

Thirdly and finally, it is necessary to note that dynamic interpersonalism as a form of pastoral psychology is the expression of personhood. In this sense, the first two observations above are subsumed under the third. Here I mean to say that like most personality theories, the author's presence remains an indelible factor. The writers of the chapters in this *Festschrift* and Paul Johnson's family, friends, colleagues, and students will easily find meaning in this statement.

The point is made clear in a very recent article written for the *Journal of Religion and Health*, where Paul outlines a confession of personal faith. It consists of the following convictions:

> *We live in a responsive universe.*
> *There is hidden greatness in every person.*
> *Persons need each other.*
> *We can learn to be one people.*
> *We cannot afford to retreat into despair.*[19]

Certainly these value claims—proceptive orientations, if you will—help to account for the selection and evaluations made of psychological theories just as such theories have helped to contribute toward the formation of the value claims. Personhood is the crucible—the dynamic mutual interaction of all systems—where all this takes place; and it is this task which still challenges the construction of a genuine and authentic pastoral psychology or psychotheology.

---

19. "What Can We Believe In?" *Journal of Religion and Health,* 11 (1972), 109-19.

Bases for a Pastoral Psychology

Judson D. Howard

Pastoral psychology as a discipline has yet to emerge. This is not surprising. Psychology itself is a young science still in the process of determining its theory and method, the nature and bounds of its inquiry. The churches have been even less interested than the public at large in the empirical study of man. Thus pastoral psychologists have been few. One of these is the man we honor in these essays, Paul E. Johnson. His pioneering work—manifested not only in what he wrote,[1] but in the scope of his enthusiasms and of what he did—is just that: the consideration of the bases for a pastoral psychology.

The need for the discipline of pastoral psychology is very great. There is not just the problem of extensive pastoral borrowing of psychological theory from other disciplines and professions;[2] there is also the absence of the contribution which pastoral psychology could be making to the broader understanding of man. The issues to be raised here have to do with pastoral psychology as a basic and not an applied science. Not that the latter is of lesser importance. Most pastoral psychological discussions occur in or have reference to situations of ministry, of pastoral care. Subdisciplines in the field of psychology are just as related to "practice": learning

1. "Bibliography of Paul Johnson," *Pastoral Psychology*, 20 (1969), 47-56.
2. Seward Hiltner, *Preface to Pastoral Theology.*

theory to the psychologist's practice of teaching, psychopatho-
logical and psychotherapeutic theory to the treatment of mental illness. Much can be said in support of the advisability of
the gradual development of psychological theory from within
the situation in which the psychologist finds himself.[3] My
purpose in dealing with basic rather than applied science issues is not to slight the latter but to underscore the crucial
role of scope or breadth of view in the churches' psychological
inquiry.

In the social sciences, the trend until quite recently has been
to narrow the scope of one's inquiry. The task of research is
far too difficult. Narrowing and specialization become a necessity. There have been other counsels for restriction. Behaviorism excluded data about human interiority on the grounds that
such were unknowable in any objective sense. Happily psychologists are now engaging in studies of language and symbols, cognition and feeling, physiognomic perception and
presence. Also, American psychologists have in the main been
very wary of admitting philosophy into their science; yet, as
John H. Flavell notes, Jean Piaget has made very creative use
of epistemology in his research.[4] The most fundamental exclusion from empirical study—of the religious and the theological
—is one in which scientists and churchmen have too often
concurred. The possibility that distortion[5] is thereby introduced needs seriously to be considered. The genius of a pastoral perspective may lie in part in the impossibility of sun-
dering the study of man into such fragments. The suggestions
as to scope which follow have to do with the empirical data
base of pastoral psychology. Although they are my own and
may not be the form in which Paul Johnson would have put

3. Susanne K. Langer, *Mind: An Essay on Human Feelings,* Vol. 1
(Baltimore: Johns Hopkins, 1967).
4. *The Developmental Psychology of Jean Piaget* (New York: Van
Nostrand Co.), p. 250.
5. David Bidney, *Theoretical Anthropology* (New York: Shocken
Books, 1967).

them, anyone who is acquainted with his thought and work will recognize his profound influence.

Bases for a Pastoral Psychology

First, the discipline of pastoral psychology should include the study of religious man. When Paul Johnson first came to Boston University, he had teaching responsibility for contemporary religions as well as for the psychology of religion and pastoral care. Such interests were deeply his own—he and Evelyn had been in China—and show in his writings.[6] There followed a long period when there were no formal relations between these fields. Now signs of a reversal in our department are appearing. Sometimes earlier insights are the best! Moreover, the study of religion is growing apace in the American universities. Claude Welch[7] thinks there is reason to divorce it from the domination of seminary faculties, to anticipate difficulty in integrating the social-scientific and humanistic approaches (he also notes that the psychology of religion has not flourished). Whatever the outcome of these issues, the setting of the university with its linguistic and other resources could provide a locus for the broadening and deepening of our understanding, scientific and religious alike.

Obviously it would be impossible to consider here the phenomenon of religious man in any extended sense, but let us look briefly at some conclusions of a few students of it. Ernst Cassirer's monumental study of mythical thinking[8] is one such, and his findings are all the more noteworthy because they in part derive from an even more monumental examination of cultural processes.[9] He finds myth and religion to be

6. For an example of this influence on his thought, see *Personality and Religion,* pp. 279 ff.

7. *Graduate Education in Religion* (Missoula: University of Montana Press, 1971).

8. *The Philosophy of Symbolic Forms: Vol. II, Mythical Thought* (New Haven: Yale University Press, 1955).

9. Also *Vol. I, Language* (Yale University Press, 1953) and *Vol. III, The Phenomenology of Knowledge* (Yale University Press, 1957).

one of several symbolic forms. He thereby discovers that the basic clue to man lies in the symbolic[10] and is best approached culturally.[11] This articulates the object-subject (world-self) differentiation in ways different from each other, each needing to be studied in and on its own terms—myth not being reduced to science, or language to mathematics, or art to any of these. The dichotomies which the mythical form articulates—of light and darkness, of good and evil, of sacred and profane—are universal dimensions of mythico-religious consciousness. Yet livingness[12] and presence—"myth lives entirely by the presence of its object" [13]—are peculiarly its domain: Thou and I, the latter finding its unity in and through ethical action.[14]

Mircea Eliade[15] comes to similar findings—the fundamental dimensioning of the sacred and the profane, the articulation of sacred space and time—and concludes that the sacred founds and centers primitive man's cosmos, putting him in touch with his origins and power and reality, thereby annulling the disintegrative and the chaotic. Arnold van Genep[16] sees the data of religious practice and experience in terms of the rites of passage—separation, transition, integration—which coincide with and have the function of negotiating periods of crisis, personal and social. Or there is Victor Turner's[17] turning from the anthropological study of the social structure of African tribes to that of their religious life and discovering the significance of *communitas* in moderating

10. *An Essay on Man: An Introduction to a Philosophy of Human Culture* (New York: Doubleday Anchor Books, 1953), pp. 41 ff.

11. *Ibid*, p. 87.

12. Livingness is a concern in art. See Susanne K. Langer, *Feeling and Form, A Theory of Art* (New York: Charles Scribner's Sons, 1953).

13. *Mythical Thought*, p. 35.

14. *Ibid.*, Part III, chap. 2.

15. *The Sacred and the Profane* (New York: Harcourt, Brace and Co., 1959).

16. *The Rites of Passage*, tr. by Monika B. Vizedom and Gabrielle L. Caffee (Chicago: Phoenix Books, 1960).

17. *The Ritual Process, Structure and Anti-Structure* (Chicago: Aldine Publishing Co., 1969).

the shock of separateness and differentness which social structure or illness or incapacity brings about. And Robert N. Bellah [18] sees individuation as an ever clearer emergent theme in the developing history of world religions.

Several observations occur to me from this all too brief excurus. A phenomenon as universal as religion can hardly be an arrant feature of man—e.g., Max Muller's observation that mythical thought is diseased. If there is difficulty in integrating the study of religious man within the social sciences, the latter's epistemological foundations may be too narrow. Scientists have, by and large, been interested in the inanimate object, actively deanimating and deanthropomorphizing the concepts they borrowed from the common cultural heritage. Though necessary for the study of the physical world and the inanimate, such is hardly adequate for understanding the personal and the animate: presence and Thou and I. Moreover, if Cassirer is correct when he claims that object and subject are always in correlation, the scientific preoccupation with the "objective" reflects a serious distortion of the knowing process. Science has often neglected to specify, indeed even to mention, the subjective or the position of the subject.[19]

The significance of religious conception begins to emerge as a concern with (a) the growth and welfare of the subject (person-in-community), who in increasing awareness stands in relation to a meaningful world, and (b) the objective source of that growth and support in the heights and depths of the cosmos. Once we become aware that religious man is very much concerned with the subjective pole—Cassirer notes that religious knowledge is distinguished from other sorts by the character of belief [20]—the many facets of religious

18. "Religious Evolution," in *Reader in Comparative Religion, an Anthropological Approach*, ed. by William A. Lessa and Evon Z. Vogt, (2nd ed.; New York: Harper & Row, 1965).

19. John Macmurray, *The Self as Agent* (New York: Harper & Brothers, 1957), p. 131.

20. *Essay on Man*, p. 101.

conception become clearer. The cosmos which the sacred founds and centers is a phenomenological one: man must live in a meaningful world, ever expanding its borders at the expense of the chaotic and foreign and unknown. The rhythms of his existence and personal growth as well as the structures of his society and the nature of his involvements therein are as much a part of that world as are space and time. Pastoral psychology must thus study both the cultural (communal-familial) and the personal (idiosyncratic-organismic). It is a social psychology which of necessity focuses upon symbol processes, for they are the fundament of religious man's cosmos.

A second area is Hebraic-Christian man. The reader may aver: Is not this a subspecies of religious man, in both the categorical and the factual sense? Though the answer is yes in both instances, the study of the Hebraic-Christian tradition launches us into issues which might not otherwise be encountered. The assessment of the role of tradition is one. As a result of our locating religious processes in symbolic activity, we see that the rather widespread contemporary view that tradition is unnecessary or dispensable is wide of the mark. Man's understanding of his world is always in the terms of his enculturation. To study one's tradition, then, is to learn more about one's self. There are paradoxes, however. Just as the fish cannot discover the ocean without out-of-ocean experience,[21] so the study of Hebraic-Christian man in part depends upon that of religious man. The Christian image of a wholly Christian world has implicit in it the destruction of its own self-understanding. Moreover, the Christian concept of missions may have sometimes erred in its assessment of the traditions it displaced—the psychic depths out of which conversions come are non-Christian in origin.

There are reasons to suppose that the Hebraic-Christian differs in basic ways from other religious perspectives. Both

21. Karl Mannheim, *Essays on the Sociology of Knowledge,* ed. by Paul Keckskemeti (New York: Oxford University Press, 1952).

Bases for a Pastoral Psychology

Cassirer and Eliade note that the conceiving of time (as linear) was different from the Indo-European (as cyclical), with the consequent valorization of history and the looking for God in the future, of all places! How great the differences are is hard to determine. In the Hindu story of Indra[22] and the biblical one of Adam and Eve, evil and social control are very differently conceived; peace and harmony are themes of one, while freedom and responsibility are themes of the other.

In recent years, and in part as the result of a concern to determine the theology of the Bible in and on its own terms,[23] several fine studies of the Old and New Testaments have emerged which are useful for their contribution to the understanding of man. According to Gerhard von Rad,[24] the mighty acts of God were early confessed by Israel, yet even from the beginning there was also a reverencing of the common life so that the seeing of Yahweh's providence in ordinary daily events represented no great break with tradition. He says that the Israelitic dealing with extensive complexes of connected history had incalculable effects upon Western spiritual development.[25] It is interesting that the concept of history and the irreversible (linear) character of some life processes underlie modern views of personality. Much has also been made lately of hope and the orientation toward the future.[26] In searching for the bond between the Old and New Testaments, Walther Eichrodt [27] finds it in the notion of covenant. Only a little reflection shows the closeness of that

22. Heinrich Zimmer, *Myths and Symbols in Indian Art and Civilization*, ed. by Joseph Campbell (New York: Harper & Row, 1946).
23. Krister Stendahl, "Biblical Theology, Contemporary," *The Interpreter's Dictionary of the Bible* (Nashville: Abingdon Press, 1962).
24. *Old Testament Theology*, Vol. 1, tr. by D. M. G. Stalker (New York: Harper & Row, 1962).
25. *Ibid.*, p. 50.
26. Thomas Oden, *The Structure of Awareness* (Nashville. Abingdon Press, 1969).
27. *Theology of the Old Testament*, Vol. I, tr. by J. A. Baker (Philadelphia: The Westminster Press, 1961).

concept to the modern ones of interpersonal relations, of status and role. Johs. Pedersen[28] presents a wonderfully detailed picture of Israelitic psychology, of the individual soul and the community and the father's house, complexly interjoined. His discussion of the role of dreams, of the unity of the soul, of the differentiation in the verb of incomplete and completed action, and of the role of ecstasy in the prophets brings to mind the theory and research of modern psychologists—e.g., Sigmund Freud and Wolfgang Wertheimer, Kurt Lewin and Abraham Maslow. How different the picture we get in reading Pedersen is from Numa Denis Fustel de Coulanges'[29] description of Greek and Roman religion as founded upon Greek and Roman family life—this in spite of the patriarchal character of both!

Though the Hellenistic church had a profound effect on the emerging Christian *kerygma*, Rudolf Bultmann[30] feels that the earliest church had a profounder one, the introducing of the concept of the people of God. So salvation history became the church's history. Undoubtedly New Testament anthropology is related to the various cultures of that period, but the concern with persons (Bultmann says that, unlike the prophets who addressed the nations, Jesus addressed individuals) and with death and resurrection seems to be transcultural in character. So also is the affirmation of the Incarnation, carrying forward the insight of the Yahwist that somehow man occupies a special place in all creation, a place which Pierre Teilhard de Chardin[31] thought should be more fully recognized within both science and Christianity. The contributions of church history to the emergence of

28. *Israel, Its Life and Culture,* Vols. I-II (Copenhagen: Branner Og Korch, 1926).
29. *The Ancient City,* tr. by Willard Small (Garden City, N. Y.: Doubleday & Co., 1967).
30. *Theology of the New Testament,* Vol. I, tr. by Kendrick Grobel (New York: Charles Scribner's Sons, 1951).
31. *The Phenomenon of Man,* tr. by Bernard Wall (New York: Harper & Brothers, 1955).

modern man are far beyond my powers to detail:[32] monasticism and its contribution to man's understanding of himself [33] and his inner life;[34] the great Christological debates in relation to human will; the defining of the sacraments and thereby the ministry to persons-and-community in crisis;[35] the development of the parish school and the university; the turning from a preoccupation with life beyond this world to life and work within it. It is curious that the centuries of development of Western thought have not been sifted more systematically for their psychological and anthropological implications. Even though Augustine has been recognized as the first psychologist, the message does not seem to get through: his work and that of many theologians and historians are symtomatic of a basic and abiding Christian concern with man and his development.

The influence of Paul Johnson's interest in biblical and church history on his psychology is extensive. In fact, his commitment has laid him open to the charge that he was not objective enough in his role as psychologist. As more is learned about the personal [36] and social foundations of knowledge, however, the force or thrust of such a charge will be less evidently true; i.e., less taken for granted as scientific common sense. A person's commitment to and participation in his tradition will also be weighed for their positive contribution, according to this view.

A third area basic to pastoral psychology is the study of pathological man. The term is not generally used in Christian discussions. More commonly, man is considered in his sinful or fallen condition. Yet the wider context of concern for

32. Williston Walker, *A History of the Christian Church* (rev. ed.; New York: Charles Scribner's Sons, 1959).

33. Bellah, "Religious Evolution."

34. Erik Erikson, *Young Man Luther* (New York: W. W. Norton & Co., 1958).

35. John T. McNeill, *A History of the Cure of Souls* (New York: Harper & Brothers, 1951).

36. Michael Polyani, *Personal Knowledge* (New York: Harper Torchbooks, 1958).

man within the Hebraic-Christian tradition reveals that the latter is far too narrow a view. Although there is ample evidence to show that in biblical and church history sin was and is a central theme, the sources of man's difficulties and plight are not limited to his failures in responsibility, as Pedersen's discussion[37] of the bases of either the weakened state or the untrammeled growth of the soul indicates. One large factor in the split between Jesus and the religious leaders of his day was their differing attitudes toward publicans and sinners. Beyond the issue of the latter's responsibility, Jesus saw their pathological condition and knew that to be the *raison d'être* and purpose of ministry. The early Christians were known for their care of the poor and the sick, the dying and the dead.

One of the remarkable developments of our time is the modern mental health movement. The church's participation in that has been and will be important,[38] yet there is reason to feel that it could have been better. The events at Worcester (Massachusetts) State Hospital provide a case study in point. It was there that Anton T. Boisen, in the early 1920s and after a severe schizophrenic episode, began in earnest his Christian ministry and his training of clergy. He worked from two basic convictions—that the crisis of mental illness could be and is best seen as a religious one with great potential for religious growth, and that the study of living documents is essential to pastoral education.[39] The resulting clinical training movement revolutionized the preparation of the clergy. Remarkable as this is, it is an eye-opener to learn of the earlier role of religious participation in patient treatment at Worcester.[40] Modeled after the York (England) Retreat of

37. *Israel, Its Life and Culture.*
38. Howard J. Clinebell, Jr., *Community Mental Health: The Role of Church and Temple* (Nashville: Abingdon Press, 1970).
39. *The Exploration of the Inner World* (New York: Harper & Brothers, 1936).
40. J. Sanbourne Bockoven, "Some Relationships between Cultural Attitudes Toward Individuality and Care of the Mentally Ill: An Historical Study," in *The Patient and the Mental Hospital,* (ed. Milton Greenblatt *et al.* (Glencoe, Ill.: The Free Press, 1957).

the Quakers, the hospital functioned on a "moral" treatment plan, which meant treating the patient as a person and providing him with all those activities that were to be had outside the hospital. The discharge rate was quite high then, especially when compared with the one-in-twenty rate of 1920. Kraeplin in the meantime had pronounced schizophrenia—the most intractable of the mental illnesses and the largest single group in mental hospital populations—to be a downward deteriorating somatic process. In consequence, relational aspects dropped out of treatment. If the churches had done some empirical study from their "moral" perspective, the case might have been different. There would at least have been a view to counterpose Kraeplin's.

All of pathology should be examined in pastoral psychology: the wish for blessing is a very ancient theme in the Hebraic-Christian tradition; the doctrine of redemption (or concern with man's pathological condition) long preceded the doctrine of creation (or concern with his normal and developmental condition). So large an area cannot be considered here, but there is one subarea I would like to raise—schizophrenia—because issues central to it (for example, trust and mistrust) have always been central in religion. Also, it was Boisen's malady and is the most intractable of all the mental illnesses.

A pioneer in its understanding and treatment, Harry Stack Sullivan[41] differed radically from Kraeplin—in being interested in the explanation rather than in the description of mental illness and in seeing interpersonal relations as the source and domain of such illness and the area in which the psychiatrist needed to be expert. By age one, the child has come to live in a world of signs (symbols) which, if they signify anxiety, lay the foundations for the self-dynamism and bad personifications resulting in a drastically reduced capacity for integrating satisfactory relationships and for high-grade learning. Opportunities for the reversal of this trend occur at the beginning of childhood and later with the same-

41. *The Interpersonal Theory of Psychiatry.*

sexed chum relation of puberty, but by and large the future does not portend well. In sum, Sullivan was concerned with the effects of people—and what they believed their training responsibilities to be—upon human development. This led him into the study of language and culture.

Harold F. Searles's[42] clinical work with this illness led him to the discovery of the fundamental place of the good early (symbiotic) mother-child relationship. Marguerite A. Sèchehaye[43] confirms this. She also found in her work with Renée, a young French girl who suffered a severe break with reality, that symbolization plays a major role in personality development. William Ronald Dodds Fairbairn's[44] work in this area led him to put object relations (a large but unsystematic part of Sigmund Freud's theory) ahead of impulse psychology. All these therapists' debt to Freud is enormous, yet each revised that theory, unanimous in being less concerned with the Oedipal period and its conflicts and more with early psychic states.

K. R. Eissler[45] has remarked that the church was once the institution which treated schizophrenics, and he wonders why it ever gave up the privilege of doing so. What has been and may be learned from this area of pathology? In its main outlines, the church's understanding of human nature is quite profound: the interpersonal basis of personhood and the place of trust and love in that togetherness and differentiation; the very great problem which evil presents and the necessity that it be overcome; the importance of presence and the animate (personification or symbol or object); the crucial role

42. *Collected Papers on Schizophrenia and Related Subjects* (New York: International Universities Press, 1965).

43. *Autobiography of a Schizophrenic Girl*, tr. by Grace Rubin-Rabson (New York: Grune & Stratton, 1951); also *Symbolic Realization*, tr. by Barbro Wursten and Helmut Wursten (New York: International Universities Press, 1951).

44. *An Object-Relations Theory of the Personality* (New York: Basic Books, 1954).

45. "Remarks on the Psychoanalysis of Schizophrenia," in *Psychotherapy with Schizophrenics*, ed. Eugene B. Brody and Frederick C. Redlich (New York: International Universities Press, 1952).

of the symbolic in the construction of reality. Yet there also appear to be deficiencies in that understanding. Emotions, particularly those around sex and aggression (Freud), are not adequately dealt with via suppression and repression.

Searles found strong emotions to be the most difficult problem confronting his patients. Socialization, understood as learning the dos and don'ts, may be permanently life-crippling at its worst (Sullivan, Sèchehaye) and shallow at its best when compared with the opportunity for the young organism to grow into responsible personhood (ego development) in relation with others. Anxiety and its pervasive effects have not been fully appreciated. And the problem of evil is far more difficult than had been envisioned—removal by exorcism[46]—even though the goal remains getting rid of bad personifications (Sullivan) or bad internal objects (Fairbairn). For what is entailed is the long and difficult work of psychotherapy and the working out of constructive relationships in family and community.

When Paul Johnson came to Boston University, he entered a setting where interest in the pathological had existed for some time. That history, though fascinating, is too complex to detail adequately here. One aspect of it, the relation of the school through Carroll Wise with Worcester State Hospital, was a portent of things to come. Under Johnson's leadership, programs for the training of clergy were started at the New England Medical Center, the Boston Psychopathic and Boston State Hospitals, and relations sustained with other clinical programs. Soon to follow was the Pastoral Counseling Service, made possible by the help of Albert and Jessie Danielsen. Paul was the first (acting) chairman of the clinical psychology program at the university.

In comparison with most other seminaries, these were pioneering achievements. What is more remarkable is the framework in which the psychological understanding of min-

46. Ida Macalpine and Richard A. Hunter, *Schizophrenia 1677* (London: William Dawson & Sons, 1956).

istry was cast—that of the interpersonal and personal, of person-in-community.[47] I take this to indicate that he and those in the personalist tradition at Boston University stood in a very ancient tradition—the religious generally and the Hebraic-Christian particularly—which had come to know and wrestle with the core issues of human existence. From the above it might seem that much has been accomplished, yet a hard look at the situation indicates it to be otherwise. Though the importance of interpersonal relations has been recognized for several years now, in comparison with other areas it is poorly mapped and understood psychologically.[48] The psychology of presence and the role of the animate object have yet to be written, although the work of several theorists (Sullivan, Fairbairn, Werner,[49] Schafer,[50] to name a few) gives us some hint of the magnitude of the task. Symbolization processes have also been neglected in a psychological atmosphere which stressed behaviorism and reality orientation. The task force mounted by all the churches and the seminaries so far is miniscule in comparison with the work needing to be done.

The life of the church is a fourth area to be included, but it presents difficulties. First, pastoral psychology becomes thereby broader than the field of psychology is generally considered to be: the person is studied in the context of his community and the ground of his being. The difficulty is more of an asset than a liability. The binding together of the religious and communal—e.g., in the Israelitic understanding of God's revelation as being to and through his chosen people

47. *Personality and Religion;* see particularly pp. 232-34.
48. Warren G. Bennis *et al.,* eds. *Interpersonal Dynamics: Essays and Readings on Human Interaction* (rev. ed.; Homewood, Ill.: The Dorsey Press, 1968).
49. Heinz Werner, *Comparative Psychology of Mental Development* (rev. ed.; New York: Follett Publishing Co., 1948).
50. Roy Schafer, *Aspects of Internalization* (New York: International Universities Press, 1968).

—is not only a fundamental theological insight but a psychological insight as well; man and his milieu are indissolubly intermixed. Second is the great diversity in church life. For example, the course in the psychology of pastoral care at Boston University has as its structure the life crises of persons in correlation with the rites and ceremonies of the church. Yet there is not unanimity among the churches as to the nature and role of the sacraments. Can there be any research of church life which does not slant its questions and findings in the direction of some sect or denomination or faith group? The danger of bias must be constantly in view. That is why the question of the analytic framework of church activity is here taken up before considering the crisis-sacrament correlation. Yet the possibility should also be entertained that the empirical examination of church life may lead to the discovery of more fundamental commonalities than are now apparent.

How, then, are the activities of the churches to be observed and analyzed within pastoral psychology? Since we have seen above that a perspective which is broader than the one usually employed in psychology is needed, we may find one in small group theory, which lies between that of the person and the community. In it, the focus is upon interpersonal activity. A common and simple mode of analysis is to sort interaction in terms of its relation to (a) the task, (b) the maintenance, and (c) the members of the group.[51] Proceeding in this way, what rough definitions might be used as an initial basis for sorting church activities so that the meaningful issues and problems are studied?

Paul Tillich's statement[52] as to what comprises the being-within the theological circle, the concern for that which is ultimate,[53] together with the concept of mission can serve as

51. Kenneth D. Benne and Paul Sheats, "Functional Roles of Group Members," *Journal of Social Issues*, 4 (1948), 42-47.

52. *Systematic Theology*, I (Chicago: University of Chicago Press, 1951), Introduction.

53. David Bakan, *The Duality of Human Existence* (Boston: Beacon Press, 1966).

a beginning definition of the task of the churches. Maintenance activities are harder to delineate, in part because they have often been derogated as the source of the church's ills. Small group research gives us a clue. In terms of leadership, these activities are less cognitive and more affective, in a word, the "caring about" activities of the group. If we include in these both intrachurch activities and those which occur in relation to the surrounding environment, we have a rough idea of what belongs in the maintenance category. Member activities have not occupied as significant a place in small group theory as the other two because they have been treated as individual and idiosyncratic, inimical to group purposes and goals. Here the Hebraic-Christian view is to be preferred, in its comprehending of the essential interdependence of the personal and the communal. The biblical concerns with redemption and creation, or with the healing and growth of persons, can serve as a rough definition of this category. It should be noted that each type of activity is as important and essential to church life as the others.

The term "church" has thus far not been defined. In Christian history there has been a tension between its use in a particularistic or local sense and a universalistic sense. Both meanings would need to be retained for the simple reason that any research of its activities must (1) take place in some specific locus, whether that be a parish or a seminary or a council of churches or some part of a hierarchy, yet (2) take into account that "that local church" is in relation to a larger whole and that that relation is essential to any analysis of its ongoing life.

Within this framework and in brief compass, are any significant issues or leads discernible? We begin to sense that church life is quite complex, in need of adequate resources and leadership. Small group research confirms this impression: leadership activity is a complex group property, no one person being able to perform all the functions involved; adequate group resources are vital to group life and growth. More

5 ०4 । ७
specifically, the cognitive character of task activities suggests
that any local church life will wither in isolation: a parish
needs academic as well as denominational and ecumenical
resources; the opposite is also true. The emotional and relational character of maintenance activity suggests that the role
of laity—those who stay and are the "interrelated" while
clergy come and go—in the enduring relations within and
without the religious community has been little appreciated
and poorly understood. Much can be done today in providing
consultation and resources for improving maintenance activity
both among its members and in the relations to its surrounding
environments. As to member activities, if the healing aspect
comprises in part pastoral counseling and the growing aspect
of religious education, we have some further inkling of how
slim the resources are in most situations.

A more traditional way to categorize church activities has
been in the terms of its worship. As the study of psychology
advances, it becomes apparent that there has been a very
sensitive ministry to persons in the churches' rites and ceremonies: infant baptism or dedication, adult baptism or confirmation, Holy Communion, the marriage service, the funeral.
We have already noted Genep's ideas about rites as negotiating critical passages. More recently in the mental health
literature, particularly in Erik Erikson,[54] there has been a
growing awareness of the significance of critical periods in
personal development and the crucial role of support during
them in strengthening the coping functions of the ego. Erich
Lindemann's[55] study of grief was greatly appreciated by the
clergy, helping them to see the processes and goals of grief
work more clearly. Recently, Gerald Caplan[56] has written at
length about the complex processes of pregnancy and birth.

54. *Identity and the Life Cycle* (New York: International Universities
Press, 1959).
55. Erich Lindemann, "Symptomatology and Management of Acute
Grief," *The American Journal of Psychiatry* (Sept. 1944).
56. *An Approach to Community Mental Health* (New York: Grune
& Stratton, 1961).

Suicide and the processes of aging and dying are other areas which are being extensively studied.

In the churches' sacramental ministry, there is a wholeness of context—of person and family and parish in relation to the ground of their being—which is marvelous in its richness yet simplicity. But there is also a growing awareness that the telescoping of these complex meanings and issues into a single sacramental act leaves much to be desired. Study of the symbolization process shows that for a symbol to be meaningful it must name or point to that which is already present or ready to be grasped. Sèchehaye's case study illustrates this. Renée was baptized in the church, but the meaning of that sacrament (according to Reuel L. Howe,[57] God's love for us in spite of our unacceptableness) was not existentially present in her family and its wider network of relations. In Erikson's schema, the foundations were being laid for much mistrust. Here an analysis in terms of task and maintenance and members may help to articulate the marvelous texture of the Christian life in which the sacraments occur, helping us better to understand human needs and the resources necessary to meet them in order that persons may have life, and more abundantly.

Paul Johson's perceptive grasp of the correlation of the life-crises-and-sacramental ministry of the churches came early,[58] before the emphasis upon crisis intervention in community psychiatry and social work. The other dimension of church life highlighted here, small group activity, was also an early interest. His eclecticism was truly remarkable. The many-faceted character of his anthropology is hard to boil down into its essence unless we keep in mind his abiding concerns with man—religious, Hebraic-Christian, pathological and normal—and with Christian life. I take this to be a sign or indication of the difficulty that any other attempts to map the domain of pastoral psychology will meet. Yet they can afford to be concerned with no less.

57. *Man's Need and God's Action* (New York: Seabury Press, 1953).
58. *Psychology of Pastoral Care.*

The Process of Symbolization

The above are four areas out of which theory in pastoral psychology should develop. Our examination of them has led to another area, however: symbols and the processes related to them. Cassirer says that man lives in a symbolic world; moreover, there are different symbolic forms, and they articulate different worlds of meaning, that is to say, different self-world correlations. Eliade's study of religious man comes to the same conclusion: the world which the sacred centers and founds and creates is not the physical but the phenomenological one; that is the cosmos which may be threatened with disintegration and chaos. Clinical data point in the same direction—the profound consequences for personal existence, estrangement and chaos, or health and wholeness—of early and continuing symbolic processes. These findings also confirm the correctness of the religious concern with the subject, both person and community.

According to Langer,[59] the clear recognition of the significance of the symbolic has come in the twentieth century. Cassirer[60] credits Heinrich Hertz with being the first modern scientist to move from a copy to a purely symbolic theory of physical knowledge. Actually, the religious discovery of the symbolic is very ancient and became a continuing theme in Hebraic-Christian and Moslem history, revolving mainly around the issue of idolatry. The alternatives were, according to Charles Williams,[61] between the acceptance or the rejection of images. Language is another symbolic form in which the awareness of the symbolic came early, the prior and apparently universal practice began the confounding of word and object. Man's use of symbols always seems to precede his awareness of them. Yet these recognitions, religious and linguistic, focused upon the symbol as such—the contrast was (and often still is) between what is symbolic and what is

59. *Philosophy in a New Key* (New York: Penguin Books, 1948).
60. *Philosophy of Symbolic Forms,* III, 20.
61. *The Descent of the Dove* (New York: Meridian Books, 1956).

real—and did not take into account the fact that awareness of reality is made possible through symbolic processes. Discussion in religion centered around whether or not to be a symbol user and in language around the nominal character of words rather than upon the processes of symbolization as such.

Here we are at the center of a whole tangle of issues that have occupied man's thought for centuries and which have radically affected knowledge-building activities. For example, symbols and symbolization have been little studied in psychology, at least in America, until very recently. The lacuna is related to the conflict between science and religion, to the former's loss, and is one more reason why the discipline of pastoral psychology is needed. In any maturing of that discipline, the symbolic could not be overlooked for long. Yet the religious appreciation of the symbolic is far from adequate, too. For example, in the church's discussion of creation there appears to be little appreciation of the fact that the Hebraic-Christian tradition—the very thought forms in which our world and ourselves are apprehended—is itself a tremendous creation, that *this* is the mighty creative act of God resulting from his worship.

The symbolic, then, is another area to be studied in pastoral psychology. It is immense, for it breaks the bounds of any field, be it the religious, philosophic, sociologic, psychologic, anthropologic, biologic, or that of the humanities. This vastness should not be avoided. Otherwise the wholeness of and the empathy with all existence, which Cassirer finds to be the central attitude in all mythical and religious thought,[62] are lost and can no longer comment upon the partiality of our visions. In its simplest definition, a symbol is something which stands for something else. Usually there is the added implicit assumption that such use is accompanied by awareness. After long wrestling with the question, I have come to the conclusion that the activity (conscious or not) which sets the

62. *An Essay on Man,* pp. 125 ff.

boundaries of the domain of the symbolic is simply: all "stand-ing-for." This definition certainly includes much that is not now included under most discussions of the symbolic, as, for example, the series of standing-for activities in vision—the images on the retina standing-for the external light patterns; the transformation leading to the innervations of the optic nerve which stand-for the image; the isomorphic pattern in area 17 standing-for the neural impulses; and the further ramifications which lead to the phenomenon Donald O. Hebb[63] calls visual "identity." Langer[64] notes that we have no psychology of plant life because sensation is absent or very rudimentary and because feeling is the mark of men-tality. This capacity for experience and for the changes which result from it, what D. E. Berlyne[65] calls epistemic behavior, is the basis of symbolic processes.

With so large a subject, what can be briefly noted about it here? First, the study of symbolization may help to integrate the disparate sciences about man. Hebb, citing Senden's study of persons born blind who later through surgery got their sight (needing a year of visual experience to recognize a triangle as such, the word triangle being difficult to retain in memory until that maturation is complete), proposes that physiological changes in the central nervous system must cor-relate with that behavior. When to this is added Jean Piaget's theory[66] about the changing nature of schemas and schematas which permit internal representation of the object and thus the solving of problems covertly, we must conclude that sym-bolization has its basis in organismic-historical process. From the clinical data we also find that interpersonal interaction is necessary to the emergence of personal identity. The self is a

63. *Organization of Behavior, A Neuropsychological Theory* (New York: John Wiley & Sons, 1949).

64. *Mind: An Essay on Human Feeling.*

65. "Motivational Problems Raised by Exploratory and Epistemic Behavior," in *Psychology: A Study of a Science,* Vol. V, ed. Sigmund Koch (New York: McGraw-Hill, 1963).

66. *The Origins of Intelligence in Children* (New York: International Universities Press, 1952).

symbolic achievement of a very high order: biologically, culturally, interpersonally.

Second, the study of symbolization may also help the churches to a more catholic understanding of religious activity and experience. Langer,[67] out of her extensive study of art, notes how narrow that point of view is which values the discursive above all else. Emphasis upon the word leads to this one-sideness. But man's spiritual life and development are not so limited. The nondiscursive forms of art—of painting and sculpture and architecture and dance and poesie and drama—have contributed immensely to that pilgrimage, and still may.

Thirdly, the study of symbolization within pastoral psychology may help to broaden the whole discipline of psychology where there has been a bias against the animistic, what Heinz Werner called the physiognomic, and the anthropomorphic. Although far too little study has been done here, there is reason to suppose that the animate is singled out for attention from the day of birth.[68] Psychoanalysts who work with children have appreciated this aspect of experience, although they have usually linked their interpretation of its significance to impulse control,[69] which is far too narrow, according to Fairbairn. The early internal objects have fateful consequences for early ego states, the foundations of the personality.

These concluding remarks about the area of symbolization only hint at its vastness. It was not an area which Paul Johnson formally singled out for discussion, although, as anyone can see, it is nascent in his thought and in religion generally. The lack is not surprising for the psychological climate in America was not conducive to its study. Happily, that is changing. Yet even in his system's incompleteness we see another feature of the emerging discipline of pastoral

67. *Feeling and Form.*
68. Unpublished paper by Gerald Stechler, Division of Psychiatry, Boston University Medical Center.
69. Selma H. Fraiberg, *The Magic Years* (New York: Charles Scribner's Sons, 1959).

psychology: an openness to growth and to the discovery of that which was from and implied in the very beginning. The churches have an image for this openness to the future and the past on the part of the present—the communion of the saints.

Part II

Pastoral Counseling

Foster J. Williams

"Even as Christ offered himself as mediator between God and man, and between man and man; so the pastor brings a mediating spirit into the world of conflict seeking a reconciling love. This ministry is known today as pastoral counseling." [1]

The pastor by tradition has been thought of as a shepherd who leads his flock to greener fields.[2] The counselor works with people in a sorting out process to discover who they are and what they are about. Pastoral counseling is a marriage of the love of God and the knowledge and skills of man. Objective observation, careful recording, learning about the normal from the abnormal have all given to the counselor, whether he be psychiatrist, psychologist, or pastor, insights about persons regarding how they work, how they grow, and how they interact. These insights are invaluable. When all is said and done, however, man finally faces the need to answer the questions about the ultimate in life. What is life's meaning and purpose? Whence did man come, and whither does he go? A pastor stands in the line of those who as theologians have gathered together the facts and drawn them into a unified, coherent, meaningful whole. In the final analysis each man is his own theologian. The pastor, however, can work with his people as they sort out their own thinking and make sense out of the facts with which they must live.

1. Johnson, *Person and Counselor*, p. 71.
2. André Godin, *The Pastor as Counselor* (New York: Holt, Rinehart and Winston, 1965), p. 12.

Pastoral counseling not only seeks to work with the individual in order to enable him to function as a fairly normal part of society, but moves through to the meaning, purpose, and values by which life is lived. Viktor Frankl calls this the "human dimension." [3] This Viennese psychiatrist insists that man is human by virtue of his spirit, by which he decides the central issues of his life and destiny.

Pastoral counseling is a dynamic interpersonal relationship where God's love becomes real to responsible persons who grow according to their choice. At least two people interact. Both grow. Each person is responsible for his own growth. Each person becomes a vehicle through which God's love is made known.

The following elements seem clearly important as a part of the experience.

The Counseling Relationship

The Context

The pastoral counselor is always related to a religious community. The American Association of Pastoral Counselors has insisted that when a man ceases to function within this context, he is no longer to be regarded as a "pastoral" counselor but instead as a psychotherapist, psychologist, or counselor without the legitimate use of the word "pastoral." [4] The American Association of Pastoral Counselors has insisted that ordination is the key to acceptance by the religious community. However, there are religious communities such as the Quakers and orders within the Roman Catholic Church where persons who perform the function of pastor may not be formally ordained. Some of the best trained and most pastorally oriented spirits in the religious community may be kept out of fellow-

3. *Man's Search for Meaning* (Boston: Beacon Press, 1963).

4. *Handbook and Directory, American Association of Pastoral Counselors* 1970-71, p. 20. Principle VIII: Statement of Private Practice and Professional Concerns.

ship with persons in the American Association of Pastoral Counselors so long as this definition of relationship with the religious community is maintained. Would it not be possible to define pastor according to function instead of ordination, and ask the religious communities to determine which persons in their community are performing this pastoral function?

It has been discovered that the context within which the counseling is done and the expectation of the person who comes for counseling make a positive difference to the outcome of counseling.[5] The pastor who is a leader in a loving community has a very important resource. This rather average, normal community of persons to whom the individual may relate both before, during, and after counseling can offer a challenge for growth, an area for practice, and support during change.

Integrity

Every counselor operates out of a value system. The ideal pastoral counselor has integrated this value system into his own life, and those who contact him experience it without any demand from him that they adopt it. St. Paul wrote, "I am what I am" (I Cor. 15:10).

A woman from New York City said that Paul Johnson impressed her the first time she met him. Why? He met her as a fellow rider in an elevator. She knew Paul. He did not know her. He was so genuinely concerned about her and her needs at that moment that she felt good for having met him. The pastoral counselor is not piously religious, but rather religiously pious. By that I mean he has a quality to his life that comes out of a kind of disciplined relationship with God that sets him free and enables him to communicate the spirit which sets men free. He feels good about being who he is. He loves himself and is able to communicate this freedom and love to his counselees. This means that he is free to be responsible.

5. Seward Hiltner and Lowell Colston, *The Context of Pastoral Counseling* (Nashville: Abingdon Press, 1961).

It does not mean that he is free to do what he wants to do just because he wants to do it.

Counseling is a very privileged position. It is important that the pastoral counselor keep in touch with the values by which he lives his life so that he does not exploit the persons who come to him and are vulnerable in the counseling process.

Respect

The pastoral counselor does not impose his own value system on others. He respects them. He respects their desire to grow and the decisions which they make that make sense to them.[6] The contract as developed in transactional analysis formalizes this respect.[7] The contract is drawn between the counselor and the counselee. The counselee says, "This is what I wish to do." The counselor says, "I am willing to take responsibility for working with you to do what you want to do." This leaves the counselee in charge of his life and the decisions which he will make.

Style

I believe in an incarnational theology. The love of God has always been communicated to man through a man who incarnated that love. Jesus of Nazareth was such a man. The gospel, the good news of God's love, is still communicated through the life of a man.[8]

An art critic pointed out that you can always tell the works of a master artist. There is something about the brush strokes, the style, which identifies the painting whether the painting is signed or not.

Characteristic of the pastoral counselor is the fact that in his

6. Carl Michalson, *Faith for Personal Crises* (Apex Books; Nashville: Abingdon Press, 1958), pp. 12-13.

7. Muriel James and Dorothy Jongeward, *Born to Win* (Reading, Mass: Addison-Wesley Publishing Co., 1971), pp. 231-37.

8. Carroll A. Wise, *The Meaning of Pastoral Care* (New York: Harper & Row, 1966), pp. 20-26.

affirmation of persons the unconditional love of God is clearly evident. In addition to this is the quiet confidence of the counselor that God (the Holy Spirit) is actively working in and through the persons involved and in every situation.[9] Tillich once declared:

> The power which makes acceptance possible is the resource in all pastoral care. It must be effective to him who helps, and it must become effective in him who is helped. . . . This means that both the pastor and the counselee . . . are under the power of something which transcends both of them. One can call this power the new creature or the New Being. The pastoral counselor can be of help only if he himself is grasped by this power.[10]

This results in a kind of indefinable something about his style which helps people understand who the Master really is.

Approaches to Pastoral Counseling

When counseling became a focus in theological education, theologians who were basically theoreticians adopted models from others, and to this day the pastor is eager to learn all he can from the behavioral scientists. It seemed that Carl Rogers' nondirective or client-centered therapy offered a protective device so that the pastor would do as little harm as possible. It became standard for most pastors to engage in nondirective counseling. However, as pastors have become better informed and have worked with and been exposed to a variety of approaches, each man tends to adopt the approach that makes sense to him. There is no one theory or technique which is uniquely fitted for the pastoral counselor. Howard Clinebell has set forth the *Basic Types of Pastoral Counseling* which are available in the many different kinds of situations which the pastor faces.

9. *Ibid.*, p. 29.
10. Quoted by Howard Clinebell, *Basic Types of Pastoral Counseling* (Nashville: Abingdon Press, 1966), p. 306.

Pastoral Counseling in the Local Church

The following are some insights gained from serving in the local church. They have been modified by working with ministers who are on active assignment. They are directed to the pastor who counsels in the local church.

Seemingly unimportant, inconsequential relationships are important. Every time the pastor relates to one of his congregation, he is either opening the door to a counseling relationship or offering support to a person who has been engaged in counseling. I believe that Paul Johnson is correct when he defines pastoral counseling as a dynamic interpersonal relationship.[11] This means there is something going on all the time. It is never static. The relationship is either growing or dying. When a man meets his pastor on the street or in a committee, he says within himself, "That's the kind of man I could talk to." When he sees the pastor preaching, he feels, "He's open, objective, and he cares. I could trust him." When he finds himself in conflict, he turns to the pastor. When the one-to-one or group counseling relationship is over, he returns to the community and, perhaps, may be intimately related to a small group. At this point he needs support. There is a sense in which every relationship is either precounseling, counseling, or postcounseling.

The performance of other tasks in the church can be enhanced by the insights which come from pastoral counseling. Pastoral counseling is essentially the development of the ability to communicate and relate to people in depth. It is the development of the ability to hear what people are feeling and to respond appropriately. It involves the development of the ability to understand what is going on within persons in groups. It is important for the pastor to learn more about how these skills can be used in the areas of organizational development, administration, preaching, religious education, etc.

Small groups save time in counseling. Many issues formerly handled in individual sessions are appropriately handled in

11. *Person and Counselor,* p. 47.

groups.[12] The group may be even more helpful. Premarital counseling groups, marriage counseling groups, personal growth groups, and groups whose focus would be areas of interest which numbers of people might share in common would multiply the contacts made in the pastor's counseling time.

Counseling is basically educational. The best education is the discovery of one's self. Content can be joined to a "leading out" of people so that they might discover themselves, their strengths, and the possibilities in life.

The church can support life by love! The church can in fact become the loving community. Persons live by "strokes." [13] This is a word which has been developed by transactional analysis to indicate the fact that all of us need the recognition that we actually exist. A "stroke" may be either positive or negative. If it is positive, it affirms the person as being worthwhile and worthy. The giver says, "I love you, you are important to me, you exist, I value you." A negative stroke may be in the form of punishment or condemnation, but at least it is a recognition that the individual exists. TLC (tender loving care) has become the prescription for life which is given by many physicians. People get well if their bank account is well stocked with strokes. People get ill and die if they are bankrupt or are living on a very narrow margin of affirmation. They can starve for love. The religious community can become a wholesome, healthy, loving community. Jesus said, "Love my people." [14] This is what it is all about!

The wise pastor will limit the number of sessions given to his own parishioners. No matter how skilled the pastor is, he will be wise to see one of his own parishioners only four or five times for counseling. There are several reasons for this: (1) If a person is going to benefit from counseling quickly, he will do so in the first four or five sessions. (2) The next seven

12. Thomas A. Harris, *I'm OK, You're OK* (New York: Harper & Row, 1969), pp. 202-12.
13. James and Jongeward, *Born to Win,* pp. 41-52.
14. John 21:17. Jesus asks Peter, "Do you love me? . . . feed my sheep." Also John 15:12, "Love one another as I have loved you."

to ten sessions are spent building trust for a deeper relationship. When that relationship is finally developed, transference may begin to take place. This means that the clergyman will be dealing with the loves and hates which the counselee feels for other people and transfers to the counselor. This is the transference neurosis encouraged by the psychoanalyst. A good deal of skill and understanding is required to handle the transference relationship constructively. The clergyman needs to be very careful lest he be drawn into relationships which do not exist or lest he minimize the feelings of the persons who are sincere in working out the feelings which they have.[15] The uninformed may naïvely hear the words of love as relating to them. What a disappointment to act on the words which are in reality a working out of feelings for someone else! And, in most cases, what a tragedy! (3) Persons who enter into long-term counseling sometimes end up by leaving the church. I recall one couple with whom I worked for about two years. When we were finished, they transferred to another church. They said, "We love you very much. We just don't wish to be reminded of all the things we have gone through together every time we sit in the church." I learned to refer long-term counselees either to professionals or to qualified clergymen from other churches whose parishioners I was seeing even as he would see mine.

The local pastor has unique resources and strengths which he needs to acknowledge and use. People do turn to him. He is regarded as the first line of defense by some mental health professionals. To borrow a medical model, the pastor is the general practitioner. He is backed up by a variety of specialists —medical men, psychologists, social workers, etc. He can find other professionals in the community with whom he can consult and to whom he can refer. He need not sell himself short. He can serve people well. He can listen to them, affirm them as important, and truly care. This is the healing relationship. Only a very few need more professional help. On the other

15. *Person and Counselor*, pp. 179-80.

hand, when they do, he needs to feel so secure within himself that he can easily refer.

The Pastoral Counselor as Specialist

Many pastors are finding a significant ministry in counseling. Some are on a church staff. Some work in counseling centers or on a mental health team. Morris Taggart studied the membership of the American Association of Pastoral Counselors and found that pastoral counselors were working in counseling services in educational settings, marriage and family counseling agencies, on the staffs of hospitals or correctional institutions, in industrial or commercial settings, or out of private offices.[16]

The position of area counselor is a full-time pastoral counseling opportunity. It is presented as an illustration of the direction one man's life has taken in a field that was virtually nonexistent a generation ago.

Who Comes for Counseling? Why and How?

In a study of one complete year's operation of the area counselor's office we see the following data:

Counselees Seen	Individual Counseling	Group Counseling
Pastors	57	74
Wives	46	64
Children	11	

Source of Referral for Counseling	
Self	69
Administration: district superintendent, bishop, or Board of Ministry	29

16. Taggart, "Membership Information Project: Preliminary Report" (Unpublished, Houston, Texas), p. 36. See the December, 1972, issue of *The Journal of Pastoral Care* for part of this study and some reactions to it.

Another minister	8
Parent	7
Psychologist, psychiatrist	6
Other	2

The fact that 57 pastors have come for counseling in the last year and only 46 wives does not adequately convey the fact that counseling is very often initiated by the wife where there is difficulty in the marriage. Couples are encouraged to attend the groups together. This is impossible where the wife works or is ill.

Several parents have asked the counselor to see their children. In two instances these parents were ministers referring their sons. This would mean that the total number referred by other ministers would be 10 instead of 8. Referrals by a psychologist or psychiatrist were for therapy provided by the church.

The majority of persons who turn to the area counselor are self-referred. This usually means that they have met the counselor and feel that they can trust him sufficiently to make a tentative approach. As rapport is established, counseling begins.

The Board of Ministry has established a testing program to screen candidates for membership in the conference. Some individuals are referred for counseling as a result of the test and interview results.

When an administrator refers an individual for counseling under threat that he must get counseling "or else," counseling is delayed. The first sessions are devoted to working through the feelings which grow out of that threat. In Indiana, we have worked out an approach to referral which, we hope, enables the person who is referred to feel good about it.

The issue of confidentiality is one of the major issues which the pastor faces in his work. We have attempted to deal with the fears of pastors and their families concerning the fact that they may be betrayed and hurt by the counselor in three ways:

(1) Geographical. The location of the area counselor's office is in the inner city, formerly in a business building, now in

an apartment house complex several miles from any administrative office such as the bishop or district superintendent.

(2) Development of philosophy. We are developing the philosophy that a person is referred to the area counselor out of pastoral concern and not because he is sick or being punished for his administrative, personal, or pastoral shortcomings. He is not branded by the use of medical terms, but rather he and we recognize that all of us need to grow. The counselor is available to those who feel uncomfortable with things as they are and wish to make some changes.

(3) The development of an understanding with administrative officers. The understanding with the district superintendents and the bishops concerning referrals is as follows:

(a) A letter will be sent to the referral source indicating the fact that an appointment has been made.

(b) There will be no communication during counseling about anything. Judgment concerning the functioning of the counselee must be made by the superintendent or the bishop on the basis of the behavior of the counselee. There is one exception. Communication with an administrator of the church can be established if, and only if, the counselee signs a release and understands in full the nature of the communication.

What Problems Do They Bring?

	Individual Counseling	Group Counseling
Marital	24	27
Personal growth	58	104
Family Relationships	12	3
Church problems	8	1
Vocational decisions	5	3
Mixed	87	33

Categories are always misleading. In the chart above, the individual has been placed in one category or the other according to his primary focus at the beginning of counseling.

Dynamic Interpersonalism for Ministry

The first category is marital. Fifty-one persons have been designated as marital since they focused largely on the relationship between the married pair.

One young couple new to the ministry came to counseling with the information that their marriage was on a shaky foundation prior to the wedding. There was a real conflict between her parents and his. The marriage almost broke up in the first few weeks. The wife was very resistant about facing any negative feelings. She wanted to emphasize the positive and "do it ourselves." The husband was very angry. He felt the need for help. Before the end of the first interview the wife was saying, "We are farther apart than we have ever been. I don't even want to try. Ours is an average marriage." The husband replied, "Ours is not average. There is no real communication. Both of us are rigid. I'm trying to find some way to work through our difficulty."

Another couple came whose ministry was drawing to an end. They were in their early sixties. The wife said, "We have only a few more years in the active pastorate, then we are going to be alone together. It seems to me that our marriage ought to mean more than it does or has."

The need for personal growth was the focus for 162 persons. These are those who need to understand themselves and learn how to more appropriately handle their feelings. Those who might be classified in one of the psychiatric categories appear here. One young preacher was referred by his district superintendent. He was described by the superintendent as irresponsible, undependable, and as one no longer able to be appointed. He described himself as "out of gas." He had a history of irrational movement and involvement in many kinds of organizations and activities. He entered school in the early sixties. By the time he came for counseling, he had been in attendance at seven schools but was not yet graduated. He had been twice married. He was once involved in civil rights activities to the point where he had been personally beaten. He had served five different churches. He had been hospitalized once. He was a very handsome young man but had a

122

way of exciting the people to fury. This need for personal growth obviously creates problems in the church and finally requires the man to face the question, "Shall I stay in the ministry?" Sometimes the individual who poses the question is not able to answer it, and the organization answers it for him.

Few who indicate a need for personal growth are so disturbed as the story above would indicate. The major concern of those participating in groups was personal growth: "This is the change I wish to make." This may be a reflection of the requirements of the contract. Many indicated they wished to identify and handle their feelings more appropriately. When people have been reared in a community where the expression of positive feelings had limited acceptance and negative feelings were denied, there can be real difficulty.

Fifteen people were involved in situations where family relationships were the basic concern. The counselee may be the child, the parent, or the couple. He may be having difficulty with either a child, a parent, or other relative who complicates life in the home. A fourteen-year-old daughter of a minister called and said, "I am having trouble with my father, can I see you?" A minister and his wife may say, "We don't know what to do with our son." Or the question may be: What do you do with parents who . . . ?" Again, "Aunt Susie just moved in. We really don't know her. She lived out West. Last Sunday night she arrived and announced that she was making her home with us."

Nine people have been listed as counseling primarily about church problems. These church problems may be organization, but they usually involve some kind of ruptured relationships with individuals in the church. A minister may be "programmed" to fail. In one way or another he manages to make the people in every church angry at him so that they get rid of him as their minister. In another instance a man was appointed to churches which he served for only one year each, over the last three charges. In his last appointment he was appointed for a second year. When he went back to the church, some of the leaders of the church waited on the district superintendent to refuse his appointment. He says that he has always conducted himself as a Christian gentleman, and he has never once spoken a harsh word, but he has his back to the wall. Obviously both these individuals have personal problems that need to be worked out before they can relate to a church. As they saw it at the beginning of counseling, however, they felt that what they needed was to learn better how to relate to or handle a congregation.

The fifth category is distinct from the category listed as church problems. This has to do with vocational decisions. It is usually phrased by the counselee in the question, "Should I stay in the ministry?" Or, "I have decided to leave the ministry. Now I feel guilty about my decision." One young man phrased it this way: "I have made up my mind I am going to leave. The only question is, when, and how angry will I be when I go?" Eight pastors wrestled with these issues in counseling.

A sixth category is named simply "mixed." When there is difficulty in one area, this difficulty usually spills over into other areas. The categories are not mutually exclusive. One hundred and twenty persons worked with problems in several of these categories.

Number of Counseling Sessions

Counseling Sessions	Individual Counseling
1-5	49
6-10	24
11-15	14
16-20	7
21-25	3
26-30	2
31-35	3
36-50	6
50 and over	3

The number of counseling sessions refers only to individual counseling. A person who has been seen for more than fifty sessions probably was active in counseling prior to the year studied. On the other hand, every file reported on has been active within the year.

Few people come only once. Many find that four or five sessions are sufficient to do what they wish. About 78 percent are seen under fifteen times. One reason for this is that many become members of one of the groups and cut short individual counseling.

Sizes of the Churches from Which Counselees Come

Under 100 members	4
101-200	19
201-300	19
301-400	24
401-500	4
501-600	3
601-700	4
701-800	1
801-900	4
901-1000	2
over 1000	11

It is interesting to note that while 69 percent of the counselees who turned to the area counselor came from churches of under 400 members, 12 percent came from churches of over 1,000 members. Speculation about what this means may be more informed if one realizes there are more than two times as many churches of under 400 members in Indiana as there are over. Does the fact that there are few counselees from the medium-size churches mean that these people are less secure and therefore unable to ask for help? Are those in the larger churches, then, more able to acknowledge their needs?

Referrals

Referrals were made to:

Psychiatrist	1
Psychologist	3
Family Service	2
Other	2

Referrals are made to other professionals who can serve persons in ways that the area counselor cannot. This may reflect one of the following conditions: the person to whom referral is made (1) has particular competence to work in a specific area; (2) is geographically more accessible to the counselee; or (3) is preferred by the counselee as a person with whom he or she would like to work. Thus, training and experience, geographical accessibility, and the very important meshing of personalities are all involved in the above referrals.

Description of the Group Counseling Sessions

One hundred and thirty-eight people have participated in sixteen small groups this year. A group meets for eight weeks. Two patterns are followed, determined largely by the amount of time available on the part of either the area counselor or the individual members. (1) The groups meet once a week for two hours for the entire eight weeks. (2) The groups meet for two weeks for two hours each. The third week is an extended session of from four to eight hours. The fourth and fifth weeks are two-hour sessions again. The sixth week is another extended session. The seventh and eighth weeks are two-hour sessions.

Extended sessions of eight hours added to the six sessions of two hours each gives twenty-eight hours of group time. This seems to be ideal, and persons involved seem to have maximum growth with this period of involvement. At the end of the eight weeks the groups dissolve, and any individuals who wish may register their intention to become a part of a new group in the future.

Each member of the group contracts with the group concerning the area of growth in which he or she wishes to work. This means that he asks the group to work with him to accomplish the task which he has set for himself. More real growth seems to take place faster in the small group than in individual counseling. However, not all individuals are ready for the group experience when they cry for help.

Transactional analysis has been found to be particularly helpful because it takes the past into account, enables the individuals involved to work in the present, and encourages the counselee to exercise his rational judgment in making decisions about where he is, what values really count, and where he wishes to be.

Conclusions

Pastoral counselors work in the local church and in settings which offer some kind of specialized ministry. In this chapter I have offered a definition of pastoral counseling and some suggestions which arise out of experience in both settings.

1. The local pastors who can develop the congregation as a support group are unique. Suggestions made to maximize the potential are:

    a. Seemingly unimportant relationships are important to build the trust necessary for counseling.

    b. The performance of other tasks in the church can be enhanced by insights from pastoral counseling.

    c. Small groups not only save time but may be even more effective to accomplish some tasks than individual counseling.

    d. The church can support life by love!

    e. The wise pastor will limit the number of sessions given to his own parishioners.

    f. The local pastor has unique resources and strengths which he needs to acknowledge and use.

2. Some of the insights which come from examining one year's work in a closely structured situation where pastoral counseling is a full-time job are:

    a. About the same number of men and women came for counseling.

    b. The suspicion of people can be faced openly and honestly allayed.

    c. The need for personal growth causes difficulties in marriage, churches, and every human relationship.

d. Leaders of medium-sized churches seem more reluctant to come for counseling than those from the small or large congregations.

e. Referral resources strengthen the quality of the services rendered.

f. Persons often benefit more rapidly from group counseling than from individual sessions.

As an area counselor, I find my work is fun. Each day is exciting. One never knows what will happen next! Growth is a glorious but painful adventure. The expressions of appreciation are sincere.

Marriage and Family Counseling

Robert C. Leslie

The contemporary counseling world has made a sharp shift from counseling individuals to working with persons in their interpersonal relationships. This shift is especially apparent in the area of marriage and the family. Increasingly, husband and wife are being seen together, often in groups; and whole families are being counseled instead of a single child. The interpersonal situations rather than the intrapsychic issues are the focus of attention. This emphasis on the interpersonal context is a validation of the orientation that Paul Johnson had advocated throughout most of his writings.

For the minister as counselor, the interpersonal emphasis is a natural one. Most of the counseling that comes to him is related to marriage and family concerns.[1] Some of it centers around a crisis such as the discovery of infidelity, or the proposal of wife-swapping, or the threat of divorce. In families, the urgent problem may be involvement in drugs, or the question of abortion, or disagreement over the stand of conscientious objection to war. In other situations the minister may work in a more educational way with couples or families who sense that the quiet desperation of their lives is inappropriate

---

1. Of 1,237 hours of pastoral counseling at the Indianapolis Pastoral Counseling Center in 1965, the problems dealt with fell into the following categories: "marital, 129; personality, 55; depression, 34; family, 34; divorce, 15; vocation, 14; sex. 8; religious, 5; juvenile, 4; psychotic, 4; finance, 3; premarital, 2; addiction, 1; and personal identity, 1." Paul E. Johnson, "Developing the Clergyman's Potential for Mental Health: Indiana Programs," in *Community Mental Health*, ed. Clinebell, p. 212.

and who seek better and deeper relations. In any case, turning to the minister for help is both an admission of failure in handling personal concerns and a plea for some immediate, positive help. There is thus an openness to counseling and, at the same time, an expectation of some sort of almost magical assistance.

In this chapter I am concerned with describing in quite specific detail how the minister as counselor can respond to the call for help in marriage and family concerns. My interest is in the kind of contribution that the counselor provides, that is, in the kind of input that he offers. I am thinking of the minister-counselor as playing a relatively active role and as functioning in a relatively short-term counseling pattern.

However else the counselor responds to the needs of the counselees, he demonstrates his concern. Here is a relationship of person, of counselees and counselor, of human beings working together for the handling of a real problem. There is no place here for a disinterested or purely objective counselor who feels none of the pain or who remains aloof from the hurt. Rather, the counselor is one who demonstrates, almost from the start, that he does care, that he is interested and concerned, that he will work toward a solution. Without losing the objectivity that comes from his disciplined understanding of personality and its various distortions, he nevertheless enters into the situation as a warm and giving and responsive human being.

One of the ways that his concern is expressed is by moving quickly into a therapeutic stance. It is my goal, very early in a counseling relationship, to intervene in a very direct way to demonstrate that I am prepared to participate actively in the work of handling the problem. This means that there is a minimum of social chit-chat and a maximum use of therapeutic opportunities. It also means that the counselor demonstrates his willingness to promote a structure in the counseling relationship within which opportunities for making some changes become apparent. It is my intent in this chapter to spell out in clear detail what the nature of these interventions can be.

Commenting on Observed Relationships

The first and often most effective tool for the marriage counselor is his own observation about relationships between a couple or within a family. One of the strongest arguments for seeing a couple together and for seeing a whole family in interaction is that the counselor then can rely on his own direct observations without needing to depend on secondhand reporting. For example, when a family enters the counseling room and the mother and daughter sit very close to each other on a sofa, but the father chooses a seat by himself across the room from them, without a word being spoken the family constellation is very clear. When the father talks about feeling excluded from the rest of the family, the counselor might say: "Then the way you are sitting, across the room from your wife and daughter, is a good indication of how you feel separated from them." Such a comment early in the opening interview makes it clear that the counselor is paying attention to what is going on, that he is using data given to him even though unwittingly.

Sometimes an observation may be made about positive factors. I recall working with one couple where obvious distance had crept into the marriage relationship, but in talking with them together I had the clear impression of a genuine desire for closeness. I commented something like this: "Although you have been talking about how separated you feel from each other, I sense a real desire in both of you to be closer. Could you express some of this desire for closeness right here?" With only a little prodding they embraced each other in a way which gave a lie to their statements of separation. Neither had been willing, or perhaps even able, to take the initiative to move toward the other until the counselor's observation opened the way. Their embrace in my office was a major step toward a resolution of their problems.

In a somewhat similar situation I recall a couple who had obvious problems and yet, when together, demonstrated a good

deal of affection and concern for each other. I commented to
them: "In spite of the very real differences in life style which
you talk about, I sense that you have a great deal more going
for you than most of the couples that I see here in marital
trouble."

Another couple talked a good deal about conflict, but as
they were leaving, the husband gave his wife a gentle slap
on her backside and said: "OK, let's go, old girl." The counselor could easily comment on the positive overtones of this
gesture which offset the negative tones of the earlier conversation.

Centering on Characteristic Behavior

A second type of counselor intervention comes when the
counselor observes several instances of the same behavior so
that he begins to get the feel of a characteristic pattern. One
of the most useful approaches I find in counseling is to check
out my observation with a comment along this line (to the
wife): "As I listen to you talk together, it occurs to me that
you have questioned the accuracy of your husband's statements several times in the last few minutes. I wonder if this
is characteristic of your relationship together." The next obvious step is a clarification of feelings about this fact which the
counselor has observed and commented on. Sometimes the
expression of feeling about this observed pattern opens up an
area for working on that has long been present but never really
faced.

It is virtually always useful in counseling to direct attention
to a person's perception of himself. To the woman who likes
to live a well-ordered and fully scheduled life, the counselor
might say: "Are you the kind of a person who likes to have
everything planned out ahead of time and who gets upset
when plans are changed?" Such a comment would be especially appropriate if the counseling session had centered on differing life styles between husband and wife over disruption
of plans by some external factor. To help anyone to see him-

self more clearly is a major goal of counseling, and self-perception is often aided by getting feedback from the spouse or other members of the family.

Sometimes the counselor himself is in a position to observe characteristic behavior under tension. I recall working with one young couple with whom it was difficult to decide the real problem area. However, when the young wife was confronted with an unavoidable conflict in schedule and made an unnecessary trip into the counseling office, she erupted in anger. Up to this point her behavior had always been so controlled and so graciously accommodating that it had been hard to sense what she was really like. The anger over the mix-up on appointments brought out the behavior pattern which her husband found so difficult to live with. Since the counselor observed her in her ugliest angry mood, he was in a position to talk with her about her characteristic response to frustration.

Group counseling of couples is of particular value in this connection. Characteristic patterns of interaction between husband and wife are picked up quickly by other couples. Thus a husband who virtually always speaks for his wife or one who consistently protects his wife in a parental way may be confronted with these patterns by other members of the group.

I recall one couples' group where the discussion of patterns of being on time or of being late was triggered off by one woman coming late. Her husband's comment before her arrival was: "She's always late." When I, as leader, asked the husband to repeat his comment in his wife's presence, her response was to admit that being late *was* a problem to her. She went on to say, however, that the group experience itself added pressures to her life, especially because her husband took no responsibility for finding babysitters to make her attendance possible. She was late because she had to make last-minute babysitting arrangements. By focusing on an observed characteristic behavior pattern, we quickly moved into a fundamental point of conflict in the marriage.

Clarifying Ambiguities

A third opportunity at which intervention is rather obvious comes whenever ambiguities are present. I recall one young wife who introduced herself to me as Patricia. Early in the initial interview I noticed that her husband referred to her as Suzie. In clearing up this ambiguity I stumbled onto a really major problem in this relationship. She used to be called by the nickname Suzie as a child, but in her efforts at breaking away from immature patterns carried over from childhood, she was presenting herself now as Patricia, using her given name. Her husband's refusal to make the transition from the name she had gone by when he first met her symbolized for her his refusal to allow her to grow up. By clarifying the ambiguity we were projected into the heart of their conflict.

The counselor can often pick up the ambiguity of a double message. When a wife demands that her husband, who has been stepping out on her, seek marriage counseling with her, and then, in the presence of the counselor, virtually gives the husband permission to do as he pleases, a mixed signal is being sent. I recall counseling in such a situation in which I sensed a double message. In role-playing the wife's alter ego (i.e., standing behind her and speaking out loud for her), I exaggerated her indifference about his behavior by saying: "You can do whatever you please. It's your life, and you can lead it any way you want. Go on and sleep with anyone who comes along. It doesn't make any difference to me." The wife very quickly disowned such words and, with only a little encouragement, spoke more directly of her feelings of hurt and anger. It turned out that the basis of the difficulty which led to the husband's hanky-panky was her inability to give him a clear message to let him know how she felt. If a counselor chose not to role-play, he could have worked on the same point, although with less direct impact, by saying: "Even though you say you don't care, that it doesn't make any difference to you, I get the feeling that deep inside you are really very hurt and very angry." If need be, the discrepancy between her insistence on counseling and her indifferent manner could be pointed out.

Ambiguities in appearance can often provide a useful key in counseling. A woman who appeared to be ten years younger than her real age responded to the counselor's observation about this fact by responding that people generally thought of her as much younger than she was and that her mother had always treated her like a little girl. How she reinforced the misperception of her age became the subject for discussion. In another instance, a woman who arrived at the counseling session dressed as if she were going out on a special date was confronted by the counselor with what seemed to be the inappropriateness of her dress. By dealing with the ambiguity of going for counseling but dressing for a date, the counselor clarified what she could expect from counseling, and thus dealt with a situation that could easily have become sticky for both. Indeed, to clarify ambiguous expectations about counseling is one good way of establishing clear understanding about profitable roles for both counselee and counselor.

Structuring for Disclosing Feelings

A fourth counseling input capitalizes on the counselor's strategic role by providing a structure within which feelings are uncovered. Most couples or families relate quite easily in terms of facts. Thus a couple that has been apart because of a business trip over which neither had any control can talk freely about what they did in each other's absence. In many instances, however, the facts of their activities do not even touch on the feelings about the absence. In working with a couple where expression of feeling is difficult, I like to invite each to role-play; for example, how each is feeling as they approach the moment of reunion after an absence. It takes only a little prodding to help them to talk, not about the events they have experienced, but their feelings about them. I would do it something like this (to the husband): "You are returning from a long weekend business trip that took you into four different states. What is going through your mind as you walk up the walk to your front door on your return?" Most men will enter easily into the situation, will simulate getting out of their car, walking up to the door, getting out their key. But usually it is hard to put their feelings into the first person. Often they need a bit of help. "Speak your thoughts in the first person. Say, 'I am feeling . . .'" The role-playing can even be extended to include the opening words that the husband might speak to his wife. A variation on this same approach is to invite the wife to role-play the husband as she sees him and then as she would like him to be. It is quite possible for a husband to gain an entirely new perspective on what expectations his wife has for him through such a role-play.

The point is that the counselor is in a good position to structure experiences which can involve considerable learning about showing feeling. I recall one husband who was lamenting the fact that he and his wife never seemed to have anything to talk about. I asked him to tell me what his day had been like that day. He reported that he had attended the funeral of the young daughter of a business associate and that he had been almost overwhelmed by the thought the young girl might have been his daughter. When I asked him if he would tell this to his wife, he said it wouldn't even occur to him to tell her because she didn't know the people concerned. I invited him to role-play telling his wife about the whole event, including especially the feelings that he had felt so keenly. It wasn't natural for him, but with a little help he was able to stumble through, and so to make more likely an actual sharing of the event with his wife.

On one occasion a mother told, with tears, of how she was unable to touch a child whom she had adopted because he had run from her when she had first tried to embrace him. Unable to risk further rejection, she had simply not attempted to touch him again. Now, literally years later, she was overwhelmed with feelings both of guilt and of longing. In a role-playing situation we played out her going to her boy's room, her knocking on his door, her stumbling efforts at declaring her longing to hold him close to her. When she left the counseling hour, she was determined to try to reach her son. That night she phoned, almost in despair, to report that she couldn't go through with it. I asked if she thought she might be able to in my office the next day. She said she thought she might. I urged her to bring the boy in. When they came together the next day, I asked her to tell him what she had told me. Hesitantly, she did so. He responded with tears. She cried, and then she moved toward him, and they hugged each other tightly. I put my arms around them both, and the three of us cried happily together!

Most communication fails because only facts and not feelings get communicated. The counselor can usually enhance the communication process by training husband and wife and other family members to speak out the feelings that are accompanying their acts. Sometimes the counselor can enter the situation himself in terms of the feelings he is experiencing: "I'm feeling frustrated in not knowing how to respond to you because I do not get a clear signal about what you are really feeling. Can you help me to know what is going on inside you right now?"

Providing Stimulus for Movement

I have been presenting the marriage and family counselor as one who takes an active role in intervening in the interest of helping people to work through their problems in relationships. Such a counselor is one who constantly works at providing a stimulus for movement. He is not one who sits back passively while the problem situation is described. Rather he is one who helps to create an environment in which progress toward a solution can be experienced.

A part of the stimulus that the counselor provides comes in linking, in typing together what might otherwise be seen as unrelated experiences. For example, the counselor might say: "You have been talking about how you feel pressured at home. Do you also feel pressured into extramarital sex?" The implication is that the problem may have more to do with feeling pressured in general than with specific sexual concerns.

The linking function is especially effective when the counselor himself experiences the tensions present in a marriage. For example, a wife manipulates her husband behind his back and now in counseling tries to manipulate the counselor by threatening to terminate counseling if her husband is brought into the picture. The counselor experiences the wife as a controlling person, and he uses the experience to help her to see how it must feel to the husband.

Another stimulus for helping the relationship to move from a nonproductive position is sometimes provided through direct information. Many couples simply need information about masturbation, or about sexual potency, or about timing for orgasm. The Masters and Johnson information that contradicts a long-held impression of a difference between a vaginal and a clitoral orgasm is often useful in clarifying misconceptions.[2] The use of vocational testing, or of reading about budgets, or of sex knowledge inventories may be a way to spur movement away from a plateau in counseling where nothing is happening.

Still another stimulus for movement is given by providing a way of conceptualizing a problem. One useful framework for understanding relationships is provided by Eric Berne in the system he calls transactional analysis.[3] By describing personality as having three parts and by labeling these parts Parent, Adult, and Child, Berne offers a way of thinking about human relationships (i.e., transactions) that is both graphic and appealing. By introducing such a system, the counselor serves as

2. For an analysis of the Masters-Johnson study, see Ruth and Edward Brecher, eds., *An Analysis of Human Sexual Response* (New York: Signet, 1966).

3. For a brief exposition of Eric Berne, see Colston and Johnson, *Personality and Christian Faith*, pp. 70-72.

educator, offering his counselees a way of thinking about their characteristic behavior and presenting a common vocabulary for talking about their relationships.

It is appropriate to conclude this chapter on marriage and family counseling with an emphasis on the counselor as educator. In many ways the minister functions best when his counseling ministry is combined with an educative function. Thus instead of being the expert who repairs broken relationships, he becomes a trainer who trains people in working on improving their relationships. In a day when change is so rapid, when the institution of marriage itself is being questioned, and when experimentation in alternative styles of family life is commonplace, the perspective of the educator is badly needed. This whole volume is living testimony to the contributions that counselor-educator Paul Johnson has made throughout the history of pastoral counseling.

Institutional Chaplaincy

David Belgum

As a novice pastor in the late 1940s, I searched for a place to study psychology of religion, pastoral counseling, and anything else that would help me cope with the personal and interpersonal problems of my parishioners. What I found was Professor Johnson's program at Boston University, around which he had clustered a variety of institutional chaplaincies and learning experiences: Boston Psychopathic Hospital and Boston State, Massachusetts General Hospital and Massachusetts Memorial, Judge Baker Guidance Center and the Boston Dispensary, to mention a few.

It was obvious that if a ministry of pastoral care were to be made available to the thousands of persons in need, it would have to take the form of *institutional* ministry. To the now generation words like "institution," "profession," "bureaucracy," and "establishment" represent depersonalization, bigness, and mass production. These impressions are quite accurate; but big problems require big solutions. Hence, large institutions have arisen to handle epidemics and widespread public health problems, like accidents and illness in our large cities, and growing population. Many years ago, when it became clear that tens of thousands were mentally retarded, each state created its "institution for the feeble-minded." Mental hospitals of two to four thousand patients were not uncommon throughout the country. Meanwhile, state and private university colleges of medicine had their thousand-bed teaching hospitals.

What fascinated me about these big institutions was the

developing emphasis on concern for the *whole person* symbolized by interprofessional cooperation. Clergymen were learning how to work as members of a team adding their perspective to that of physicians, social workers, nurses, and others. Interdisciplinary case conferences demonstrated time and again how the wholistic approach to the patient or client contributed to a more thorough diagnosis and a more realistic and comprehensive treatment plan. Such ministry was not only a service, but a constant learning experience. Those institutional chaplaincy programs in the Boston area became the laboratories in which we tried out the theories and principles of pastoral theology and psychology of religion. And throughout ran a red thread of dynamic interpersonalism.

Depersonalization? Obviously, persons are admitted to such large institutions not because of personal or friendship connections but because the patients or inmates fall into certain categories. There is something arbitrary about such assignments to the eye ward, the surgery ward, the psychiatric ward. They are removed from their home communities and from all the natural kinship and mutual support systems upon which they have counted in everyday life.

It is precisely this abnormal situation which provides the constitutional justification for institutional ministry. Soldiers in their military camps and sailors in their naval bases are likewise arbitrarily removed from their home communities and placed in artificial groupings. They would be denied the right and freedom to practice their religion unless provisions were made through some kind of ministry within the institution or camp itself. Army and navy chaplains operated under this principle long before hospital chaplains were appointed fulltime to hospital staffs as they are today.

Growth in Numbers and Acceptance

The plain statistical growth of chaplaincy has been impressive. In February of 1952 I presented the findings of a doctoral dissertation, which I wrote under Paul Johnson at

Boston University, *The Role of the Chaplain in the Care of the Patient,* at a chaplains' convention in Cleveland. There were about fifty-five present. My study was based on a survey of chaplains who belonged to the Chaplains' Association of the American Protestant Hospital Association. There were fifty-one accredited, active chaplains of that group serving in hospitals at the time of the study.

Contrast that group with the situation today, twenty years later. Chaplain conventions fill large hotel ballrooms to overflowing. There are about three hundred clinical pastoral education training centers accredited by the Association for Clinical Pastoral Education. Practically all the state mental hospitals in the nation have one or several chaplains, and the same may be said for prisons and reformatories. More recently the Roman Catholic chaplains have created their own organization for strengthening, coordinating, and setting standards for the specialized ministry of institutional chaplaincy.

Numerical growth has been accompanied by diversification. Beyond the medical-surgical and mental hospitals, other institutions have seen the benefits of including chaplains on their staffs. These include alcoholic treatment centers, community mental health centers, schools for the retarded, and geriatric facilities, to mention a few specialties. College and university chaplaincy arose from another basis, and although these ministries have much in common with the others mentioned above, they have their own history and present organization. The pastoral counseling and group work functions of campus ministers provide common ground with other institutional chaplains. The need for cooperation with other professions, such as student personnel workers, student health services, professors, etc., and the educational setting in which they work would seem to lend their field naturally to the purposes of clinical pastoral education. Two years ago I made some preliminary plans to initiate such a program through the School of Religion at the University of Iowa, but they are still on the drawing board. It seems that what holds the basic core of institutional chaplaincy together is the fact that the constituency is viewed as "clients" needing "treatment" or "care."

How well have chaplaincy services been accepted in the institutions where they have been introduced? Many specific examples of acceptance could be cited. Recently, I heard that at Billings Clinics (University of Chicago School of Medicine) chaplaincy service was requested for the dialysis unit and its kidney patients. A chaplain intern was assigned. It was clear that the usefulness of chaplaincy services had been demonstrated in order to warrant this request. The seminar on dying conducted by Dr. Elisabeth Kübler-Ross and the late Chaplain Carl Nighswonger had shown that the chaplain could definitely bring a dimension of care needed to supplement the therapy of the rest of the health team. Another example of hospital acceptance of chaplaincy is the program of the Department of Pastoral Services at Rockford Memorial Hospital (Illinois). Community clergy were welcomed and integrated into the hospital's program through the channel of the chaplain's role. A dozen workshops at each annual meeting of the College of Chaplains document such innovations throughout the country. Nothing succeeds like success. Chaplaincy is becoming widely accepted in various places in different shapes and according to different models suitable to each institution.

Professional Certification

Each new profession, or an old profession redefining its role, spends a great deal of energy on clarifying its identity, function, status, and interprofessional relationships. Social work has gone through this phase in recent years and so has institutional chaplaincy. At the University of Iowa Hospitals, the profession of occupational therapy was instituted, thrived for a short while, and has already been phased out. Newcomers have to prove themselves and make their place in any group. Will they be allowed by their elders to stake out a territory, to "get into the act"? This is not just neurotic concern for status; it is a legitimate test. In institutions there is usually a premium on space and quite a scramble for a piece of the limited budget. Others do not automatically move over to create a position in the table of organization.

The above pressures put a new program or new professional service on notice to prove itself. Is it worthy to be included among already validated services, such as those of the physician or nurse? What evidence can an administrator look to for judging whether a candidate for such a position is qualified? What are the standards? If the profession itself does not know, how can the administrator or board of directors be expected to make a judgment?

Prior to the professional institutional chaplaincy there had been a wide range of competence, capacity, and performance. As often as not, an elderly clergyman was retired to such a post under the assumption that it would not be as demanding as parish ministry. It often lacked economic support commensurate with more regular ministries, and it also lacked professional standing, so that such persons were considered by their peers to be on a vocational sidetrack.

Social workers had to live down the image of "lady bountiful," the wife of the company president who brought apples and other goodies to the poor at Thanksgiving and Christmas. Chaplains had to live down some of the reputations of hospital "visitors," who had seen the institution as a field for evangelism and patients as fair game for proselytizing from one religious loyalty to another. Some saw the task as a kind of "cheering up," which any well-meaning and sincere person could do. Meanwhile, it was assumed that the other roles of the health team required a sizable body of theory, careful training under supervision, and the mastery of certain techniques and skills. Who was to say that it took more than a friendly attitude and heartfelt sincerity to be a social worker or a chaplain?

The Association for Clinical Pastoral Education, Inc. is the present nationally recognized organization to provide professional training for institutional chaplaincy. These credentials are looked to by hospital administrators as well as denominational agencies and others who wish to employ full-time institutional chaplains. They can safely assume that persons completing such a training program have been exposed to a minimum understanding of the institutional process, client or patient therapy, the role unique to the chaplain, and the factors that lead to good interprofessional cooperation. Such a chaplain should be expected to fit into the health team as well as a nurse, physician, or physical therapist who has undergone corresponding rigorous discipline in his respective specialty. A very large number of chaplains have had at least four quarters (twelve months) of such training divided among several training centers. Although such training dates back to the middle of the third decade of this century, trained chaplains were not certified in any large numbers until after World War II. That makes institutional chaplaincy a relatively young profession in the specialized form it has today.

The College of Chaplains, a division of the American Hospital Association, has assumed a large role in the past twenty-seven years in giving professional recognition to chaplains who have been enrolled in clinical pastoral education programs. Candidates must submit materials reflecting their work, recommendations from chaplain supervisors under whom they have trained, and, finally, appear before a review committee for an oral examination and an interview in depth.

The Association of Mental Hospital Chaplains, established twenty-five years ago, has fostered and solidified the gains of chaplaincy as a distinct profession in mental hospitals in the United States and Canada. State after state established policies and accepted standards for chaplaincy service in all their institutions. Many of these hospitals and mental health institutes also have training programs as part of their function.

The American Hospital Association (as well as the College of Chaplains mentioned above) has issued a manual describing the various arrangements and alternative plans for establishing, staffing, equipping, housing, and programming a department of chaplaincy in its member hospitals. Clearly, institutional chaplaincy has arrived as a distinct and professionally established function today. Professional growth is always necessary, but its place is secure.

Impact on Ministry

Increasingly, theological education has turned to chaplain supervisors of clinical pastoral education programs in hospitals, prisons, and other institutions, to provide the "laboratory" in which the theory of pastoral theology and other theological insights can be tested out and experienced in the lives of seminary students. A large and increasing number of theological schools require one quarter (often a summer) of CPE. Thus the institutional chaplain becomes, indirectly if not formally, an adjunct instructor in all theological seminaries which send him students. Other seminaries send their students to institutions one or two times a week for field work or practicum experience. Frequently it is while studying the "human documents," as Anton Boisen phrased it, and trying to relate the theological perspective to the patient's real life situation of suffering that the student finally "gets it all together." Religion is seen as relevant as it becomes apparent that the characters in biblical stories wrestled with some of the same issues as patients in the hospital's case histories. Love, grace, forgiveness, sin, reconciliation, faith, hope, and much more cry out for application in the lives of patients in mental hospitals, patients facing surgery or terminal illness, and prisoners facing punishment and rehabilitation. If religion cannot speak to these persons in the midst of their need and distress, their suffering and depression, then it is less meaningful to present these great doctrines and principles in sermons, books, hymns, etc.

Theological students have come back to their second or third year of seminary studies with a new involvement because they have been "dunked in life and have come up dripping," as Reuel Howe has put it. This decade of students has spoken much about the need for "involvement." Here is their chance: at the bedside, beside the bereaved, sharing the disappointment and inferiority feelings of a person stigmatized by a ghastly blemish or defect, sharing the dilemma of a physician as he is confronted by the question of when to shut off the machinery and stop all heroic efforts to prolong life (or dying). Back at the seminary courses in theology, scripture, and even church history take on a new dynamic dimension as fresh questions are brought back from the laboratory of human suffering to the lecture room of academic discourse. Institutional chaplaincy has helped to make such an impact.

Clergymen who have been out in the parish ministry for ten or fifteen years are using clinical pastoral education as their form of continuing education, professional improvement, a shot in the arm. A pastor of seventeen years' experience stated in a CPE group that when he went out into the ministry he was at sea, unable to handle his stresses, and ended up with the major part of his stomach removed after several bouts with ulcers. He was supportive of the new ordinand across the table from him, who was in tears struggling with his beginnings. The pastor said, "I'm glad you are getting some of these things worked out now so they won't need to hinder your ministry like they did mine."

A new departure in some centers is to bring clergymen into the hospital on a part-time basis over a thirty-week period, which is equated with a quarter of standard CPE. These clergymen integrate their parish perspective with the institutional experience and find both foci of their ministry enriched.

The initiator of religion and medicine conferences or meetings between the local religious leaders' association and the county medical society is often the hospital chaplain, and the setting may be the hospital staff dining room. Thus the institutional chaplain reaches out into the community to build bridges of interprofessional understanding, cooperation, and challenge. The kind of relationships Professor Johnson and others were demonstrating in the institutions mentioned at the beginning of this chapter are now commonplace throughout the country in hundreds of institutions.

Institutional chaplains have contributed their fair share of writing and research in pastoral theology, pastoral care and counseling, religion and mental health, and related subjects.

Impact on Medicine

At the beginning of this new era of institutional (especially in hospitals) chaplaincy, the main project was to become accepted, to draw insights and inspirations from other members of the staff. Physicians, nurses, social workers, psychiatrists, psychologists, pathologists, administrators, were on the agenda, of clinical pastoral education programs. The direction of contribution was mostly one way in the beginning. As chaplains grew in confidence, they saw that they had much to teach the rest of the staff, and the rest of the staff was willing to listen. One of the signs of adult maturity is the capacity and willingness to give and take, to contribute as well as to receive.

To return to the example of the seminar on dying (conducted by Kübler-Ross and Nighswonger) at the University of Chicago medical center, there is a case in point. In the beginning the physicians did not want to talk about dying, did not even like to admit they had terminal patients under their care. It was not medical students but divinity students who came to the hospital concerned about this question. The impact was electric. The seminar was crowded with many kinds of students. In a few years Kübler-Ross and Nighswonger were both in great demand, speaking and lecturing, conducting workshops, and serving on panels dealing with the understanding and care of dying patients. Kübler-Ross's book *On Death and Dying* became very popular and quickly went into a paperback edition. Articles appeared in major popular magazines. Television programs covered the subject, and today many educational films are available on this issue.

Medical ethics questions are becoming increasingly com-

plex, and scientific medicine is beginning to recognize the
need for input from the humanities, social sciences, law, and
religion. Instead of just dumping the freshman medical student into gross anatomy, we now have a series of interpretive
sessions during orientation week. There is an explanation of
the motivation behind the "deeded body program" indicating
how persons from all walks of life come to decide to give
their bodies to the medical college, thus adding another
dimension of meaning to their final illness and death. A
professor of pediatrics discusses care of the dying and dealing
with the families of dying children. A professor of religion
sets death in a larger perspective related to the meaning of
life. This is all part of the new curriculum. Later the freshman
class requested two chaplains to discuss "Euthanasia: Pro
and Con." The point is that there is a trend to pay more
attention to the nonmedical, nonscientific aspects of medicine.
It is in this context that institutional chaplains are making
their impact on medical education.

With new and heroic measures of treatment come new
ethical questions, which are generally conceived in religious
terms. Heart and kidney transplants involve the families of
the donors and the attitudes of the recipients. On what ethical
grounds does the father of three young children decide to give
one kidney to his brother if his wife is ambivalent about the
gift? Is an ameliorating surgery justified in the case of an
elderly and near-terminal patient? How long should you try
to keep a defective child alive via heroic measures? Abortion
laws have changed the situation in many hospitals, but the
patients still struggle with the decision and need help in the
moral sphere of their lives. Physicians have not been trained
in this aspect of patient care and turn to chaplains whom they
can trust and respect not only for guidance on specific questions, but for help in training interns and medical students so
that they will be more aware of these factors in their later
careers. Sterilization, genetic counseling, the growing concern
for the right to health care, and other similar matters go
beyond the scope of the field of medicine because they involve

the ethics of choice and social responsibility. Religion has traditionally concerned itself with the quality of life. Physicians have a natural right to turn to chaplains for help in these matters.

Pastoral Care of Institutions and Staffs Within Them

Is it possible to raise the morale of a whole institution? Do institutions have personalities like people? Yes, in a strange way one can sense the deep concern for, or the cold disregard of, persons in a hospital by everything from the architectural layout of the wards to the procedures for admission to the clinics. Decor, maintenance, and traffic patterns all tell one whether the patient's needs are at the top or bottom of the priority list. Who should be especially sensitive to the question of human values in institutional life? Who should call a conference on "humanizing the patients' hospital experience"? It may well be the chaplain. Administrators have the access to blueprints and the resources to hire consultants; but who will raise the pertinent questions? A respected and sufficiently aggressive chaplain could have an influence. How often does it happen? It might be a challenge to try.

Patients are not the only human beings of value in institutions. A thousand-bed hospital might well have two thousand employees, trainees, students, and assorted staff members. Many of these come under stress and temptations unique to hospital life. The research physician works in his laboratory checking animals and specimens at odd hours. He is thrown together with a young female technician or research assistant under intimate and prolonged working relationships. She "understands" him and his work better than his wife, or so it seems. There are pressures and insidious factors in these situations which go beyond the common boss-secretary situation which develops into an affair in the business world. Physicians and nurses are thrown together in personal ways that can try an already shaky marriage.

A sensitive chaplain can be available for marriage counseling of staff members in ways which the person's own clergyman might not be. He is on the scene and grasps the pressures of the institutional life. If staff members come to have confidence in the chaplain and see the tangible benefit his counseling provides for their patients, they may be quite willing to turn to him with their own problems. Referral by word of mouth can make the chaplain's availability known among the staff. Such a ministry is doubly valuable, because not only does it help the staff member personally, but it frees him or her to be a more effective member of the health team, and thus it benefits the patients indirectly.

Medical students also have their problems: with vocation, with girl (or boy) friend, working wife, identity crisis, finances, personality problems, etc. Again, if the chaplain is seen as a caring and effective pastoral counselor who can be trusted and respected, there will be opportunities to serve.

Hospital chaplains have a long-standing tradition of lecturing to classes of nurses on the spiritual and emotional needs of patients. These teaching opportunities also open channels for pastoral care of nursing students and nursing staff.

Interpreting topics of "religion and health" to the public through speaking engagements, panel participation, and other contacts with the public constitute another aspect of service of the institutional chaplain.

Many chaplains have developed a ministry of writing on such themes and thus have extended the services of their institution to a broader public.

These are a few ways in which institutional chaplaincy moves beyond direct care of patients, working in, through, and beyond the walls of the institution.

Changes on the Horizon

Rapid social and institutional changes characterize the decade of the seventies. What lies ahead for institutional chaplains?

Changes in the role and status of the clergy in society at large cannot help but affect the way in which chaplains are perceived. Should they be agents of social change in the role of prophet? This was hinted at in the previous section. In a prison, should chaplains represent the inmates in their desperate plea for protection from homosexual assault, or should they represent the warden and the establishment? Perhaps they should be ministers of reconciliation. One of the criticisms leveled against pastoral care and pastoral counseling types of ministry was that such ministers were not in evidence in the civil rights movement and the anti-war protests. They were supposedly too busy "accepting" and "understanding" people. "Peace of mind" and "symptom relief" can be bought at too high a price, say some. Perhaps a profession that is young and insecure hesitates to rock the boat. Institutions and their administrative delegates like a smooth operation. This is not the place for a full discussion of this question; it is enough to note that the future may differ from the past in this regard.

What will nationalized or socialized medicine bring in its wake as far as chaplaincy is concerned? We could have a strange role reversal. Let us suppose that physicians finally go on straight salary (or nearly so) under a vast nationalized medical program, hired and paid like schoolteachers, judges, and other civil servants. We have, on the other hand, a new trend in pastoral counseling in which this service is being rendered by some on a fee-for-service basis. Formerly, it was assumed that a priest or pastor was on some kind of salaried support, and that his sacramental and pastoral care functions were just part of his total ministry, his calling.

Support for chaplains still follows a great variety of patterns in institutions. I know of at least the following types of financing: a departmental budget account, an administrative line, support by one denomination, sponsorship by the state council of churches, proceeds from a private endowment fund, support by the National Institute of Health or some other governmental research or training grant. Then there is the range of volunteers, including local parish clergy with a special interest in the municipal hospital, and part-time chaplains, to name a few peripheral categories. Perhaps a mark of maturity of the profession will be a more regularized relationship. One cannot easily imagine nursing, radiology, or surgery being related to hospitals in such a variety of fashions. Note, even the private-duty-nurse ranks have been eroded by intensive care and coronary care units, staff "nurse specialists," and other established programs.

Institutional chaplaincy should be flexible enough to adapt to new forms, needs, demands, and possibilities.

Will chaplaincy continue to be thought of as an "arm of the church," a "call to special service" within a denominational context? Perhaps that will be considered too parochial by the end of the century. Will a chaplain serve all regardless of denominational or faith group loyalties? A few years ago, clinical pastoral education students called on patients in their wards of their own group (e.g., Protestant students calling on Protestant patients). Those distinctions are fading out fast. In our clinical pastoral education summer program, it is almost impossible to tell whether a Protestant or Catholic student is conducting the chapel service Sunday mornings. This goes for dress, theology, and liturgy. And on the wards and corridor rooms the question of denominational identity of the student chaplain is seldom of interest to the patient. It seems that the trend will continue in that direction.

When we contemplate the future, however, we should bear in mind that history does not go in a straight line. Frequently there is a pendulum pattern with action and reaction, a swing in status from high to low and back to high again, a downgrading of some function and then a resurgence of interest. Recently we have seen this take place in the scientific fields. Sputnik, a Russian space achievement, scared Americans into a crash program for training scientists and aerospace research. Now there is an oversupply, and Ph.D.s in physics and chemistry are driving taxicabs.

Specialization and emphasis on training could have adverse

effects on institutional chaplaincy. Many are very much interested in becoming chaplain supervisors because they like the excitement of the group dynamics process, the interaction with students, and the role of teacher-therapist; but they would not want to do daily what they are training their students to do: namely, call on patients on the wards. Some administrators may say in effect, "Your clinical pastoral education program sounds exciting, but what we really need is a floor chaplain." Will we be aware of the signs that we have reached the saturation point? We will need to dignify the role of chaplain to the extent that an institutional chaplain will not need to feel he has not really arrived unless he is a chaplain supervisor with his own training program.

Conclusion

We have come a long way since Anton Boisen began a program to train hospital chaplains at Worcester State Hospital in Massachusetts in 1925. There has been growth not only in numbers but in stature and professional identity. Significant and lasting impact has been made on the ministry and theological education, as well as on medicine and medical education. Our capacity to predict the future is definitely limited; but one thing is certain, the future will be as exciting as my first encounter with this movement in the late 1940s.

Career Counseling

James H. Burns

Colston and Johnson have defined personality as the dynamic mutual interaction of all systems—physical, social, political, economic, ecological, etc., which comprise and affect the organism.[1] Career counseling approaches a person and his work on all these levels, viewing the task as a psychological one in which personality and occupation are vitally intertwined.

The dynamics of personality are important factors in career development. However, career counseling does not attempt to bring about personality changes, but fosters growing understanding and insight and acceptance of reality as it touches a person's life. The stages of career development are based upon the stages of life.

At the present time there is more than the usual amount of unrest in the middle-aged group of ministers. This unrest is characterized by emotional instability, physical complaints, boredom, a form of calendar neurosis (that is, an irrational fear of aging), and an urgent desire to be doing something different.[2]

When a group of Protestant ministers described themselves as "profoundly distressed, disturbed, frustrated, and in a state of utter disquietude about the nature and mission of the

1. *Personality and Christian Faith.*
2. Seward Hiltner, *Ferment in the Ministry* (Nashville: Abingdon Press, 1969).

church in a time of revolution," [3] we can believe they were deadly in earnest and were voicing the feelings of many pastors.

A half century ago, thoughtful men observed that great socioeconomic changes had begun to take place. Giant business corporations had begun to appear. Worldwide commercialism was developing. Barriers to communication were rapidly breaking down. There was a new complexity and centralization of organization in many spheres of man's life. Men dared to hope for a brave new world. These processes continue like Noah's ancient flood. But the brave new world has not been realized; it seems farther away. Men, including ministers, feel overwhelmed and desperate.

Every pastor at some time in his life becomes discouraged or confused about his calling.[4] There may be misunderstanding between him and members of his church, or between him and his colleagues or his denominational leaders. Perhaps he is worried about members of his family. Sometimes he hardly knows what to think about himself and his future.

He may feel he is sick in body, mind, or soul. Maybe his feelings have been deeply hurt. He may feel terribly ashamed because of something he has done or failed to do. Maybe he is having trouble making a decision or needs help in making up his mind about what he should do next. He may feel trapped. When a pastor has these or similar problems, he needs someone to talk to—a person or persons he can trust and whom he can respect.

Some pastors would rather not talk about these things with family or personal friends. Usually the pastor feels he ought not to talk about his own problems with members of his church. Most avoid going to colleagues or denominational

3. Gerald J. Jud, Edgar W. Mills, and Genevieve Welters Burch, *Ex-Pastors: Why Men Leave the Parish Ministry* (Philadelphia: Pilgrim Press, 1970).

4. Laile E. Bartlett, *The Vanishing Parson* (Boston: Beacon Press, 1971).

officials for this kind of help. A number of pastors hesitate to seek help from persons in other professions.

Where, then, can the pastor go to talk about all these things which vitally affect his work in his chosen calling? Growing members are enrolling in career development planning programs in church career centers located in scores of cities in the United States.

Most clergymen find career development planning a strange new concept to apply to their occupation. However, the idea that a career is the total pattern of jobs held during a worker's lifetime is not particularly theatening.[5] It follows that career development is that succession of jobs a person holds during his working life. Career development must then be viewed as a process. The end product of career planning is a series of occupational experiences rather than a final occupational choice. Career decisions are based on information about occupations plus the way in which an individual reacts to this information. Success in any given occupation, including the ministry, depends about 15 percent on training and 85 percent on personal qualities.

There are some basic working principles which underlie satisfaction, fulfillment, and self-esteem through an occupation or career. A person who has clear objectives in his career is helped to maintain a strong sense of direction and purpose.[6] This gives a feeling that progress is being made toward goals. The resulting satisfaction from his work gives the person assurance that he has control of the situation. Also, the job or work is a realistic place to find satisfaction for dependency needs as well as a place where assertion of independence can take place.

It is primarily on the job where a person learns to cultivate the capacity to accept talents as well as limitations. Career

5. James B. Hofrenning, ed., *The Continuing Quest* (Minneapolis: Augsburg Publishing House, 1970).

6. E. S. Ginzberg, *et al., Occupational Choice: An Approach to a General Theory* (New York: Columbia University Press, 1951).

development assures a growing capacity to function more fully according to one's talents and limitations. This fosters self-esteem. The ideal work situation helps develop in a person the capacity to desire, to like or dislike, and to trust or fear. This augments the feeling of being a real person. The above only briefly hints at the 85 percent personal qualities which are a part of effectiveness in a given occupation.

Career development planning offered in church career centers provides a unique opportunity for employed church workers to obtain help in professional and personal growth. The centers provide a nonthreatening environment and program which is readily acceptable to most church workers. It is hoped that the career programs aid in the prevention of more severe disturbances in the lives and careers of church professionals.

It is possible the career programs contribute to a new level of personal and professional health of pastors and other leaders. If so, they may have a health-giving impact on their churches, which in turn may have a health-giving influence on their neighborhoods and communities and possibly on society in general.

Beginnings of Church Career Counseling

Career counseling for professional church workers was first formed into a structured three-day program by the United Presbyterian Church in the U.S.A. It was devised as a service to ministers in that denomination.[7] The director of the Interboard Office of Personnel Services for the United Presbyterian Church had been impressed with the unrest of Presbyterian clergymen during the early years of the 1960s. He took particular notice of the growing number of pastors in the prime

7. Edward S. Golden, director of the Interboard Office of Personnel Services of the United Presbyterian Church, U.S.A., private conversations and a talk before the Commission on the Ministry of the American Baptist Convention, 1968.

of life who were apparently significantly effective in their ministry and were pastors of large, strong congregations; yet they were deciding to leave the ministry of the church for positions in business, industry, or in other secular positions in public or private institutions and agencies.

Inquiry regarding the motivating factors revealed a growing unrest and disenchantment with lifetime service in a church occupation. The director reported he was impressed with the high professional quality of the men interviewed. Nevertheless, he was appalled at the circumstantial, haphazard, and almost accidental manner in which nearly all of these persons had gone at solving their problem of vocational dissatisfaction. The director knew there was a better way because he knew of organizations and agencies in business and industry which had developed programs through which executives could obtain help and guidance as they made life-changing career decisions. He began to develop, in the United Presbyterian offices in Philadelphia, a similar program for Presbyterian ministers. The need was great and the response so large within a year that it was necessary to move into separate quarters in Princeton, New Jersey.

The service was named the Northeast Career Center. It was sponsored by the United Presbyterian Church and was responsible to that denomination. In the beginning most of the funding came from the United Presbyterian Church. Nevertheless, from the beginning there was an ecumenical openness on the part of the staff of the Northeast Career Center. The first year in Princeton was a year of experimentation. The real beginning can be equated with the appointment of Thomas E. Brown as the director-counselor of the Princeton center.[8]

Among American Baptists a similar development was taking place. As early as 1961 a study was made of the professional problems which were pressing upon American Baptist pastors.

8. Thomas E. Brown, "Career Counseling As a Form of Pastoral Care," *Pastoral Psychology* (Mar. 1971).

It was found that Baptist pastors were confused about their duties and roles and in general felt beleaguered.[9]

In 1962 a more comprehensive study was made.[10] It was reported that the ministers themselves expressed a need for pastoral care. They were asking, "Who ministers to the minister?" A third and even more definitive study was concluded in 1965.[11] It was conducted by the Ministers and Missionaries Benefit Board of the American Baptist Convention. Most of this study focused on the American Baptist placement system.

Early the next year, the Commission on the Ministry of the American Baptist Convention suggested three possible alternatives for the current unsatisfactory placement methods. First, the present system could be maintained but efforts made to improve it. Second, placement could be handled by newly created regional offices of the denomination, making use of an automated matching system. The third proposal was that the denomination create five to eight regional Centers for the Ministry which would perform a variety of services for the churches and the ministers. It was suggested that each center would have (1) a regional director of placement; (2) a career development counselor; (3) a continuing education counselor; and (4) a regional administrator for a national minimum salary program. Thus was born the concept of a denominational Center for the Ministry.

The center concept arose out of widespread recognition of the need for more adequate undergirding structures for the professional leadership of the American Baptist Convention.[12]

9. Donald F. Thomas, "Report of the Mission to Ministers of 1961," sponsored by the American Baptist Home Mission Societies and the American Baptist Board of Education and Publication, 1961.

10. Oren H. Baker, "The Conservation of the Ministry—A Profile of the American Baptist Pastor" (New York: The M and M Board, American Baptist Convention, 1965).

11. Otto Nallinger, H. Victor Kane, and Yoshio Fukuyama, "Placement Study" (New York: The M and M Board, American Baptist Convention, 1965).

12. Charles N. Forsberg, ed., *The Pastor*, Vol. XI, No. 1 and No. 4, The Ministers' Council of the American Baptist Convention, Valley Forge, PA 19481, 1967.

Most important of all, there was a desire for a more person-oriented utilization of the professional leaders of the denomination. This was expressed by the ministers themselves.

Career counseling as a planned, formal program designed by church leaders for professional church workers has a brief history. The entire development is less than ten years old.

As plans for the centers began to take shape in the spring of 1967, it was thought three to five regional centers would be sufficient. Later that year the first center was opened in Wellesley Hills, Massachusetts. In mid-1970 a second center was established in Oakland, California.

In the original proposal reference was made to career direction, uncertainty, felt and unsuspected continuing education needs, plus frustration with the church and unrest in the ministry as needs which might be met in a Center for the Ministry. It was pointed out that some of the existing resources for dealing with the deeply personal nature of the minister's self-doubts, professional incompetencies, and personal or family conflicts were frequently rendered inoperable by their link with persons responsible for placement and advancement. It was concluded that career development counseling was essential for the ministry and should become a vital segment of the more general category of pastoral care. It was thought that the center's contribution, including that of career counseling, would be in helping persons review the course of their ministry, opening up other possible career tracks within church occupations, and generally acting as the conserving factor of one of the church's most valuable resources—its professional leadership.

The Career Counselor

In career counseling the counselor is the key person in the process. It goes without saying that the career counselor should have a broad, rich formal training in many fields—psychological, sociological, and vocational. He should be a person who has previously demonstrated his ability as an advisor and leader among his ministerial peers. In addition he must be trained and experienced in the principles and practices of career assessment and career development planning, particularly as these relate to bringing out the best in a person and to helping the individual know himself. He must understand career process. Also, he must be alert to the differences between the collection of knowledge or facts and the expression of wisdom.

The career counselor must believe there is a spark of excellence in each person. Without this belief, the counselor cannot appreciate a person's potential for excellence and, therefore, will be unable to look for it.

He must be solution-oriented. He must be convinced there is a solution to every situation and aware that only the person with the concern can really know the solution. The career counselor is, therefore, concerned with the use of procedures which will help the person find, in the most efficient manner, the solutions which are right for him. He avoids becoming involved with problems. He starts with discomforts, not problems. He tries to recognize only obstacles which are seen as realities to be overcome or surmounted. He keeps his eyes on the right or optimum solution for the person. Identification of the solution is the counselor's first concern, not discovery of problems or their causes.

He must be competent as a communicator, by tongue and on paper. At the same time, he must avoid being in love with the sound of his own voice or the use of his own phrases. He must be the listening type, not simply a talking advice-giver. He should understand both the meaning and impact of words. He must show patience, perseverance, perception, and awareness.

He must be persuasive and tough-minded, resistant both to the biases of the person and to his own. He must be aware of the maneuvers frequently used by people who seem to prefer the uncomfortable ruts with which they are familiar to the challenges of change and progress. He must prove his real interest in bringing out the best in the other person by actively educating and reeducating the other person in the sense of helping him develop himself and his career.

He must have the conviction that all good guidance is God-given. He must never try to "act God" or be the wise man. He must be conscious of being a channel or a catalyst through which others come to appreciate more clearly what they can do with themselves and their career. The counselor who is tense, tired, or concerned with personal troubles cannot be a clear channel through which others can receive good guidance.

Some Instruments Used in Church Career Counseling

Since the first two denominationally related church career centers were founded in the mid-sixties, nine more centers have been established and accredited by the Church Career Development Council, Inc.[13] Of the nine, one was the second American Baptist center. The other eight were each incorporated as a cooperative service sponsored and funded by church judicatories in an area or region.

Although the first American Baptist Center for the Ministry emerged from several studies and was the result of much planning, the Career Development Planning Program leaned heavily on the Princeton center for techniques, methods, and operational procedures. Before taking up his duties, the first Baptist career counselor[14] spent the last four months of 1967 working and studying at the Northeast Career Center.

Some of the services of the American Baptist Center for the Ministry had been inaugurated in the spring of 1967. Career counseling began January 1, 1968. Both of the Baptist centers were founded as a service primarily for Baptist professional church workers. However, following the lead of the Northeast

13. A current list of centers accredited by Church Career Development Council, Inc., may be obtained by writing to the Council at 815 Second Avenue, Suite 515, New York, N. Y. 10017.

14. James H. Burns, "The Minister's Profession: How Does He Plan?" *Nexus,* Nov., 1969.

Center, ecumenicity has been practiced. During the first three years, slightly more than 10 percent of the persons enrolled were other than American Baptist. Since those enrolling have been predominantly Baptists, this has influenced the development and growth of the style of career counseling done in the Baptist centers.

The personal history document (Career Development Questionnaire) was borrowed partially from the Northeast Center. Much of it was rewritten, rephrased, or rearranged to make it seem more informal and nonthreatening. American Baptists seem to have resistance to anything that smacks of structure or the exercise of authority.[15] Also, because of the Baptist distrust of psychology in general and tests in particular, many of the tests used at the Northeast Center were not introduced at Wellesley. The Kuder has been used instead of the Strong because it seemed to produce more general findings. From the beginning, two religious tests were included. They seem to have some real usefulness in the program, but they may be more valuable as visible evidence to Baptists that career counseling is a religious experience rather than another bit of psychological mumbo-jumbo.

Warner's Index of Social Characteristics[16] has been used from the beginning. Its impact on some persons is considerable. Nearly all American Baptist professional leaders grew up in the middle class or below. Currently, nine out of ten are to be viewed as lower-upper-class persons. This means that most American Baptist leaders have had upward social mobility of one, two, three, or even four social classes. Use of the Warner Index visualizes and highlights this upward social mobility. Some persons consider the revelations of this simple instrument to be the major key to their understanding of who they are. Verification of who a person is opens the door to

15. Paul M. Harrison, *Authority and Power in the Free Church Tradition* (Princeton: Princeton University Press, 1959).

16. W. Lloyd Warner and Marchia Meeker, *Social Class in America* (New York: Harper Torchbooks, 1949).

self-acceptance. For some persons these simple ideas take on the explosive quality of a conversion experience.

A standard Sentence Completion, borrowed partly from the Northeast Center, is regularly used. The value seems to lie partly in the process of filling out the instrument. Many Baptists have never heard of Sentence Completions, let alone seen or written one. In the career counseling program the Sentence Completion is used as the springboard for a form of free association. Some view the process of associating to items selected from the Sentence Completion as a stimulating game. Others are unbelieving and astonished at how much they reveal about themselves "by answering those silly sentences."

The Capability Analysis was compiled from many sources. In "What Color Is Your Parachute?" [17] a dozen different titles are listed for similar instruments. All endeavor to analyze a person's achievements. American Baptists generally find this instrument to be a hard one. Nearly all take a minimum of two hours to do it. Nevertheless, almost everyone declares great satisfaction in doing it. Some assert they have found a whole new way of seeing themselves. They are confident they will think and feel differently about themselves from this time forward.

Introduction to Career Counseling

When the person, usually plus the spouse, arrives at the center at 9:00 A.M. to begin the three-day program, he is greeted by a member of the staff, shown around, and taken to the office of the coordinator of the center. He engages the person in a friendly fifteen-minute conversation about the programs at the center and then brings him to the career counselor's room.

As soon as he and the counselor are settled, a sheet titled Introduction to the Career Development Planning Program is

17. Richard N. Bolles, *What Color Is Your Parachute?* (627 Taylor St., San Francisco, Calif. 94102, 1971).

presented. There are thirteen statements on the sheet. Each one is read and discussed. The first is, "The purpose of Career Development Planning is to focus on the interests, resources, attitudes, preferences, motivations, and capabilities of the person in the program." It is explained that during the three days, focus will be on the positive factors in each person. Many work experiences tend abundantly to point up a person's faults, failures, weaknesses, and limitations. In the Career Development Planning Program, the negative or unsatisfactory aspects of personal performance are not ignored. However, emphasis is placed on what a person does and on the results which are acceptable and useful.

It is suggested there is always pressure on a person to face failures and mistakes, but rarely is an individual in a situation where there is a planned, organized effort to take an objective look at things done well and with considerable satisfaction to all concerned, including the performer. It takes courage for people to take a close look at their achievements. This seems to be particularly hard for professional church workers.

The next statement is, "The approach is to examine what the person has done and the results, rather than the individual's feelings and thoughts." The counselor explains that some test instruments are used to assist in this process, but that the test findings are considered contributive rather than definitive, exploratory rather than predictive, and that they will open up possibilities rather than narrow them down.[18] If there is reason for believing the persons have at least modest psychological sophistication, the counselor explains that, broadly speaking, there have been three streams of development in psychology. Counseling psychology is the oldest with its emphasis on feelings and emotions. This psychology has influenced ministerial thought and practice greatly in the last half century. The second stream is educational psychology with its emphasis on the mind and its development,

18. Arthur Liebers, *How to Pass Employment Tests* (New York: Arco Publishing Co., 1964).

the learning-teaching process, and the cerebral-thinking exercise. The third stream has been management psychology.

The beginnings of management psychology can be traced to the Western Electric study forty years ago which focused on understanding and management of employee morale. It resulted in the human relations approach to personnel problems. One of the goals was to discover how to manage or manipulate the worker so he would be more cooperative and less resistant.[19] Over the years management psychology has developed within business and industry and has been instrumental in developing understandings of the productivity of workers, supervisors, and executives.[20]

The first two psychologies have concentrated on sick or developing persons. The third has worked with supposedly normal adults in terms of effectiveness in their employment. Management psychology has not neglected feelings and thoughts.[21] However, there is a deliberate reordering of the emphasis because of the conviction that persons are essentially functional animals. Most often, feelings and thoughts flow from function or behavior rather than the reverse. It is assumed a person can fully find his identity only when he has also found his place in society.[22]

The next two items indicate that the career program at the center has borrowed heavily from the secular organizations which began developing career planning programs in business and industry several decades ago.

The fifth item is a statement of philosophy as follows: "The counselor subscribes to the philosophy that every individual is a very special person, a child of the universe, and has a right to be in the world. He believes persons can

19. Everett L. Shostrom, *Man, the Manipulator* (Nashville: Abingdon Press, 1968).
20. Peter F. Drucker, *The Effective Executive* (New York: Harper & Row, 1966)
21. Donald E. Super, *The Psychology of Careers* (New York: Harper & Row, 1957)
22. Donald E. Super and Martin J. Bohn, Jr., *Occupational Psychology* (Belmont, Calif.: Wadsworth Publishing Co., 1970).

unfold and grow as God intended they should, and he believes this process can be fostered by various means including the Career Development Planning Program." The response to this statement is nearly always a sigh of relief and visible relaxation. Later in the program individuals often refer to the above statement as a turning point in their experience at the center. Before that they were apprehensive, uncertain, and with limited positive expectations.

The next two items restate that persons enrolled in the program should be in reasonably good health—physically, mentally, and emotionally—and that the program is not a short course of personal therapy. At this time the counselor brings up for brief discussion particularly significant items in the health history, especially those which might influence the way the person works. It is emphasized that although the three-day program is not designed as therapy, it is thought of as "therapeutic," as are all valid interpersonal relations such as a friendship, a good boss-employee relationship, or a pastor-parishioner relationship. It is stated the three-day experience will be a cooperative peer relationship and that the counselor will endeavor to be a friend, not a psychiatrist.

Beginning with the eighth item, the working contract for the three days is spelled out. It is explained that the counselor has already carefully studied all the written material prepared by the person and sent to the center before his arrival. It is stated that because of this, the counselor already knows the person to some degree. Further it is indicated that the personal history document (the eight-page Career Development Questionnaire) will be used as the basis for two or more hours of conversation, during which time the individual's growth and development as a person will be reviewed. Reference is made to the fact that it is generally agreed among persons in the helping professions that any time a person reviews his life in a connected way—using almost any theme and having as his questioner a trained, competent, concerned listener—it is a liberating, integrating, "getting-it-together" experience.

It is then stated that during the three days, this reviewing type of exercise will be done in three different ways. First, the Career Development Questionnaire will be the basis. The second day a Sentence Completion will be used, and the third day the Capability Analysis will be the vehicle. About two hours will be spent with each instrument.

Another of the "contract items" makes the point that during the first day, the persons enrolled will do two test instruments at the center and four others in the evening at their home or motel. They will do the Capability Analysis the evening of the second day.

At this time the reference to an hour-and-a-half session with the consulting clinical psychologist is interpreted. It is explained that the primary purpose is professional supervision. It is stated that the persons in the program are professionals, and the counselor is a professional. Nevertheless, it is valuable to bring in another person for a short time to look at what is going on and its direction.

It is explained that the counselor will share the Career Development Questionnaire with the clinical psychologist and will brief him on test results and developments before he sees the person. Normally the session with the clinical psychologist is during the afternoon of the second day. He brings his sandwich and sits with the counselor and the persons at lunch.

It is stated the person will receive feedback from the psychological consultation in at least three ways. First, during the session itself the person may ask the clinical psychologist any questions he wishes. Second, the psychologist will brief the counselor immediately after the hour-and-a-half session is finished. The counselor will take notes and discuss this material with the person. Finally, the psychologist will later submit a written psychological report. The counselor will in due course write a personal letter to the individual either restating some of the psychologist's remarks at the center or interpreting additional statements in the psychological report.

Sometimes there are sentences or short paragraphs in non-technical language which can be quoted.

Another item provides an opportunity to set the stage for the many hours of face-to-face conversations which will go on during the three days. It is stated that there is nothing mysterious or magical about the program. It is referred to as an experience and as a process. It is emphasized that the test findings and the three kinds of personal reviews serve as a means of putting before the person and the counselor a great mass of data and information which relates to the person in the program. It is stated that the person is more important than information; therefore, the primary focus will be on the individual and his concerns.

This leads easily to a statement regarding goals or results. That statement is, "Professional church workers are able to make their own career decisions and implement them if they have sufficient knowledge and understanding of themselves; an appropriate image of themselves; and realistic information about job opportunities." The counselor interprets this to mean that the three-day program will give the person some new perspectives on himself, perhaps a few new insights, and almost certainly confirmation of many things which were more or less already known. It is declared that the individual will surely have a better answer to the question "Who am I?"

It is also clearly stated that the career counselor has no direct responsibility for placement of persons in church or church-related positions. Nevertheless, it is emphasized that at a time when the person is negotiating for a job, upon request the counselor will telephone anyone named by the person. The point is made that all that goes on during the three days is professionally confidential and will be discussed with a third party only if the person names the third person and requests the counselor to contact that individual.

The final item is a reference to the summary letter. It is explained that at the end of the third day, before the person leaves the center, an outline and a sample summary will be provided. It is stated that writing the letter is done after the three days. However, the person will want to save copies of test results and other materials and make notes on some of the conversations and consultations. It is suggested the person plan to write the summary letter within a couple of weeks after leaving the center.

The Summary Letter

Review and discussion of the outline for the summary letter is done near the close of the third day of the program. The counselor reads the items of the outline and comments upon them while the person looks on. It is suggested in the outline that the writing of the summary is optional. But it is stated nine out of ten persons do write summaries, and almost all claim this final task is essential to obtaining the greatest benefit from the center experience.

It is suggested writing the summary letter will (1) aid the person in evaluating the career assessment experience, (2) crystalize and bring into focus insights and understandings, and (3) provide reference material for recall and use in the future.

The person is instructed to address the summary to a real person who knows and cares about the writer. Sometimes the letter is prepared as a formal report to a denominational or church official. In any event, the personalizing of it sharpens the focus, forces clarity of reporting, and tempers any tendency to euphoria. When the summary letter is in its final form, it is the person's property which he can use in whatever way he wishes. Even if requested by the person to do so, the counselor will not normally send or give a copy of the summary to a third party. This is policy because the personal nature of the summary, coupled with the recording of growing insights, requires face-to-face interpretation by the person in order for it to be fully understood and appreciated by another individual.

The outline urges the person to write in his most natural person-to-person style. He is asked to interpret the findings and his experience in an open, positive manner. Attention is called to a sample summary letter attached to the outline. It is suggested that his summary should more or less follow the pattern of the sample. However, it is emphasized that his letter should in all respects be characteristic of himself. The sample is there to serve only as evidence of how another person wrote a summary.

The person is reminded to review and interpret the findings on the half-dozen instruments used. He is invited to include any insights gained about himself, any new understandings of his professional strengths, any decision made, and any short- or long-range plans developed.

The outline asks the person to write the summary letter in rough draft form and to send it to the counselor for his editing and contributions. The counselor usually spends about two hours working over a summary letter. The counselor normally takes out a number of words which impede the flow of thought, adds words to smooth connections, takes out repetitive sentences, adds parts of sentences to complete thoughts or ideas, and sometimes adds a paragraph where a part of the letter seems incomplete. The summary letter becomes a document produced by the person and the counselor. It is typed in its final form at the center. The person receives the original and one copy. A copy is kept at the center in the person's file.

At the time the finished summary letter is returned to the person, the counselor writes a private letter to the person in which important items in the summary may be referred to and emphasized. Also the counselor often reiterates some of the significant insights gained during the three-day program. Sometimes there is general information or personal detail included in this private letter. Always there is an interpretation of and possibly quotations from the psychological report.

174

Findings, Conclusions, and Questions

A study of 117 ministers seen in the three-day Career Development Planning Program provided some interesting data. There was a constellation of major motivated capabilities (talents) which was characteristic of the persons studied. The combination of talents often found in the pastors included a knack for conceptualizing facts and information into plans. Generally they had a natural inclination to lead and guide people, but they preferred to lead and guide through a teamwork relationship. It was found that many ministers are fairly strong on the indirect type of soft-sell persuasiveness.

It could be said the prototype of the minister is a person whose style is to gently lead people to cooperate in the implementing of ideas which the minister has helped form into plans. This is not to say that a pastor with this style of work is the ideal minister. It only means that a significant number of ministers who remain in religious occupations do have this working life style.

Other research has established that those ministers who stay longest in church occupations are extroverted-intuitive-feeling-judging types. This finding was confirmed in this survey.

The following findings are tentative. In general it can be said that ministers are less likely to be extroverted than are people in the total population. At the same time they are more likely to be intuitive than nonclergy. Clergymen marry women who are likely to be more intuitive than women in general, but they may be less intuitive than the minister himself. In spite of the image ministers have of themselves as thinkers (scholars), they are much more likely to be feeling-oriented. The women they marry are not only feeling-oriented, but they tend to be more feeling-oriented than both the minister himself and other women. Clergymen are twice as likely to be judging (doing) types than are most other persons. There is a strong tendency for ministers to marry women who are judging (doing) types like themselves. One in ten clergymen marries a woman who has the same typology traits he has.

One in twenty-five is likely to marry a woman who is his opposite in the four major trait categories.

During the first eighteen months in the first American Baptist Career Center, a total of 179 persons were seen. Of this number, five were at the center one or two days. Thirty-three came for a single consultation an hour-and-a-half long. Forty-one persons came with their spouses for a half-day of testing and consultation. A hundred persons were enrolled for the full three-day Career Development Planning Program.

As a part of a detailed study of all the services of the center, seven special questions were directed to the hundred persons who had experienced the three-day career counseling program. Seventy-nine responded.

Question 1.   To what degree did the program assist you in recognizing the areas of your professional strengths?

Response: 35 very much, 35 considerably, 8 somewhat, 1 very little.

Question 2.   Was your awareness of your personal identity enhanced by the program?

Response: 53 yes, greatly enhanced; 26 yes, slightly enhanced.

Question 3.   Did the experience help you to increase objectivity regarding your current job situation?

Response: 23 very much, 33 considerably, 18 somewhat, 4 very little.

Question 4.   In what ways has your process of decision-making been affected by the experience?

Response: 21 significantly changed my decision-making style, 44 reinforced my style, 12 affected my style very little.

Question 5.   Did a particular personal or professional decision grow directly out of your career assessment experience?

Response: 42 yes, 29 no.

Question 6.	How much did the center assist you in discovering answers for the questions you brought to the center?
Response:	18 very much, 43 considerably, 14 somewhat, 2 very little.
Question 7.	As you reflect on your visit to the center, do you feel that the staff understood your reasons for coming and adequately dealt with them?
Response:	59 definitely yes, 14 probably yes, 4 somewhat, 2 very little.

The writer of the evaluation report stated the following conclusion: "In summary regarding career assessment, it would seem that the persons who utilized this service are highly positive in their reactions to it. This conclusion is reinforced by the written comments which the respondents often added to each question." [23]

Because career counseling is a new service for professional church personnel, many crucial questions still need to be researched carefully. Some of the most pressing questions are: (1) Does church career counseling increase the minister's self-understanding in relation to his occupation? If so, how, how much, and in what ways? (2) Does career counseling increase role clarification as related to tasks in the church as well as other sectors of a person's life? (3) Does career counseling clarify a pastor's self-image as a person, and if so, how does this affect his work style? (4) Does career counseling affect or alter personal dynamics? If so, in what ways? (5) What does career counseling show regarding the adequacy of emotional rewards in professional religious work? (6) What does career counseling suggest regarding the use of, stimulation, or impact on, the intellectual capacities of professional church workers? (7) What questions does career counseling raise regarding the relationship between theological education and effectiveness and/or contentment in pro-

23. Robert D. Rasmussen, "Evaluation Committee Report Concerning the Center for the Ministry of the American Baptist Convention" (Valley Forge: Commission on the Ministry, 1969).

fessional church work? (8) Does career counseling say anything about the need for and ways and means of balancing the personal and family needs with the demand of the clergyman's church work? (9) What effect does career counseling have on placement or advancement in church or church-related work? (10) How does church career counseling relate to placement of clergymen in part- or full-time secular jobs?

Teaching Ministry in Seminaries

Vernon L. Strempke

In response to an inquiry about "new mathematics," a high school teacher said, "In my opinion it isn't new, and it isn't math!" An assessment of the teaching ministry of many seminaries might suggest a similar harsh conclusion, "It isn't teaching, and it isn't ministry!" Rather than debate the validity of such a judgment, there is more potential value in considering the identification, correlation, and application of resources inherent in the church's ministry and the seminary teacher's profession.

The Church and Its Ministry

An understanding of a teaching ministry in the seminary can begin with some brief observations about the church and its ministry. What is the nature of the church? What identifies the church's ministry? What are its characteristics? Who is a minister?

Christ: The Dynamic Norm of Ministry

A Christian's ministry is derivative of the church and its ministry, and the same is true for the ministry of a seminary. The church consists of those persons who by the Holy Spirit are faithful to Christ through their response to the Word and sacraments. The *Church* is the faithful people of God; the *church* is an institution of society. A people has institutions, but it never itself is an institution.

The church's ministry is the communication of God's Word

and the administration of his sacraments. Traditionally this means that ministry includes such functions as preaching, baptizing, and administering the Lord's Supper. However, these functions are supplemented by many others which identify the church and its ministry.

The intent of the church's ministry is to make it possible for people to encounter Christ and to experience reconciliation. Christ is the divine Word of reconciliation; he is God's sacrament. The church is Christ's continuing presence in this world. For this reason the church is spoken of as the body of Christ and as the primal sacrament (*Ursakrament*). The sacramental presence of the church among and through human beings is based on the understanding of a sacrament being that which "partakes fully of the immediacy of human life and yet communicates a meaning that transcends human life." [1]

The church's ministry, in other words, has a transcendent impetus, which is derived from Christ and not from society or its culture. The purpose and dynamic of the church's ministry are expressions of divine will and creative activity. Without this involvement of Christ, the church's ministry would become introverted and demonic. The sacramental presence of Christ is a dynamic norm for the church and its ministry. This is to be remembered when assessing the teaching ministry in a seminary.

God's Word: The Mark of the Church and Its Ministry

The apostle Paul in his epistles reports the meaning of ministry for the early Christians. The most exact definition of ministry is provided by Paul according to Walter Lowrie in *Ministers of Christ*.[2] Paul writes, "One should regard us as ministers of Christ and stewards of God's mysteries" (I Cor. 4:1). Paul also writes about "ministers of a new covenant" (II Cor. 3:6), and "ambassadors of the gospel" (Eph. 6:19).

1. Urban T. Holmes III, *The Future Shape of Ministry* (New York: Seabury Press, 1971), p. 5.
2. Lowrie, *Ministers of Christ* (Cloister Press, 1946).

These and other descriptions are reflected in the traditional expression "ministry of the Word," or "the ministry of God's Word."

"The Word of God" is a metaphor by which Christians commonly refer to God's revelation to man. This *Word* is of Divinity in contrast to the *word* of humanity. It conveys the implication that God speaks to man and that man listens as well as hears! The Word of God focuses on a message that God has given and continues to give to man. This message is an essential ministry for man's salvation.[3] For Christians, Jesus is God's Word in human form. He is the incarnate Word. Being the Word of God, Jesus is the message of good news which man needs. This Word, therefore, is a ministry of God to man; it is personalized in Jesus, the Christ.

During the course of the church's life and ministry, there have been confusion and controversy about the words of the Bible being the Word of God. There have been honest differences among Christians about what constitutes God's Word in reference to the holy writings known as the Scriptures or the Bible. Some Christians have been heretical in their literal use of the Bible. Martin Luther spoke clearly on the subject. The literal words of the Bible did not constitute God's Word for Luther, nor did he limit the Word to the Bible. Luther strongly emphasized that spoken or proclaimed words have the potential of carrying the message of the Word. The message of the Word is what drives Christ into the heart of a person; it makes him think seriously and respond. As a consequence of the Word's activity, a person repents, is forgiven, and lives his life accordingly.[4] This activity identifies the ministry of the Word.

All Christian denominations of today in some measure share the conviction that ministry should be in conformity with the

3. Seward Hiltner, *Theological Dynamics* (Nashville: Abingdon Press, 1972), p. 166.
4. Martin Luther, *Letters of Spiritual Counsel*, ed. and tr. by Theodore G. Tappert. Library of Christian Classics XVIII (Philadelphia: The Westminster Press, 1955), 15.

Scriptures. Though this statement is accepted as true, it is somewhat platitudinous. The Scriptures for Christians are the primary source of inspiration, teaching, and guidance for living. But the Scriptures don't have answers for all questions. They have much to say about the church and its ministry which is descriptive and normative, but they do not answer some questions about ordination, succession, women and the ministry, the pastoral office, etc.[5] The church, therefore, faithfully minds the Scriptures in support and guidance for its ministry, and it is at the same time alert to the possibility of additional assistance from the perspectives of traditional church practice and contemporary circumstances. The Scriptures in this way are the central focus for the church, and they are consequently the mark of identification and the norm to which it conforms.

Rigorous efforts in self-evaluation for conformity to the Scriptures were exercised by the prophets, the apostles, and also Jesus. Their self-questioning recognized the necessity of bringing their message and lives under the scrutiny of God's Word.[6] When such scrutiny confirms conformity with the gospel of the Scriptures, there is vital continuity with Christ's ministry. Evidence of confusion and frustration regarding the church's ministry suggests the necessity of taking more seriously God's Word. That Word speaks with authority to the faithful minister of the church; it is that Word which he serves, regardless of his particular ministry.

The Christian's Ministry

Christ through the Word and sacraments is the normative mark of the church's ministry. Through these means a person becomes a Christian and is empowered by God's Spirit for ministry. The individual Christian becomes a participant in that ministry through baptism and a public confirmation of

5. J. Robert Nelson, "Styles of Service in the New Testament and Now," *Theology Today*, 22 (1965), 85-88.
6. Daniel Jenkins, *The Gift of Ministry* (London: Faber and Faber, 1947), pp. 29-31.

his faith in Christ. The Christian is a privileged servant or, more literally, a slave (*doulos*); his ministry is a service (*diakonia*) for Christ. Old and New Testament meanings are interwoven into this heritage of servanthood.

This heritage of servanthood belongs equally to laity and clergy. Though the Scriptures provide for some persons to be called by God through the church to fulfill particular responsibilities, nevertheless the essential ministry is consigned to God's people. The Scriptures do not assign exclusively the ministry of Christ to ordained clergy. The significance of the ministerial office of every Christian is the basis for the importance of the ordained clergyman's office. There are no distinctions of rank among Christ's servants, but there are distinctions in the nature of their services or ministries.

The Gospels specifically refer to the Christian's identification as a servant and his understanding of ministry. "Whosoever will be first among you must be your servant" (Mark 10:44). Nothing less than genuine service is ministry; it is that which is beneficial for those being served. Christian service is not merely a work of philanthropy, but a true sharing in suffering or need. The imperative rule for the Christian is to serve "just as the Son of man has not come to be served, but to serve" (Mark 10:45).

The Ministry's Unity and Diversity of Functions

In the Gospel of Matthew (25:31-46) Jesus includes a broad variety of activities in his discussion of ministry or services. They are: giving food and drink, offering shelter, providing clothes, visiting the sick and imprisoned. This passage communicates the thought that ministry is basically "being for others," even to the point of giving one's life for another. As a consequence "early Christianity learned to regard and describe as *diakonia* all significant activity for the edification of the community."[7] This understanding of min-

7. Gerhard Kittel, ed., *Theological Dictionary of the New Testament*, II (Eerdmans Publishing Co., 1964), 87.

istry contributed to unity in commitment, thought, and function of the original fellowship of Christians.

In contrast to the early church, the contemporary church is involved in emphasizing specialized ministries; thereby, it confronts the danger of conversely deemphasizing the unity of its ministry. This danger sometimes appears within a seminary community. The various curricular disciplines and skills often become isolated fragments of varying importance in the experience of the seminarian. Such divisive emphases may encourage consideration of specialized ministries but may also discourage or prohibit an appreciation for the ministry's unity. This potential danger is supported by the attitudinal and behavioral incompatibility which is too often observable among seminary teachers, parish clergy, and other professional leaders of the church.

The ministry of the church is viewed by the apostle Paul (Eph. 4) as an organic unity; each part is essentially related to all the other parts. Specialized ministries can be advantageous and even necessary, but they are never independent of the church's corporate, unified ministry.

The Ministry of Teaching

The teaching function belongs to the essence of the church's ministry.[8] The church must teach, or it will not be the church. Just as the function of teaching was emphasized in the ministry of the Israelites as reflected throughout the Old Testament (Lev. 10:11; Deut. 6:4-9; Prov. 1:8; Neh. 8; Ezek. 44: 23), so also was it emphasized in the ministry of Christ and his disciples throughout the New Testament (Mark 1:22; Matt. 4:23; Luke 4:15; John 3:2; Acts 1:1; 5:42; I Cor. 12:28; Eph. 4:11; Col. 3:16; I Tim. 4:11; 6:2). All Christians comprising the church have responsibility to teach, but specific teaching assignments are given to selected persons or agencies. The teacher in a seminary is an example.

8. James D. Smart, *The Teaching Ministry of the Church* (Philadelphia: The Westminster Press, 1954), p. 11.

The Church's Teaching Ministry in the Seminaries

The very nature and purpose of theological seminaries relates them fundamentally to the church and its ministry. The term "seminary" comes from the eighteenth canon of the Council of Trent (1545-1563). This canon directed bishops of the principal sees in the Catholic Church to establish educational institutions for the preparation of ministerial candidates. Each seminary was to be a "perpetual seed-plot of ministers of God" *Dei ministrorum perpetuum seminarium* (Session XXIII, July 15, 1563, Canon 18).

Since the Council of Trent the seminary has had the primary responsibility of preparing clergy for the Roman Catholic Church. It replaced the medieval system, whereby ministerial candidates first gained mastery of theological disciplines at a university and then served an apprenticeship of pastoral practice under the guidance of local clergy. In some instances it was advantageous after the Council of Trent to continue utilizing the faculties of universities for theological studies. Where this occurred, the Tridentine seminary emphasized ecclesiastical understandings and practices in addition to training in piety. The name Tridentine refers to the Tridentine Profession of Faith to which all Catholic priests and public teachers since 1564 must subscribe as decreed by Pius IV.

The Protestant seminaries in Europe followed a pattern of development similar to that of the Roman Catholic Church. Though dependent initially upon clergy with a European theological education, American Protestantism during the seventeenth and eighteenth centuries established colleges primarily to prepare ministerial candidates. Such "higher education" often supplemented programs of apprenticeship for the candidates. At the beginning of the nineteenth century, Protestants were responding to the rising standards for theological education and founding their own seminaries. Protestant denominations and the Roman Catholic Church, through the teaching ministry of their seminaries, have directly influenced the characteristics and qualifications of their clergy.

Correlations Between the
Ministries of Church and Seminary

The assumption made at the beginning of this chapter was that an adequate and valid consideration of the teaching ministry of the seminary necessarily includes understandings of the church and its ministry. It can be said that the seminary is a microcosm of the church. That which uniquely identifies the church can be expected to be identifiable in the seminary. Whatever the church is to be doing through its ministry in the world must also be occurring in its ministry within the seminary. The goals, methods, and resources for achieving the church's mission in the world need to be analyzed, applied, experienced, and evaluated as well as those of the seminary. The scope and depth of the seminary's ministry may be more than the church's ministry in the world, but can it justifiably be less?

This discussion about church and seminary in respect to ministry, more specifically the ministry of teaching, involves correlations. Correlations can lead to deeper insights and meanings, and thereby are exciting and refreshing, stimulating and penetrating, dialogical and communicative. Correlations focus on connections, mutualities, commonality of implications, and reciprocal relations in respect to nature and process. In the following sections the church's ministry and the teaching ministry of seminaries will be correlated in respect to these basic functional factors of Christian ministry: (1) responding to the Holy Spirit; (2) encountering Christ; (3) serving persons; (4) maintaining community; (5) conforming to the liberating Word.

Responding to the Holy Spirit

Theological systems consistently acknowledge that the Holy Spirit creates the church and affects the work of ministry among people. However, conscious awareness of the Holy Spirit is often conspicuously absent or distorted in the minds of clergy and laity. This lack of sensitivity to the Holy Spirit is reflected in attempts to be religious or Christian by relying on human resources or potentials or by depending on being imitations of Christ. If the Holy Spirit is given consideration, too often it is in terms of only being a helper who facilitates, supports, and completes human effort. God's Spirit is usually thought to be a participant in the enterprises of good people. This is in contrast to the reality of the Holy Spirit being present and active in accomplishing God's purposes with or without human participation. The Spirit brings humans into relation with God and gives them an openness and responsiveness to his presence, thus an opportunity to participate in his continuing creative activities.

The Holy Spirit is essential for a theology of relationship. The Holy Spirit is already in relation with the person who begins the search for God. Theology is not a series of speculations about a lonely God removed by infinite distance. God is not "Wholly Other" or an inaccessible *Ding-an-sich* as described by Kant. If man gains a relation with God, it is achieved by the Holy Spirit who encounters him.

The neo-personalism of Paul E. Johnson is consistent with a theology of relationship which finds man being directly encountered by the Spirit of God.[9] God's encounter with many, according to Johnson, is not mediated through a "rational structure of conscious experience," but it is an immediate, personal experience. The Holy Spirit's coming to man is not an idea, a doctrine, or a mediated apprehension of God; it is the person's experience of the Divinity relating to humanity.

Human oversight, blindness, and rejection of the Holy Spirit's initiating presence make for a dull, discouraging, and tragic existence. Responsiveness to the Holy Spirit enables a person to escape his isolation, his closed conceptual and interpersonal systems. He discovers the whole meaning of existence emerging from this experience of God meeting him on the road to nowhere.

9. "The Trend Toward Dynamic Interpersonalism," *Religion in Life,* 35 (1966), 758.

A demonstration of the Holy Spirit's invasion of daily life would radically change attitudes, participation, and activities among members of the church. Activated convictions to be instruments or agents of God's Spirit would release new creative energies for worship, administration, education, and other functional ministries. In fact the Spirit's guidance could release Christians from obsolete forms of ministry and call them into new and beneficial ministries.

The limited role acknowledged for the Holy Spirit in the church is paralleled in the seminary. The teaching ministry of the seminary seems to evidence greater reliance on intellectual and will power than dependence on the Holy Spirit for living the Christian life as well as fulfilling responsibilities of ministry. Insensitivity to the Holy Spirit encourages exclusive concentration on human resources and ingenuity which breed anxiety, competition, defensiveness, and separateness. The consequence of depreciating the Holy Spirit's activity in the seminary is a crippled educational ministry which handicaps other ministries of the church.

When the Holy Spirit is central in the seminary's teaching ministry, faith in Christ is then instilled and nurtured within teachers and students. They are able to achieve community through the Spirit's creativity by relating significantly among themselves and with others. By this creative power the teacher can become very real as a Christ to the student. The same divine power makes possible responses of the student to the teacher in directions of personal affirmation, intellectual insight, and behavioral achievement. Teacher and student thus constitute the nucleus of a learning community in which there is mutual acceptance, respect, trust, and appreciation for one another's roles and contributions. In this dynamic context the Spirit can teach through either the teacher or student; obviously such an achievement of the Spirit is humiliating for some teachers.

A teaching ministry with the involvement of the Holy Spirit is identified primarily with the teacher-learner relationship and secondarily with theoretical content. The seminary teacher is first a minister of the Holy Spirit who incarnates the Christ; and second, he or she is a teacher of a particular subject which at best may be about Christ.

Encountering Christ

Jesus' teaching ministry for the disciples inescapably involved them in confrontations with God and the reality of his kingdom. Through these confrontations they were called into a relation of faith with Christ and consequently into a new life which was revolutionized by his presence. When Jesus taught his disciples, they gained more than a new religion, or new religious ideas, or new principles for moral life. He gave them himself. His giving of himself was the giving of his life, which he lived in oneness with God. Jesus' ministry was sacrificial and confrontational.

The teaching ministry of the apostles and early Christians was a continuing, conscious emphasis on the reality of encountering the living Christ. The apostle Paul's life and ministry illustrate this fact; Paul was converted when he encountered Christ on the road to Damascus. Following his conversion Paul lived with and for Christ rather than against him. The intensity of Paul's relation to Christ prompted him to speak about the "Christ who lives in me" (Galatians 2:20). Faith in Christ for Paul wasn't acceptance of a doctrine, but it was confrontation with the reality of God's presence through Christ.

The church throughout its history has discovered and rediscovered that the role and function of God are to encounter and to reveal. The Christian faith is the fruit of God's action in confronting and encountering man through Jesus Christ. Divine revelation is, therefore, not a concept or doctrine about God but a personal dynamic relation with him.[10] This conscious awareness of Christ's encounter and involvement in the totality of life characterized the lives of the early Christians.

10. *Ibid.*, p. 759.

They lived in the continuity of Christ's presence by the gift of the Holy Spirit, which produced revolutionary changes in their thoughts, attitudes, and behavior.

Dynamic interpersonal psychology as developed by Paul E. Johnson helps illuminate the meaning of God encountering man. Johnson as a psychologist begins with the experience of "I," but he asserts that the "I" is known only to itself in relation to "Thou." [11] He concurs with Martin Buber that real life is meeting in address and response. For Johnson this is more than psychological theory; it is life! If a person is fully alive, he is sensitive and aware of persons encountering him. It is the encounter of others and the ensuing relationships which hold the meanings of life.

According to Johnson, therefore, revelation is relational and not propositional. God's revelation to man does not consist of linguistic symbols or other abstractions, but it is God giving himself totally to man in relationship. The ultimate revelation and expression of God for man is the incarnation of Jesus Christ. Christ is the mediator of God, whose reconciling and loving presence is known directly and not by inference. This revealing, forgiving, and loving presence of Christ encounters man and enables him to love God and man in response. The experienced reality of encountering Christ's presence is the very essence of the church.

This heritage of encountering and being in Christ's presence is reflected in today's church. It legitimately has the valid objective of enabling people to encounter Christ through its ministries. Since the seminary is the church's seedbed for ministers, its teaching ministry necessarily aims to involve students in a continuing, personal encounter with Christ.

Theological education, like all education, must be personal; "it must take place in a personal encounter, *and only secondarily is it transmissive.*" [12] The seminary teacher encounters the person of the student and solicits a response. In this con-

11. *Ibid.,* p. 757.
12. Reuel Howe, *Man's Need and God's Action,* p. 114.

frontation the teacher communicates meanings by his being and doing. This process is reciprocal for teacher and student. Though they do not give up their roles, nevertheless the mutuality of their dynamic relationship provides new, emerging meanings.

St. Augustine discussed the relation of teacher and student in "The Teacher." According to Augustine the teaching-learning process for teacher and student approximates "dwelling in each other." Reciprocity, mutuality, and empathy are involved in living together and are expressed in communicating, listening, and feeling. Augustine indicates the teacher-student relation has significant dimensions for him because of his awareness that Christ, the Master, dwells within him.[13] Christ's presence within Augustine influenced his personality and his encounters with others. This presence participated in Augustine's teaching-learning activities and made them a ministry.

Although the teaching ministry of the seminary must essentially be a significant personal encounter, it must also provide for the transmission of subject matter. The elements of encounter and transmission are complementary in this teaching-learning process. This is also true for other aspects of the church's life. It is a community of encounter, but also of tradition. Both are important to the church, and one is not to be subordinated to the other.

> When the content of the tradition is lost, the meaning of the encounter is lost, and in the end even encounter itself. And when encounter is lost, tradition becomes idolatrous and sterile. Both are necessary to the faith community, and both are dangerous and meaningless if separated. And Christian teaching must depend upon both.[14]

The teaching ministries of seminaries in the United States and Canada are becoming increasingly personal and student-

13. Roy Joseph Defarrari, ed., *The Fathers of the Church*, Vol. 59 (Washington: Catholic University of America, 1968), p. 51.
14. Howe, *Man's Need and God's Action*, pp. 114-15.

centered. This trend is confirmed in a study of theological education made by Charles R. Fielding.[15] This trend is encouraging, but it is long overdue. Unless candidates for the church's ministries experience meaningful encounters with Christ, teachers, and peers, they cannot be expected to duplicate such experiences for the benefit of others.

Serving Persons

Christians are called to be servants for others in achieving God's purposes. As servants they respond to the needs of others. The Christian's service or ministry as motivated by Christ aims to be person-centered. The service corresponds to a person's needs. It affirms him and makes it possible for him to exercise the option of becoming what God intended him to be. When this person-centered ministry is implemented in the educational context, the "centered" person is the student.

The purpose of the seminary can be defined in personal terms, namely, to prepare the student for ministry. This preparation is intended to be a ministry, and therefore has as its focus the whole person of the student. This theme is familiar in studies about theological education. The study reported by Bridston and Culver emphasizes the cultural, professional, and vocational growth of theological candidates.[16] Niebuhr's study acknowledges the importance of rational structure in theological education but even more "the facilitation of the process of personal growth and maturity in Christian faith and church commitment."[17] Fielding in his study of theological education discusses preparation of the whole person in terms of "ministerial formation."[18] Such formation is the result of

15. *Education for Ministry* (American Association of Theological Schools, 1966), pp. 109-13.

16. Keith R. Bridston and Dwight W. Culver, *The Making of Ministers* (Minneapolis: Augsburg Publishing Co., 1964), pp. 30-115.

17. H. Richard Niebuhr, Daniel Day Williams and James M. Gustafson, *The Advancement of Theological Education* (New York: Harper & Brothers, 1957), p. 173.

18. *Education for Ministry*, pp. 159-62.

a comprehensive ministry which combines emphases on human growth, professional competence, and growth in Christian life. By giving primary consideration to the total needs of the student, a teacher honors God by reverently respecting God's supreme creature. Man bears God's image, and his potentials are unpredictable. A teacher's sensitivity to the reality of God's involvement in human life makes him respectful and expectant of the student's potentials as well as of his own. The teacher with such an orientation to persons serves God by serving students. He tries to fashion his relationships with students in accordance with God's relationship to man. Without this commitment to practicing ministry through his teaching, the seminary teacher either demonstrates his lack of understanding, or he is denying for himself the validity of the gospel. Unless the teacher becomes the best of his ability the truth he teaches, he is merely dispensing information. Such teaching is apt to be content-centered, and this can be idolatrous.

Teaching, which ministers to the whole person in the Spirit of Christ, has the potential of significantly changing the student and qualifying him for ministry. The effected changes in a student are described by Charles R. Stinnette, Jr., in terms of transformation and transfiguration.[19] Changes of such a pervasive nature in a person are results of more than a socialization process. Socialization is a process of designed change through the stimulus-response program of learning. This process fails to provide meaning. The comprehension of meaning is the significance of history. The meaning of divine and human action leads to discoveries of identity, values, and potentials or alternatives of choice. These kinds of discoveries can constitute for a person the awareness of God participating in life. In responding to this awareness of Christ, a person can be transformed. Such transformation can enable the person to progress in consciously becoming a minister and in effectively fulfilling responsibilities toward others.

19. *Learning in Theological Perspective* (New York: Association Press, 1965), pp. 12, 68-88.

Various measurements have been developed for assessing human capacities and abilities for responding helpfully to people. These measurements can be employed before and after a program of learning experiences for the purpose of indicating degrees of change in thinking, acting, and feeling. For example, teachers for student nurses desire to increase empathetic capacities. R. W. Hyde has demonstrated that particular kinds of training in psychiatric faclities do increase empathy.[20] Similar changes have been discovered in ministerial students as a consequence of participating in programs of clinical pastoral education.[21] These and other measurements tend to support the conclusion that a person-centered ministry in the seminary does prepare students more adequately for responding to the needs of people through ministry.

The emphasis on the person has encountered and continues to encounter considerable resistance from scholastically oriented theological educators. Their "mind set" originates from medieval university education, which was based on authority and reason.[22] The classical tradition of antiquity was the authority for the sciences; biblical tradition was the authority for theology. Reason had the task of resolving contradictory elements of tradition, resisting heresies, and making conclusions relevant.

As a consequence of its scholastic heritage, theology is assumed to possess the knowledge of man. Theological doctrines of man tend to be absolutistic, and their advocates are prone to deny the need for correlating and confronting the interpretations of the social sciences regarding human existence. For example, Barth fails to consider adequately psy-

20. Harriet M. Kandler and R. W. Hyde, "Changes in Empathy: A Student Nurses During Psychiatric Affiliation," *Nursing Review*, 2 (1953), 33-36.

21. Orlo Strunk and Kenneth Reed, "The Learning of Empathy: A Pilot Study," *The Journal of Pastoral Care*, 14 (1960), 44-48.

22. Aarne J. Siirala, "Implications of the Personalistic Era for Theological Education" (mimeographed paper, Waterloo Lutheran University, Waterloo, Ontario, 1965).

chological, sociological, anthropological, or even medical understandings of man.

The resistance of theological education to deal with the person, as distinct from the person's mind, is characteristic of the Western world's education. Reinhold Niebuhr makes this observation in his essay "The Person and the Mind in Modern Education." In speaking about modern Western culture's confusion about person, self, and mind, Niebuhr laments that "it does not see that self at all!" [23] The naturalistic, empirical sciences are strongly dominated by the scholastic tradition. This means the scientific understanding of man is derived from his understanding of nature. If these sciences provide new understandings of nature, adjustments are correspondingly made in the knowledge of man, but the basic dichotomy between mind and person remains unchanged.

This background explains the general opposition of the naturalistic-empirical sciences and theology to depth, analytical, personalistic, and interpersonal psychologies. This opposition is apparent in theological education which readily accepts without serious question the identification of mind and person, considers human feelings of little importance in comparison to theological and biblical truth, and reverences the principle that "knowledge is virtue."

The purpose of the church and its ministry as presented in the preceding sections requires identifying and serving the whole person in the totality of his situation. Scholastic patterns of theological education, which cogently offer brilliant abstractions of man but arrogantly ignore the whole person, are woefully inadequate for the personal and functional era. Such theological education shares in the demonic depersonalization of man, God's creation.

So long as mythological and ontological systems of scholasticism shape theological education, the so-called "academic"

23. Boyd H. Bode, Richard R. Niebuhr, *et al. Modern Education and Human Values*, Pitcairn-Crabb Foundation Lecture Series (University of Pittsburgh, 1948), v. 2, p. 24.

and "practical" curricular elements will remain separate and problematic. The solution is not in making the "practical" academic or the "academic" practical. Though cognition is a very important element in theological education, the teaching ministry of seminaries must include in its focus more than the rational powers of the person. The focus must be the whole person because the giving and receiving of ministry involved the totality of the human being and his situation. For this comprehensive ministry of teaching, the seminary must consequently be a context of openness and dialogue for resources from all disciplines which address themselves to man and his situation, as well as to the relation God establishes with man.

Maintaining Community

The church as a ministering community is crucially important for the individual Christian. The Christian becomes a minister and is received into the church through baptism. The church equips and nurtures the Christian for the implementation of his individual ministry and for his participation in the corporate ministry of fellow Christians. Just as a person's identity and continuing existence are dependent upon relations with other persons, so also the Christian is dependent upon other Christians who constitute the Christian community.

The preceding statements stress the fundamental relation of church and ministry. Neither ministry nor the minister can be considered in isolation from the church, which is an extended group of persons in communion with one another and with God as revealed in Christ. This community must be taken seriously if the seminary's teaching ministry is to achieve maximum benefits.

The Group: A Serving Community. What is said about church and ministry has correlations in discussing the seminary and its teaching ministry. Educators are generally agreed that advantageous group situations facilitate the teaching-learning process. Such a group includes the teacher(s), student(s), and others who may be involved in the teaching-learning. The group as a serving community holds considerable power and authority for the individual participant by influencing his sense of identity, authorizing his role, and approving his rewards. The group is not merely an economical way to teach; it is the matrix of the teaching-learning process.

The many educational values which reside in a group have not been generally recognized or thoroughly understood by most seminary teachers. The forces of a group, latent or active, among persons in and out of the classroom can be very supportive of individual learning. This extended group can be a valuable resource for the teacher rather than a handicap or roadblock. Skillful employment of a group's interests, needs, and assets avoids paralyzing struggles between teachers and students regarding what and how to learn.

A full exploration of the biblical record cannot be undertaken here to highlight the role of group fellowship in the history of God's people. Most sections of the Bible give proof for the conclusion that no personal religious life occurs without community or the fellowship of a group's members. Paul Tillich in referring to the biblical record observed there is no personal being without communal being.[24]

The New Testament takes for granted interpersonal brotherliness, mutual love, and common efforts of help as essential marks of the church being a community. The image of the church as the body of Christ implies the "many made one," each one a member-in-community and functioning together for mutual benefits (I Cor. 12:12-27). New Testament descriptions of the church in its infancy are frequently images of the family, households, and small clusters of people such as Jesus' disciples who met "all together in one place" (Acts 2:1). The community experienced in these small groups and the ministries to the individual members were intense and beneficial. The goals for this group life of community and ministry are stated by the author of Hebrews: "Let us consider

24. *Systematic Theology,* I, 176.

how to stir up one another to love and good works, not neglecting to meet together . . . encouraging one another" (Heb. 10:24-25*a*).

The Group: A Teaching-Learning Community. Seminary teachers, like many others in and outside their profession, often assume learning is an individual affair which may occur somewhat accidentally in the context of community. If a teacher does accept the group situation as the best context for learning, he or she may be referring to social, spatial, or economic aspects rather than the dynamics underlying learning. Too few seminary teachers can develop a class for effective participation in the teaching-learning process, because their education omitted skills for building and maintaining productive learning groups. The educational background of most seminary teachers doesn't include the principles and practices of teaching, because the knowledge of a discipline is erroneously assumed to qualify a person to teach it.[25]

Seminary teachers, as a consequence of their limitations as educators, rely heavily on the rational organization of material and upon their verbal behavior. Teaching from this perspective is largely a solo performance of the teacher, rather than an orchestration by teacher and students. Fielding, in his review of theological education, concludes that the seminary's ineffectiveness in preparing persons for ministry can be attributed in part to the domination and indiscriminate use of the lecture method.[26] The typical seminary professor is more ready to speak than to listen and is thus a poor model for ministry. Candidates for ministry in this kind of educational environment are apt to remain personally unchallenged and unexposed to the critical thinking of peers. As a result they can become crippled and dependent thinkers, or they can become insensitive, unresponsive, or rebellious because of their unvented thoughts and feelings. Usually overprotected students like these are incapable of continuing their own edu-

25. Fielding, *Education for Ministry*, p. 102.
26. *Ibid.*, p. 108.

cation, which is recognized as a widespread deficiency among clergy.[27]

A teacher-centered orientation to teaching in the seminary is unfortunate for the reasons already cited and because it violates the nature of ministry as interpreted by the church. Ministry emphasizes doing something with and for people rather than to people; ministry cultivates and draws out the talents of all the involved persons. When the resources of a group and its members are optimally appropriated for the teaching-learning task in the seminary, then the church's heritage of ministry is more fully realized.

The experience and research of educators support the distribution of teaching and learning responsibilities among persons who function as a group in pursuing a common educational endeavor.[28] When teaching and learning become the responsibilities of a group's members, individual learning is enhanced by the release of the group's varied resources and potentials. Difficulties in teaching and learning then become the concern of more than the individual teacher or learner. Members of the group provide acceptance, emotional support, factual input, feedback, and corrective information. Experience with these and other facets of a group's teaching-learning activity prepares participants for future ministries involving groups such as committees, organizations, task forces, and teams of staff members.

A variety of educational group methods have been developed of which "team learning" is among the most recent.[29] The educational experiences of students are centered in their learning team with the involvement of the teacher as a participating supervisor. The main objective of team learning is to respect the uniqueness of each person and encourage ex-

27. Niebuhr, *et al. The Advancement of Theological Education,* p. 209.

28. Leland P. Bradford, ed., *Human Forces in Teaching and Learning* (Washington: National Training Laboratories, National Education Association, 1961), pp. 34-47.

29. Gerard A. Poirer, *Students as Partners in Team Learning* (Berkeley, Calif.: Center of Team Learning, 1970).

pression of individual differences. Team learning is based on the assumption that by diversifying teaching and learning, ways may be devised to reach and teach all the group's participants most of the time. This educational model for teaching and learning is highly structured in design but very flexible in operation. It individualizes teaching and learning by more actively involving students and by exercising more strategically the teacher's diagnostic and resourceful responsibilities. Team learning commends itself for seminary teaching because of its philosophy, principles, and applicability in the ministries of churches.

The Expanded Group: A Context for Professional Education. Seminaries are gradually recognizing the disadvantages of being bipolar, involving only students and teachers.[30] The number of participants in the seminary's teaching-learning group is increasing through clinical courses, action training centers, field education, clinical pastoral education, internships, and similar teaching-learning experiences. The expanded group of participants includes professionals of various disciplines as sell as representatives of the church's clergy and laity. While granting the value of these belated developments, nevertheless these educational experiences too often continue to be "additives" rather than integral elements of the total curriculum. This circumstance is partially explained by the schizophrenia of seminaries regarding their character as graduate, professional, or trade schools.

A professional orientation to theological education most advantageously makes available and integrates the insights of scholarship and the skills of practice. The seminary which divorces scholarship from practice, or vice versa, has a debatable justification for existence in the interest of the church and its ministries. Professional education by its very nature involves theoreticians and practitioners; thus its teaching-learning community tends to be inclusive rather than exclusive. In addition

30. H. Richard Niebuhr, *The Purpose of the Church and Its Ministry* (New York: Harper & Brothers, 1956), p. 117.

to social and cultural orientations, contemporary education for professionals offers interdisciplinary courses. The design for this kind of professional preparation not only permits but requires the infusion of varying interests and diversified talents of persons from different professions.[31]

In recent years many professions have developed "group practice." Professional education's expanded group of involved persons has undoubtedly encouraged group practice among professionals. Doctors relate to clinics, lawyers join law firms, architects and engineers become associates in a consulting agency. Today's public generally expects the availability of resources provided by a professional team or cluster of professionals except in respect to the professionals in the church's ministries. Teamwork among professionals in the church's ministry is proving to be difficult in most instances and is developing slowly. More favorable developments can't be expected unless seminary education becomes more professional and group-oriented.

In *The Academic Revolution,* Jencks and Riesman[32] discuss a decided shift among professionals from being client-oriented to being colleague-oriented. A client orientation can be seductive in the direction of gaining approval, a larger practice, and more income rather than gaining professional expertise. A collegial orientation can be evaluative in the direction of identifying weaknesses, strengths, failures, and alternatives. Until theological education and the church's ministries become more decidedly collegial in orientation, their identification as professional will be questioned by many.

The possibility of theological education and the church's ministries becoming more professional is intertwined with the need for intensified and broadened group involvements. The potentials of the group have been discussed in reference to the preparation of ministerial candidates. Similar potentials await

31. Algo D. Henderson, "Social Change and Education for the Professions," *School and Society,* 98 (1970), 92-98.

32. Christopher Jencks and David Riesman, *The Academic Revolution* (Garden City, N.Y.: Doubleday & Co., 1968), p. 201.

realization in continuing education for clergy through a greater emphasis upon the group and professional criteria. Peer group activities can become professionally constructive and supportive rather than competitive and destructive.[33] Some clergy are assuming these responsibilities for themselves and colleagues through the Academy of Parish Clergy.[34] Other clergy recognize the possibilities of professional development through their involvement in groups of ministers from the local community. Such groups aim for the professional improvement of the church's ministries and solicit the participation of representatives from various professions and the church's laity. The viability of theological education "in the field" of "on the job" for ordained clergy as well as ministerial candidates has been demonstrated in some overseas younger churches and missions.

These trends and potentials suggest seminary teachers need to become more professional in the sense of integrating and balancing scholarship with practice as required by the church's ministries. Teachers in a seminary are easily tempted to become overly involved in a discipline at the expense of its application in professional practice of ministry. If they succumb to the temptation, their seminaries deserve the accusation of being discontinuous with today's ministry.[35] Seminary teachers can benefit professionally by serving periodically in the ministries of the church other than the teaching ministry. A sabbatical leave could be invested in professional experience, or specific professional services could be rendered on a part-time basis while fulfilling concurrently some teaching responsibilities. The ministry of many seminary teachers can be upgraded by their acquiring and applying skills for group-oriented teaching. Evaluations by peers and others in the extended teaching-learning group can stimulate professional

33. James D. Glasse, *Profession: Minister* (Nashville: Abingdon Press, 1971), p. 146.
34. The Academy of Parish Clergy, Inc., 3100 West Lake St., Minneapolis.
35. Fielding, *Education for Ministry*, p. 15.

growth and heighten the professional standards of other ministries in the church. Seminary teachers need freedom to gravitate toward graduate schools, research, or other ministries in the event their interests or commitments incline them in these directions. Decisions like these regarding the professional quality of the teaching ministry need to be made in the interest of the immediate group being served and thus also the total ministry of the church.

Conforming to the Liberating Word

The ministry of the church is the ministry of the Word, Jesus Christ. This Word is also the essence of the seminary's teaching ministry. By faithfully responding to the Word, students and teachers in the seminary are liberated in thought, word, and behavior for ministry. The Word is normative for the church and its seminaries. The seminary's teachers and students are expected to conform their personal and professional lives to the Word; the teaching and learning activities are intended to help achieve this conformity. Though the authority of the Word validates the seminary's teaching ministry, teachers and students aren't necessarily safeguarded from vexing ambiguities and conflicting interests or commitments.

Confusion and frustration are well known to many ministers of today's institutional church, including those in the teaching ministry. Seminary teachers, parish pastors, campus, military, and institutional chaplains, plus others, often feel caught in a network of opposing demands and loyalties. This is illustrated by comparing the circumstances experienced by the seminary teacher and parish pastor.

The pastor is committed to being a minister of the Word; he has a responsibility to his denomination; he is sensitive to the expectations of the congregation he serves; he confronts the specific needs and problems of parishioners. The seminary teacher's situation is similar to that of the parish pastor. Whether ordained or not, the Christian with responsibilities for teaching in a seminary is committed to being a minister of the Word. He relates responsibly to his denomination; he responds to the expectations of his faculty peers, the seminary's board members, and representatives of the supporting constituencies. He confronts the specific needs of seminarians and their families in and out of the teaching-learning situation. The seminary teacher's maceration can be as painful as it is for parish pastors and many other Christians of various occupational involvements.

How can this dilemma of the seminary teacher be resolved? How can he be liberated? Isn't the seminary teacher, like the pastor or others, wise in looking for liberation from the source of authorization for his ministry? Isn't his ministry, like every Christian's ministry, derived from Christ? The Christian's ministry isn't derived from the institutional church. This can't be an "either-or"! This *church* isn't equivalent to Christ! This is clear to most members of the Christian family, Roman Catholics as well as Protestants. The origin and authority of the teacher's ministry does not emerge from the lives of those who constitute the seminary community, nor from the seminary's community of students, faculty, and staff. The authority of the teacher's ministry isn't derived from the seminary's supporting constituencies of alumni, laity, congregations, or other groups and agencies. This community of persons and agencies can only confirm in Christ the authority and validity of the seminary teacher's ministry just as it does the ministries of others. The ministry can only be derived from Christ. Therefore, the seminary teacher, like the parish pastor, makes his priority the communication of God's Word when responding to his own concerns and to the needs of other persons.

The teacher's ministry in the seminary of all places needs to conform to God's liberating Word! How can seminarians become ministers of the Word except through liberating educational experiences which confront them with the Christ? Unless the ministry of seminary teachers conforms to the liberating Word, the ministries of students will lack conformity to the Word as well as its gifts of liberation. How can the liberation of God's Word be appropriated most meaningfully through the seminary's teaching ministry?

Reuel Howe states that "the function of the Church is to be in dialogue with the world." [36] He therefore proposes a dialogical method for seminary teachers in which the authoritative function of the Word can be experienced. The objective of this method is to recognize and engage in the dialogue between the meanings of the gospel and the meanings of people's lives. Howe insists that participants in theological education need to identify and relate the meaning of contemporary symbols to the meanings of traditional symbols. This is *doing* theology and not just *talking* theology.

The dialogical approach to seminary teaching concentrates on formulating questions of the *now* in preparation for hearing and understanding answers of the Word.[37] Experience with the dialogue between the Word and human phenomena clearly demonstrates the impossibility of discovering *the* answer but instead the possibility of responding with *an* answer of faith. This refreshing orientation to the meaning of human existence in dialogue with the Word makes the study of the Bible an equally exciting dialogical experience. After all, the Bible is the record of the dialogue between God and man which is continuing through the present moment.

Seminary teaching which conforms to the authority of the Word can be creative and informative. By contrast, teaching which conforms to theological propositions tends to be rigid, defensive, and destructive. Under the authority of theological orthodoxy, students and teachers can become inhibited and intimidated by their fears of heresy. They are frustrated in courageously exploring the meanings of the gospel for daily living. The meaning of the Word to love, to forgive, and to be free encourages participants in theological education to think and to experiment without being frustrated or immobilized by the possibilities of unorthodoxy. The Word in

36. Bridston, *The Making of Ministers*, pp. 220-21.
37. Reuel Howe, "Training for a Time of Change," *The Christian Century*, 87 (1970), 477-80.

the ministry of teaching can thus be an authoritative, liberating guide in discovering theological insights and formulating theological conclusions about the issues of life.

Accountability in the Teaching Ministry of Seminaries

This discussion of the seminaries' teaching ministry in relation to the church and its ministry is in principle a study of accountability. The preceding pages express implicitly the question: To whom or to what is the teaching ministry in seminaries accountable? There are also other related questions. What is the basis or the justification for such accountability? How can accountability be defined and identified in a seminary's teaching ministry? Some answers have been suggested which clarify the nature of the seminary's accountability in respect to its teaching ministry. Several ways have been indicated as to how seminaries can demonstrate their accountability through teaching ministries. The following paragraphs about accountability summarize some of the thoughts expressed in this chapter.

Seminaries no longer enjoy the halo of former years which made suspicions, investigations, and evaluations inappropriate on the part of supporting church constituencies. Segments of the public have lost faith in educational institutions, and so also, segments of the church have lost faith in seminaries as a realistic answer to the need for adequately prepared religious leadership in our day. For some people the seminary has credibility, but serious questions often are raised about its teaching program.

Educational accountability is comparable to other abstract virtues, such as loyalty and honesty, which are universally acknowledged but often difficult to describe and to apply in specific situations. Part of the difficulty stems from the multidimensional character of accountability. Three types of accountability in education are often delineated, and they are proposed as being applicable to the seminary in the context of this discussion.[38] They are: goal accountability, program accountability, and outcome accountability.

A seminary is accountable to the church through an institutional commitment or administrative relationship to a denomination or denominations. As a consequence the seminary is accountable to the church for selecting goals which are in accord with the church and in support of its ministries. The board of a seminary, which is charged with the operation of the seminary, is usually accountable to the church through a denominational agency. The accountability of a seminary's teaching ministry can be judged by the correlation of its goals with those of the church and its ministry: namely, by the power of the Holy Spirit to communicate God's Word and administer the sacraments, to be agents for encountering Christ and experiencing his reconciliation.

A strategy and design for a teaching ministry is developed in accordance with selected goals. This teaching ministry or program is usually the joint responsibility of a seminary and its faculty. Teachers are accountable for the outcomes of their teaching activities, but they can only be held accountable within the parameters of the program, which is formally approved by those who have ultimate operational responsibility for a seminary. Administrative staff are specifically accountable for maintaining the adopted program which is appropriate for achieving a specific set of goals.

By baptism a Christian is a minister and is responsible to Christ and his church for living a life of ministry. A Christian's ministry may be realized through teaching in a seminary, which is an agency of the church with responsibility for an educational program. The program accountability of a seminary's teaching ministry can be assessed in terms of correlation with the church's ministry in respect to such functional factors as responding to the Holy Spirit, encountering

38. Marvin C. Alkin, "Accountability Defined," *Evaluation Comment,* University of California, Center for the Study for Evaluation, 3 (May, 1972), pp. 1-5.

Christ, serving persons, maintaining community, and conforming to the liberating Word.

Outcome accountability for the teaching ministry of a seminary relates most directly to those in the roles of teacher and student. Although teachers and students have joint responsibility for the outcome of their common efforts, the teacher has in addition an administrative responsibility. The teacher is responsible for administering the sequence of educational experiences in such a way as to satisfy specific objectives and criteria for the program.

The ministry of the seminary is more adequately described as a teaching-learning process for which the community or group of teachers and students have a shared accountability for the outcome of their efforts. In recent years an increasing number of church representatives with a variety of professional qualifications has contributed primarily to the teaching process of the seminary's ministry. This trend is in harmony with the nature of the church and its ministry; it also makes the outcome of the seminary's ministry more directly accountable to the church's constituency. When the teaching ministry of a seminary is viewed as a Christian context of dynamic interpersonal responsibility, it correlates favorably with the nature of the church and its ministry.

The Ministry of
Educational Administration

James Edward Doty

Paul E. Johnson has stated that interpersonal psychology has certain emphases that one needs to note. Succinctly he has summarized his position on the uniqueness of interpersonal psychology as he enumerates the following areas:

1. Persons are the central focus of this psychology.
2. Persons confront each other in I-Thou relationships.
3. Personal motives are responses to significant persons in one's social orbit.
4. The desires and efforts of persons are aimed toward goals valued by other persons.
5. Persons work for values in order to share them with, or keep them from, other persons.
6. From defensive tactics come fear, rivalry, and poverty; from sharing come mutual confidence, cooperation, and growth.
7. The health of persons and societies depends upon the kind of relations persons develop toward each other; when interpersonal relations are insecure, hostile, and predatory, the society declines, and its members suffer nervous disorders; when interpersonal relations provide security, love, and mutual aid, the society prospers, and its members mature in creative wholeness.[1]

1. *Christian Love* (Nashville and New York: Abingdon-Cokesbury Press, 1951), pp. 6-7.

The importance of Johnson's interpersonal psychology emphases can readily be seen in their application to the educational opportunity in academia. Johnson in a later publication wrote, "My desire is to be a responsive person meeting you as a responsive person. This is what we mean by responsive counseling, where each is continually listening and responding to the other." [2]

As Johnson developed responsive counseling further, he maintained:

> Dynamic interpersonal psychology will give a larger place to the whole context of relationships in which the person is involved. The unconscious life is continuously engaged with the conscious in supportive and conflicting ways. The transactions with time, space, and objects in the world belong to the whole conscious-unconscious life of the person as he interacts with them to pursue his course of life. The community of persons around him provides the matrix of his desiring, in the give-and-take of mutual address and response. Among persons there is an interchange of experience by verbal and nonverbal communication. [3]

Johnson has maintained that the counselor fulfills his responsibility by responding "with my whole being to the person before me at this moment. He may be a stranger but he has full claim upon me. For this hour and this person I am called to give my best." [4]

It is obvious that both Frankl and Buber have influenced Johnson in his synthesis of what it means to be a responsible person. Buber maintained that "genuine responsibility exists only when there is real responding. Respond to what? To what happens to one? To what is seen and heard and felt—each concrete hour alloted to the person with its content drawn from the world and from destiny it speaks for the man who is attentive. . . . Responsibility presupposes one

2. *Person and Counselor,* p. 9.
3. *Ibid.,* p. 47.
4. *Ibid.,* p. 173.

who addresses me primarily, that is, from a realm independent of myself and from whom I am answerable. He addresses me about something that he has entrusted to me and that I am bound to take care of loyally. [5]

For the past half decade on the university campuses, one has heard the student not only in his plea for responsibility but in his desire to be an authentic person. This for the student is the individual free from sham, from pretense, an honest individual who is open and free of defensive reactions. The student is aware of the professor who is nonauthentic and is quick to judge him by not taking his course offerings. Authenticity shines through, and the student is aware of the relationship that has meaning and purpose.

It is in the Christian context of *agape* that one theologian has defined it as "simply being present when there is a need." Helmuth Thielicke says in his superb book *The Ethics of Sex* that

> *agape* therefore penetrates beyond the superficialities of the momentary adequacy or inadequacy of the other person and addresses itself to his ultimate mystery. And this is precisely what makes it creative: the other person knows that he is being addressed and respected at the core of his being, at that point of human dignity which is unconditioned by, and independent of, what he in actuality and which has its own hidden history with God. In this way *agape* brings out, "loves" out, as it were, the real person with the other human being. This is why all those who came into contact with Jesus—and especially the dubious characters, the harlots and publicans, the outcasts, the outsiders, the insulted and injured—were dignified by his *agape* and grew up into that dignity. They did not first have to qualify themselves in order to become worthy of his love; rather they were qualified by this love; and if this is not misunderstood in the sense of idealistic philosophy, one might even say that under the warmth of this love they grew to be something beyond themselves. This love addressed itself to the child of God within

5. Martin Buber, *Between Man and Man*, tr. by R. G. Smith (New York: The Macmillan Co., 1947), pp. 16, 45.

them, and therefore it also liberated that child of God within them. It was a creative breath that blew upon them.[6]

During the Congo uprising in 1964 I was invited by the Methodist Board of Missions to do emergency counseling for missionary personnel who had been evacuated from the central and northern parts of the Congo into the comparative safety of the southern sector. One afternoon as I was lecturing at our Methodist Theological Seminary at Mulungwishi, I was using the Greek word *agape,* obviously meaning "God's love." I was attempting to delineate the uniqueness of *agape* in a time of massive hostility such as the Congo was facing during that very week. An African pastor was translating my English into the Swahili and misunderstood the word *agape* and used the Swahili word *ngape.* After the mistranslation had been going on for a period of several minutes, one of the missionary pastors interrupted. "Pastor Joab, the speaker is using the Greek word *agape* meaning 'God's love' and you are translating the Swahili word meaning 'how much.' "

Obviously, for the rest of the address the mistranslation was corrected. However, the more I heard it, the better I liked the mistranslation. Each person asks himself ultimately, "How much is God's love?" The responsive counselor searching for authenticity and meaning enables the person to know that God's love is unfathomable, as the counselor now personifies his willingness to give time and effort to the counselee.

Johnson maintains that there are three moving actions in the search for authenticity. "(1) I seek to be as fully aware as I can be at the moment. (2) I choose how I will invest my life. (3) I take responsibility for the choice I have made, whatever may come, whether tragic suffering or joy, from my actions and my limitations." [7]

Whether one is hearing Thielicke's concept that the other

6. Helmuth Thielicke, *The Ethics of Sex* (New York: Harper & Row, 1964), p. 98.

7. *Person and Counselor,* p. 195.

person knows that he is being addressed and respected at the core of his being, or whether in Johnson's terminology, "I seek to be as fully aware as I can be at the moment," the individual is aware of this kind of relationship. This relationship nurtures growth and support and enables the person to know that goals can now be viewed in a supportive and mutually helpful manner.

Vicktor Frankl has influenced Johnson in a considerable manner since Johnson spent a sabbatical with Frankl, at the time the director of the Neurological Department of the Poliklinik Hospital in Vienna. At Baker University, where I serve as president, our new core curriculum entitled "Man's Search for Meaning" picked up the Frankl theme.

Indeed, Frankl himself came on campus for the opening lecture in the establishment of the unique core curriculum. His *Man's Search for Meaning* had then sold more than 600,000 copies, a book he had written in nine days in 1949.

Frankl maintained in his lecture at Baker:

> The pursuit of happiness proves to be self-defeating and not only contradicts the self-transcending quality of human existence, because the more a man sets out to gain pleasure, to attain happiness, the less he is capable of arriving at happiness. This is due to the fact that happiness is the effect of having a reason to be happy, be it that I have fulfilled a meaning or lovingly encountered another human being. Happiness is not something to be pursued but something which ensues from the pursuit of meaning.[8]

Later Frankl stated:

> We have to arrive at the true meanings conscientiously, responsibly. The only capacity of man which is capable of finding the unique meanings inherent in all his life situations is what is called conscience. Conscience shows us what is the meaning of a given situation and what this situation means to us. In an

8. Frankl, "Youth in Search of Meaning," *Students Search For Meaning*, ed. by James Edward Doty (Kansas City, Mo.: The Lowell Press, 1971), pp. 2-3.

age pervaded by feelings of meaninglessness, education today, rather than confining itself to and being content with the transmission of traditions and traditional values, should see its principal assignment as developing conscience. Thus, although all the universal values might be on the wane, man still is equipped with the faculty to find meaning in his life, in the unique life situations confronting him. [9]

Frankl has argued that of his German-speaking students attending lectures on neurology and psychiatry, 25 percent admitted they knew only the feeling of meaninglessness. However, among his American students that figure was not 25 percent but 60 percent!

A responsible counselor, as he searches for authenticity and meaning in his own life, enables the counselee to know that here is an individual who has struggled and has found answers for his own identity crisis. This assurance communicates itself more nonverbally than verbally as the counselee is made aware of the fact that "I feel I am being treated humanely in this relationship. There is creativity and support, and I feel that I can divulge the area of my life to this person who listens with empathic concern."

The search for meaning is an endlessly exciting process. The counselor is not making the decisions for the counselee, but rather is providing the framework in which the counselee can then see his growth potential and the way in which he faces new decisions, not with trepidation but with assurance and challenge. If a mistake in the choice has been made, this is not the end of the road. It simply means that one alternate has been explored, and there are many other alternates which can be seen in the light of changing needs and responses.

The College and Education

Reuel L. Howe, director of the Institute for Advanced Pastoral Studies, Bloomfield Hills, Michigan, has argued that education should not only help people learn, but it should

9. *Ibid.*, p. 10.

also teach them how to learn from experience. He maintains that one of the evidences of the ineffectiveness of the educational process is that after men finish their schooling and go to work, they stop reading books and feel guilty about their failure to study. They have not associated the reading of books with the real business of living. However, in his continuing education studies, Howe has come to the realization that once a man is taught to study the human document and the meaning of human experience, he turns to books to help him to understand what he is experiencing; and he becomes a person who has learned how to learn from doing. "The purpose of education is to release the powers of a person for learning, for growth, for service to others, and, finally, for acknowledgment of the ultimate meaning of his experience." [10]

The college today experientially is providing a new context for educational challenge and response. In a brief four-year period, fifteen of our sixty faculty members at Baker had spent a minimum of ten weeks in Southern Africa with student groups. In a three-year period, fifty-eight faculty and students had been in newly independent Botswana bordering Rhodesia and South Africa. Fifty students and three professors during two consecutive Januarys spent the interterm in Vienna studying German and fine arts. Seventy-one students and five faculty in two summers have enjoyed Baker University in England at Exeter University. Students are at work in oceanographic interterms in Florida; premed students at Mayo's in Rochester, Minnesota; drama majors in London; students moving into social work living in inner-city Kansas City and the south side of Chicago; journalism students working in newspaper offices in Topeka, Kansas City, and Chicago; political science majors at the United Nations and at state legislatures. This is a new world, and the students are aware of it.

What Howard Mumford Jones, Harvard professor of the humanities, said on the occasion of the inauguration of the

10. Howe, ". . . In Continuing Education," *Pastoral Psychology* (Feb., 1970), p. 60.

president of Wellesley College is particularly applicable to the college scene: "The college should be in the world but not of it. It is a vantage point, not a billboard, a house of intellect through whose wide windows the turmoil and the violence of even this violent age can be appraised on principles more lasting than the shifting passions of the hour."

When the student faces his world in this kind of challenging context, he raises the searching question: If we can land men on the moon in this blending of science and technology, and the miraculous can be accepted as commonplace, why cannot the same kind of thoroughgoing attacks be launched against the evils of our day which make life miserable for so many?

The teacher is a large part of the answer as the student faces himself in his own identity crisis. The identity crisis is a real one as the teacher works with the students in late adolescence and early adulthood. Obviously, some form of identity crisis occurs in everyone.

James A. Knight, associate dean and professor of psychiatry at Tulane University School of Medicine, has defined identity crisis as "a struggle to achieve direction while suspended between the child of the past and the adult of the future." [11] He quotes Erikson as indicating the location of the identity crisis "in that period of the life cycle when each youth must forge for himself some central perspective and direction, some working unity, out of the effective remnants of his childhood and the hopes of his anticipated adulthood; he must detect some meaningful resemblance between what he has come to see in himself and what his sharpened awareness tells him others judge and expect him to be." [12]

The church-related institution with 1,000 students will say it differently from the State University of New York with 65 campuses and 314,000 students. If the secret comes back to

11. "Confrontation in Counseling With Special Emphasis on the Student Setting," *Pastoral Psychology* (Dec., 1965), p. 53.
12. Erikson, *Young Man Luther*, p. 14.

the uniqueness of the professor in the process of communication with the student, Buber described the difficulty of creative resolution of conflict between teacher and student when he argued that the professor must use his own insight wholeheartedly and must not blunt the piercing impact of his knowledge. He must at the same time have in readiness the healing ointment for the heart pierced by it. "Not for a moment may he conduct a dialectical maneuver instead of the real battle for truth. But if he is the victor, he has to help the vanquished endure defeat; and if he cannot conquer the self-willed soul that faces him, then he has to find the word of love which alone can help to overcome so difficult a situation." [13]

Educational administration must be administration with fairness, justice, and creative love, as seen through the relationship of mutual concern of the teacher and the student. The administrator must have good institutional goals individualized by the particular institution in the total community involved. The functions of planning and development must be institutionalized within the university, as the university has its own identity crisis and needs to find out who it is and where it needs to go and what it needs to become.

College administrators today are looking at the management task, as one insightful wag has suggested it, the same way one leaves as one enters the challenge, "fired with enthusiasm!" With a tenure of only four years and three months on an average and with more than three hundred college presidencies open, a college administrator needs to understand what the identity crisis becomes for the institution, as well as the constituencies that compose that institution.

In 1960 the late Harold C. Case argued that if we were to have education with an ideal, if we were to condition the generation of our youth to feel deeply about the plight of mankind, if they were to care deeply for the worth of every person, then the Christian colleges should go to their knees

13. Quoted by James A. Knight, "Confrontation in Counseling," p. 48.

praying for wisdom and strength equal to their tasks. [14] These tasks have been accomplished in many cases because our youth do feel very deeply, not only about the plight of mankind but the plights as well. We have accomplished these tasks exceedingly well. The apathy of the 50s led to the revolution of the 60s. Let us trust that the 70s will be a time of synthesis, of judgment, and of creative tensions that will bring new resolutions in responsibility and insight.

I was in the Cleveland airport recently when I saw a young man oblivious that an "out of order" sign had been placed on his back by his friend who was walking with him along the airport corridor. His so-called friend had obviously seen the sign and had simply taped it to his back unbeknownst to him. In a real sense this is exactly the way many young people feel today—alienated, out of order with the order— and they are rebellious and hostile at a time when they and certainly we do not always know why.

Dean Colin Williams of Yale Divinity School has pointed out that

> my world of the over 40's finds it desperately difficult to understand this revolt amongst our affluent progeny. What we see are the obvious inconsistencies: the search for meaning beyond the death of the present institutions, while living parasitically on the fruits of the present institutions, the preaching of a need for a *new being* beyond the present world of bourgeois *having*, with the use of all the technical skills of the having world as the media for the expression of that rejection.

Seward Hiltner, in a provocative editorial for the December, 1960, issue of *Pastoral Psychology*, affirmed that the great need today among adolescents and adults is to work with young people in the communication "which is a genuine encounter or meeting between teen-agers and adults, which is at a deep rather than a superficial level, and which respects

14. Case, "The Christian College and the Concourse of History," *A Perspective on Methodist Higher Eudcation*, ed. by Woodrow A. Geier, 1960, p. 76.

rather than violates the emerging self-respect of the adolescent." [15]

Who is this adolescent about which so much has been written in the past two decades, and how do we understand him? Anna Freud put it succinctly:

> It is normal for an adolescent to behave in an inconsistent and unpredictable manner; to fight his impulses and to accept them; to love his parents and to hate them; to be deeply ashamed to acknowledge his mother before others, and, unexpectedly, to desire heart-to-heart talks with her; to thrive on imitation of an identification with others while searching unceasingly for his own identity, to be more idealistic, artistic, generous, and unselfish, than he will ever be again, but also the opposite; self-centered, egotistic, calculating. Such fluctuations between extreme opposites would be deemed highly abnormal at any other time of life. At this time they may signify no more than that an adult structure of personality takes a long time to emerge, that the ego of the individual in question does not cease to experiment and is in no hurry to close down on possibilities. [16]

The questions these students today are asking on the college campuses are questions concerning the morality of war, the values implied in academic progress, questions concerning new sexual freedoms which they are currently enjoying. Very often the adult in middle life is unwilling to hear the questions raised by the adolescent, because traditional answers from us will not suffice in this time of confrontation. The question concerning vocation, "What are you going to do?" is raised; however, "What is it that you want to be?" is more relevant.

Henri J. M. Nouwen, staff member of the Pastoral Institute, Amsterdam, Holland, writing in the March, 1969, issue of *Pastoral Psychology,* states with understanding: "We know that the most common form of mental suffering on campuses

15. Seward Hiltner, "Adolescents and Adults," *Pastoral Psychology* (Dec., 1960), p. 7.
16. *The Psychoanalytic Study of the Child.* (New York: International Universities Press, 1951).

today is depression. Depression is caused by questions which cannot be asked and which are swallowed and inverted into the experience of deep guilt. The question, 'Why do I live?' is turned into a castigating self-doubt, 'Is it worthwhile to live?' " [17] As he has asked certain questions, he is aware of different answers from former generations.

The valedictorian of Haverford College in 1970 was asked upon his graduation what he planned to do. His surprising answer—"I am planning to be an auto mechanic in New Hampshire."

Rationalization for those who have not found their way is indicated in a poignant vignette in the award-winning musical *Promises, Promises!* adapted from the motion picture *The Apartment.* A young woman in her early twenties is asked, concerning her broken compact mirror which she carries in her purse, why she hasn't gotten it repaired. Her classic comment: "I like it that way, because it makes me look the way I feel."

Elmer N. Witt, director of youth work for the Lutheran Church, Missouri Synod, Chicago, Illinois, said in 1964 what prerevolution youth were really saying:

Within the foreseeable future, we are going to have a *silent* revolution which will make our political upheavals look like bird-watching excursions. There will be no mass meetings, the explosive generation will not chase some dictator down the street, nor will any bricks or molotov-cocktails be thrown at the current Big Brother. The revolution will be far more than sexual, but will have plenty of sexual manifestations. Repression as we now know it, along with its curious pattern of conscious controls, will go down the drain. People are going to go back to sex, in loud rebellion against the sterility in our society. Miss America is polished marble taking her cues and dues in a sterile fertility rite. For all our freedom, we just cannot let go. But there will come a day. And it will be soon. And I also venture

17. "Training for the Campus Ministry," *Pastoral Psychology* (Mar., 1969), p. 29.

to say that the church will again be out-to-lunch, probably discussing whether the symbolic motif has anything to do with weight lifting.[18]

Perhaps we as older adults have a tendency to generalize on the basis of a few particulars. During the period 1968-71, when campus upheaval was the primary newspaper story and the 6:00 o'clock news showed campus riots almost nightly, a recurring question which we college presidents would hear from the leaders in business and industry was: "Well, what's happened on your campus this year?" When we would indicate that confrontations were not taking place on every campus, that buildings were not being burned, and presidents' and deans' offices not taken over, it seemed to present a degree of surprise to the questioner. Indeed, when we pointed out that 4,896,700 college students in 1969 took no part in riots or demonstrations, this did not seem to tell enough of the story. Two percent of the student body in rebellion capturing the headlines would not tell the complete story of other students searching for meaning in less dramatic and violent manners.

Resolving the Youth-Adult Alienation: A Place for Dynamic Interpersonalism

There is a generation gap existing in homes today, whether it is in Sarawak or Salisbury, in Botswana or Buffalo, in Denmark or Denver. It is as old as the prodigal son and as new as the recent movie *I Never Sang for My Father*. John Quincy Adams once recorded in his boyhood diary concerning a day he and his father had spent fishing. "Went fishing today with my father—the most wonderful day of my life." Interestingly enough, his father had also recorded the same day in his diary. "Went fishing today with my son—a whole day wasted!"

18. Witt, "Youth in the Flesh," *Pastoral Psychology* (Oct., 1964), p. 23.

The generation gap is inevitable because parents have lived two or three times longer than the child in sheer chronology of time. It is inevitable because I can in no way communicate to our two sons and our daughter what it was really like to live in the days of the depression. But I remember as a youth the bread lines and the soup kitchens and the days when many spent every waking moment wondering where the next meal was coming from. But to my children—food, clothing, and shelter? What are they? They are there for the taking! Yes, it is inevitable that there be a generation gap in background, in wisdom, in patience, in experience, in change versus status quo, in freedom versus conformity.

And this leads to many kinds of conflict between youth and adults: conflict in the concept of race, the use of money, what music says and does, beliefs about change, differences in attitudes about sex, worship, politics, hair, dress, status, education, drugs, marriage, premarital sex, abortion, environment, equality, peace, service, the poor, the migrant, words and more words, relationship, and God. In fact, the sum total of our life style.

Haim G. Ginott has wisely stated:

A day comes in any parent's life when there is a sudden realization: "My child is a child no longer." This is a unique moment of elation and fear. There is joy in seeing our seed— a sapling. There is also apprehension: No longer can we protect him from all winds. No longer can we stand between him and the world, to shield him from life's dangers. From now on he must face unavoidable challenges unaccompanied by us.

There is also conflict. As parents, our need is to be needed; as teenagers their need is not to need us. This conflict is real; we experience it daily as we help those we love become independent of us.

This can be our finest hour. To let go when we want to hold on requires utmost generosity and love. Only parents are capable of such painful greatness.[19]

19. *Between Parent & Teenager* (New York: Avon Books, 1969), preface.

Paul Tournier, probably one of the world's most insightful Christian physicians, has written an absorbing book entitled *A Place For You.* Our family read parts of it aloud in the car on our recent vacation, and we had a superb discussion about what it means to have a place. Dr. Tournier's thesis is that every man has to have a place where he is accepted and loved just for what he is, no matter what, and I underscore *no matter what!* Like a tree, if we are to grow tall and mature, we have to have our roots deep in the ground—a place. The ideal place for the child is the family. When the family is such that the child cannot fit himself into it properly, he looks everywhere for some other place, incapable of settling down anywhere. He bears about him this constant, restless, impelling nostalgia to find his place. On the other hand, the child who has grown up in a healthy, harmonious family finds welcome everywhere. For him life becomes not a matter of always searching, but rather of choosing!

So man attaches great importance to place, both significant and insignificant: places of singing, places of crying, places of hurt, places of reassurance; the place of the first kiss, the first great decision; places of struggle, and many minor places. Man's real place consists of all the many places he incorporates into his being and his experience, and once he has established his real place, he is free to change from one place to another and find himself at home anywhere—without anxiety, without injury, without pain.

This is the way a person establishes his identity. The ideal original place for the child is the family, and from that, if he is fortunate, he is able to extend his place to the whole family of man under the care of a loving Heavenly Father. It is like the little boy sitting forlornly on the steps of his house that burned to the ground a few days before. A passerby said to him, "I am so sorry you've lost your home." And he quickly replied, "Oh, we still have our home—we just don't have a house to put it in!"

If a person finds his identity, his place, in his color, or in his race, or in his culture, or his country more than he does in his personhood, he will never be as secure as the person who finds his identity, his place, in God and the whole family of mankind. We are given our place primarily by parents who have nurtured us with love. The greatest trench for the child is deprivation of love, deprivation of a place; and the greatest bridge is the giving of love, the establishing of the child in his place. A Baker student once said to me: "My professor loved me when I didn't love myself!"

Frankl tells about treating a seventeen-year-old girl. Although the girl had sought help from him for a problem concerning a love affair, Frankl helped her most in her search for meaning. She wanted to find reasonable, honest answers to her questions. She was troubled over not finding a clear sense of meaning and purpose in life. Her boyfriend ridiculed her search for something more than mere pleasure in sex and life in general. But Frankl emphasized the human quality of her search: "Who searches for meaning? Certainly an ant will not, neither will a bee." A girl of seventeen, however, posing such questions and involved in such a quest proves to be a truly human being struggling for meaning. "You are right," he told her, "in contending that pleasure cannot be the most important thing in life. Struggling for a meaning in life, at the risk of floundering in the search with questions and even doubts, is the prerogative of youth. A truly young person never takes meaning for granted—he always dares to challenge it!"

There is a ministry of educational administration, and Paul Johnson has helped me find it at Baker University. It is in the context of pastoral care in the parish as I came to know it for ten years in New England. It is the same context during nine years in the Indiana area as director of pastoral care and counseling for The Methodist Church.

Pastoral care training brought me to three distinct challenges in the area of educational administration:

1. Initially, in order to learn who the faculty and staff were at Baker, I scheduled hour-long interviews in my study as we explored together who they were, what they were about in their assigned tasks, information about their families, what

were the areas of fulfillment and disappointment, and what goals did they envision. This helped me prepare a realistic agenda for the years that were to follow. We included the workers in the kitchens, housemothers, maintenance personnel, and secretaries. It was a rewarding series of encounters.

2. In order to learn the real feelings of Methodist clergy in the Kansas East Conference, through the assistance of the bishop and the district superintendents, I spent thirty minutes with each pastor in his own church or study. More than 250 interviews were conducted in the first four months of my Baker ministry. I learned about hostilities and loves toward Baker, the institutional church, problems of communication with the hierarchy and laymen, family illnesses, children, and bereavements.

3. For six years I have spent large portions of the second semester in thirty-minute interviews with the graduating seniors in my office. This has given us an opportunity to talk about the four years on the campus, including the high points and the lows. We have done role reversals where I ask the soon-to-be alumnus or alumna, "If you were in my chair and had unlimited power (which I don't have!), what changes would you institute at Baker in the next one to five years?"

This elicits helpful responses as the senior honestly shares his feelings. We talk about his plans, whether it is graduate school, a job, marriage plans, and the faculty members who have turned him off or on.

Out of these conversations we have striven to hear the student articulate his needs and struggles, his victories and achievements. Through these conversations and others, three students are now on the Board of Trustees, seven students attend faculty meetings, two are on the Trustee Committee for Long-Range Planning. In addition, every faculty committee now has student representation.

As we prepare the incoming freshman for his orientation, I write a personal, handwritten letter to each student in the four months' period prior to September. This pastoral care enables him to know through the Admissions, Deans' and

Treasurer's offices that he is a person, and we are catalysts assisting him in his growth toward maturity and the reaching of academic, psychological, social, and spiritual goals.

Paul E. Johnson said it well in his preface to *Christian Love* that interpersonal psychology is "to me a social and religious psychology, therefore qualified to find meaning in Christian love."

This he has done eminently well. This we are challenged to do in the ministry of educational administration.

The Ministry of Supervision

Charles W. Stewart

Interpersonalism has been developed as a personality theory, but it also provides a context for understanding supervision, particularly the supervision of students in preparation for professional ministry. Paul Johnson has uniquely developed the interpersonal theory of personality in relation to religious psychology. According to Sullivan, interpersonal relations are the "processes that involve or go on between people." [1] Personality can never be isolated from the complex of interpersonal relations in which the person lives and has his being. Therefore, in the developmental process one understands the individual not simply in terms of the satisfactions of his drives but also in terms of security in relation to significant others, with empathy and anxiety being the primary emotions.

As Paul Johnson has shown, interpersonalism provides us with a context for understanding the church, the leadership of the church, and the congregation as the living, sustaining fellowship. In addition one sees the church as the interpersonal system in which the student learns the tradition of the faith and the ways in which the minister and laymen accomplish the mission of the church in the world. Paul Johnson has been a pioneer in developing our understandings of interpersonal social system, and in his contributions to clinical pastoral education, the development of the pastoral counseling center, and the seminary as a context for learning pastoral

1. Harry Stack Sullivan, *Conceptions of Modern Psychiatry* (New York: The William Alanson White Foundation, 1946), p. 4.

care skills. In the interpersonal context of the church, he gave us—his students—the frame of reference, the motivation, and the direction in which to develop new insights and understandings concerning training for ministry.

In this chapter I shall present the interpersonal context for the supervision of seminary students in theological professional training for ministry. I shall first define supervision; develop the interpersonal context for supervision—the structure, training situation, contracts for work and learning; the role of the supervisor; and the parallel processes of supervision and work.

A Definition of Supervision

First, let us define supervision, as we have developed it in American theological education. Supervision represents a relationship between a teacher professional and a student in training, established in a social system of work and responsibility, where a student may learn the roles of the profession through the controlled and guided enablement of the teacher. Supervision is not psychotherapy, since psychotherapy focuses on character change—i.e., change in the personal self in one's interpersonal relations. Supervision more narrowly focuses on changes in the professional self in the context of work. It is not, therefore, academic learning, in that learning does not take place through the laws of association and insight. It is rather skill learning and role learning which takes place through conditioning and role identification.

The early clinical pastoral trainers often operated on the mistaken notion that raw experience is the best teacher. One exposes the student to the shock of sick people in clinics or back wards of the hospital, and he therefore learns. Action training in its early stages was also guilty of this shock treatment of the student. Leave the middle-class young man without money in an inner city ghetto and let him experience hunger, joblessness, and no place to sleep, and he will learn. But he needs more than exposure; he needs reflection on his experience with the help of a trained supervisor who can guide him in reflection on interpersonal responses, positive and negative, and how he incorporates his exposure into role responses. The academician has held a similar mistaken notion that the student needs biblical, theological, and historical content to balance his exposure to the human situation. Unless the content is existential—i.e., unless the student is able to be met where he is and to wrestle with the meaning of his life and work in relation to the questions posed by the patient, the counselee, the parishioner—he cannot correlate his knowledge with the situation he is facing. The supervisor-teacher is unique in that he works with the student in a controlled professional exposure and supports, guides, confronts, directs the student so that the student himself may understand his responses, learn by his mistakes, be guided into more relevant responses and ways which will be helpful, constructive, and enabling to the person with whom the student works.

The Interpersonal Context

The interpersonal context for supervision implies first the use of the clinical rhombus. Ekstein and Wallerstein developed this in relation to the teaching and learning of psychotherapy, but it applies equally well to the learning of professional ministry in interpersonal relations.[2]

The chaplain-pastor or teacher-supervisor relates to the student, who relates in turn to the parishioner, counselee, or patient. The supervisor needs to distinguish between his work as supervisor and administrator. If this is a pastor who works with the student as a member of his staff, he may have administrative responsibilities which are shared with the student through the staff conference. However, when he is exercising the role of supervisor, he meets with the student explicitly for the concerns of supervision, relates to him now as teacher

2. R. Ekstein and R. Wallerstein, *The Teaching and Learning of Psychotherapy* (Basic Books, 1958), p. 11.

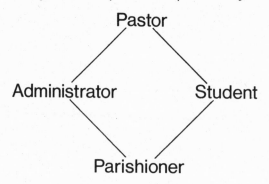

rather than as employer. He is concerned in discussing various work responsibilities which the student is carrying out, but now not specifically to see if the responsibilities are met, but how they are met, and what can be learned from them in the interpersonal context. The student is aware that he may make mistakes, but the mistakes are not now the occasion for incurring the wrath of his senior pastor; rather they become the materials for learning how he may do things differently.

The clinical rhombus is also helpful to show us that the pastor may relate to the parishioner or the chaplain to the patient within the larger interpersonal context of the parish or the hospital. He knows the parishioner or patient through other associations; he has experience within the social system of parish or hospital where the student operates; he knows the other professionals with whom the parishioner or patient is having relationships. Therefore, it is not simply the fact that the supervisor is more seasoned in ministry, but that he knows from firsthand experience the interpersonal context in which the student is learning ministry. This, it seems to me, is most important to stress. The theological teacher who teaches a Bible class at the church or an expert in marriage and family relations who runs a workshop does not have the same sense of the setting as the pastor or chaplain who works with the student as his supervisor.

The interpersonal context is one in which the contract for work and the contract for learning are negotiated. The student, whether in a hospital setting or a pastoral counseling service or a parish, negotiates with the personnel committee in order to understand his contract for work. Unless this contract is in writing and understood fully by the employing or training committee and the student being employed or taken for training, there are possibilities for misunderstanding at the very beginning. Dr. Karl Menninger first used the term "contract" in relation to the working agreement reached between psychotherapist and patient. Ekstein and Wallerstein, while at the Menninger Foundation, enlarged the usage to include the interpersonal relationship of supervisor-supervisee. The contract for learning differs from the contract for work in that the training student may understand that he has been employed to make hospital calls, to preach, to work with groups, etc., but not understand the context for supervision as one in which he is to learn to modify his ways of working with people. The training supervisor needs to establish this learning contract in addition to the contract for work before the supervisory relationship becomes a reality.

The interpersonal context for supervisors needs a natural situation in which the student can practice his profession. These natural situations began in hospitals, prisons, and state schools with people in crisis. Clinical pastoral education developed the supervisor-pastoral role. It waited upon pioneers like Seward Hiltner, Paul Johnson, Carroll Wise, Wayne Oates, and others to bring the insights from clinical pastoral education into the seminary classroom. Through the use of verbatim interview, role playing, and reality practice, students were given the opportunity of participating in the pastoral care role while being related to the rest of their seminary training. The development of the pastoral counseling center, of which the Albert V. Danielsen Pastoral Counseling Center at Boston University was a pioneer, enabled the student to obtain supervision through other professionals, such as psychiatrists, psychologists, and social workers, as well as the kind of peer supervision which is possible through the clinical case conference. Finally, by utilizing the insights of clinical pastorial education through the field education setting, it has been possible to develop pastoral supervisors through the total role of ministry and allow students to reflect upon their experience with the help of a skilled and experienced minister.[3]

What is common in all of the settings is that the place is natural to the development of the professional self. It is an interpersonal context in which people may be related to by the student and understanding may be developed regarding this professional relationship. There have been differences among writers regarding the quality of this relationship. Should it be a relationship in crisis? Should it be one in which a critical incident develops around the student-counselee relationship? Tom Klink and the Menninger group have emphasized the critical incident as the means by which one understands what happens between the student and the one whom he is helping. Hilda Goodwin and Emily Mudd have taken a similar point of view—that the student will reveal his "nuclear problem," i.e., his unique mode of relating to others, through some critical incident in the helping operation. My experience has shown that the student needs to look at his everyday modes of relating to others professionally along with those incidents which challenge his customary modes of professional involvement and enable him to ask questions which direct him toward new patterns more in harmony with his role image and identity. *The formation of a professional identity and style are central to the supervisory experience.* And this formation is not limited to critical incidents, to crisis experiences. I feel it involves the student more directly in examination of his professional image and identity if he looks at both his successes and failures in the light of a developing understanding of how he wants to perform ministry, and whether or not what he is doing coincides with his particular image and identity.

3. Charles W. Stewart, "Training Pastoral Supervisors for Field Education," *The Journal of Pastoral Care*, 24 (1971), 24-32.

Role of the Supervisor

What is the supervisor's function in relation to the student in professional training? First, the supervisor, as an experienced professional, takes the student seriously as the student attempts to forge his pastoral identity in his work. This implies neither a condescending approach nor one in which the experienced person has become so case-hardened that he communicates cynicism to the student. My experience in training pastoral supervisors reveals that older men fall quite naturally into a father-son relationship with the student and that the student generally resents this and may withdraw or rebel.

Second, the supervisor helps the student manage his anxiety surrounding the new situation in which he finds himself so that he can begin to assume the professional roles within the work context. Hilda Goodwin calls this phase of learning "working through a period of unknowing," [4] i.e., the student does not know what others expect of him and how he can adequately meet their expectations. The supervisor supports the student through this anxious period until he knows the ropes in his job and can adequately fill the roles which he has thrust upon him.

Third, the supervisor keeps his interest focused on the student's work responsibility and counsels with him regarding its preparation, enactment, and evaluation within the interpersonal context. The focus in supervision is upon work, and the supervisor enables the student to go about his work in a professional manner. John Patton calls the supervisor an "interpreter of professional function." [5] I would agree that this is his job *par excellence,* and at this stage of the student's development, where he is on trial and entering the profession, he needs this kind of person as he needs no one else.

4. "Supervision as a Catalyst for Growth," *Professional Growth for Clergymen,* ed. by Robert Leslie and Emily Mudd (Nashville: Abingdon Press, 1970).
5. John Patton and John Warkentin, "A Dialogue on Supervision and Consultation," *The Journal of Pastoral Care,* 25 (1971), 167-74.

Parallel Processes

Finally, the interpersonal context for supervision focuses on the parallel process: the parallel between problems in learning and learning problems. The debate in clinical pastoral education concerning whether one should focus on the student-patient relationship or the student-supervisor relationship demands not an either-or but a both-and answer. Armen Jorjorian says it depends upon where the student is, and is individually determined.[6] I would follow Ekstein and Wallerstein, who see a parallel process going on; that is, the learning problems are caused by the characteristic, and at times inappropriate, patterns of interpersonal response of the student toward those under his care. The problems of learning are the ones which emerge in the relationship of the student with his supervisor, as well as the problems surrounding the choice of profession, etc. Both sets of problems are dealt with in supervision; however, it is important to understand that what the student's concerns are in his professional roles parallel the problems which he experiences with his supervisor.

An example of this occurred with the group of pastoral supervisors which I coordinate at Wesley Seminary. The student and the pastor were presenting the job description and reporting the kind of problems which the student experienced in the church, where they were the only staff. They reported no problems at all in their staff relationship, although I knew from private conversations with each one that the student was having problems accepting the authority of the pastor, who acted toward him with strong demands but with little enforcement of those demands. When some of the other pastors began questioning the student, the student became angry and accused the pastors of trying to psychoanalyze him. His senior pastor remained passively in the background while this was going on. The student became aware of his authority problem only when this was uncovered with the group of

6. Jorjorian, "The Meaning and Character of Supervisory Acts," *The Journal of Pastoral Care*, 25 (1971), 148-56.

supervisors; and the senior pastor became aware that he was handling the student in too "passively aggressive" a fashion and so was not getting anywhere with him in the teaching-learning sessions. In other words, the student's difficulties in his parish work, where he could not meet the demands put upon him to do parish work, paralleled the difficulties which the student faced in the supervisory session, where he could not accept the criticism of the rest of the group.

The student, therefore, explores the professional self with the supervisor—he does not undergo psychotherapy—and is enabled to understand the difficulties he is having with parishioners, with groups, with administrators, etc., in relationship to the kind of professional image which he desires and the kind of professional identity which he is trying to establish. The supervisor does not ask the student to duplicate or imitate himself. In our work with pastoral supervisors in field education, we have discovered basically three styles of relationship: (1) Father-son, in which the student relates to the senior pastor in a dependent and passive fashion and in which there is a tendency to imitate the traditional model of pastor-preacher; (2) elder brother–younger brother, in which there is still some tendency of the senior pastor to force his own image and identity on the younger man, but with more independence and more possibility of the student to form his own pastoral identity; (3) peer-peer, in which the supervisor allows the student the freedom to choose his own image and identity and gives him the kinds of responsibility to allow this, supporting him as he grows and develops in his own fashion. The problems in learning which the student faces surrounding interpersonal relationships are paralleled in the supervisory hour. The student's tendencies to resist change, to resent authority, or to form a symbiotic relationship are looked at both in the context of his work and in the context of the supervisory relationship. The supervisor works out with the student a mutual contractual relationship which enables him to utilize his potential and develop his skills into a growing, maturing, professional self.

Conclusion

Supervision is a skill representing the relationship between a teacher-professional and a student-in-training. It is developed in a social system of work and responsibility. It allows the student to learn the roles of the profession, and it takes place through the controlled and guided enablement of the teacher-supervisor. More research needs to be done concerning the nature and function of supervision in a variety of roles of new ministry and new contexts of theological education. However, this kind of education is at the center of professional training for ministry on the current American scene. And it holds the key to the renewal and relevancy of the professional ministry in the decades to come.

Missionary Ministry

John W. Johannaber

Mission is grounded in interpersonalism. Isolationism is the death of mission. Psychologically, neither introversive perspectives nor analytic, individual, or factoral concepts contribute significantly to an understanding of a missional stance and involvement. Theologically, it is in the correlative interrelationship of God and human beings with human beings that the foundation of mission is established.

Mission is sometimes understood as proclamation of the gospel and witness to Christ. When these are carried out as tasks to be performed rather than as occasions when the proclamation of the gospel really involves the truth that has claimed one person being brought into deep interpersonal reality with the truth that has claimed the other, it becomes static and formal.

Likewise, mission is sometimes construed as changing environmental circumstances and conditions so that the quality of life may be improved. But if this is done impersonally, it can become manipulative, or one can be caught up in changing structures; unless there are profoundly personal transforming experiences which grow out of genuine mutuality, new structures can be as demonic and oppressive as the old.

The church came into being in a missional situation. Pentecost was a dynamically communicative experience. That the mighty acts of God were shared by those who had perceived in language even strangers understood suggests the disinclination of the "missioner" to allow preoccupation with "objective" reality to take precedence over the reality which occurred in the genuine communicative relationship. Privatism and mysticism were subordinated to that kind of conscientiousness through which the situational or cultural context of the potential believer could actually become the ground in which faith could take root and flower.

Currently, the understanding and practice of mission in the church, to which Paul Johnson's teaching and ministry have contributed so significantly, is seeking to fulfill the implications of interpersonalism. The old charge of paternalism, with its static and manipulative transplantation of culturally "superior" forms and structures, has been heard with telling effect. New relationships of partnership and mutuality have brought in an era of self-determination, autonomy, and cooperative work. Ecumenicity has been the hallmark of deepening respect and more productive involvement with the diverse forms of witness to the gospel, as well as with the efforts to humanize and to minister to human need through secular efforts. Internationalization of mission has been the rubric through which broader ranges of relationships of mutuality might be achieved. It is also the rubric through which the pervasiveness and universality of the problems that place humanity in jeopardy might be dealt with on a more wholistic basis.

Dr. Johnson has stimulated the development of pastoral care ministries, not only in the preparation of clergy in the United States, but also through participation in study and educational programs with missionaries, national pastors, and church persons in many areas of the world. His was a short term of service in China in the early twenties. Yet, as with so many of the "China hands," the association with this ancient culture and dynamic society was deep and lasting, even as his commitment to relevant ministry has been vital.

The personalistic dictum enunciated by William Stern, that the person is open to the world around him, characterizes both the goal and process of missionary activity, as well as the criteria by which missionaries are selected. We grow into personhood through vital experiences with other persons. In spite of our ego defenses, the way to health and wholeness is through open boundaries between the conscious and the unconscious and from person to person. All living organisms are open systems participating in a larger context of relationships. Revelation is relational, not propositional. The "I-Thou" relationship is suggestive of the dialogical nature of our relationship. It is suggestive, as well, of the fundamental character of the way in which persons, in their very being as well as in their full functioning, are not isolated entities but living beings in relationship. This reality is basic both to the missional understanding of the Christian faith and to the interpersonalistic understanding of persons.

Any enterprise risks ossification after an early period in which personal involvement is intense and personal concerns move quickly to arouse others in a movement that seeks to fulfill ideal aspirations. Institution-building in the earlier days of the missionary movement was a sign of that personal commitment to a cause or program which was clearly to improve the life of people who were being served. Missionary support was increased by funds to build buildings needed for the institutional care of and service to persosn. Although there have been elements of ecclesiastical imperialism in the sweep of missions, there has also emerged as a testimony to the health of the relationships between the missionary and nationals—peer relationships of openness, trust, and mutual benefit. Currently, missionary dominance is clearly past. National church leadership has grown in many parts of the world to assume primary responsibility for the ongoing life of the church. The missionary's role, then, is not to be pioneer, initiator, leader in any dominating or patronizing way. It is to be lived out within the context of real mutuality.

The one-way pattern of mission sending has given way to profound cultural and religious encounters. Dialogue with persons of other faiths characterizes the approach of thoughtful and mature missionaries. Study centers for the meeting of persons of different faiths in genuine and mutual exploration exist in many countries. Theological training for the ordained clergy is complemented in many countries by lay-training programs which help laymen in engagement with persons of different faith stances. In it all, too, new respect and appreciation for the diversity of cultures and the richness of the varied contributions that each can make to all are experienced.

Respect for persons requires an instrumental perspective on mass culture and technology. Monolithic communication and production systems can have a tyrannical dominance over human life and values. Even in the traditional missionary situation institutional processes can be given a priority and significance which reduce the possibility of personal growth and development. At the same time, organizational relationships can not only achieve conditions conducive to justice and liberation for people involved internally, but they can also be instrumental in the missional penetration of societal structures and the effecting of environmental change. Perhaps this is even more true in the secular world in which massive systems proliferate and expand the possibilities for unjust and inhumane exclusion or oppression. To keep the institutions of government, business and industry, education, and the church sensitive to the full development of persons becomes an increasingly complex task. The emergence of consumerism as a protective divide may make some contribution to health, safety, and fair play in the marketplace, but it may be more of a symptom of the reality of human beings being overwhelmed by a gargantuan economic system than an effective means of realizing justice and realizing the good life for all. It may alleviate some of the conspicuous exploitation of conspicuous consumers. But for those who cannot buy, life may be as conspicuously bleak.

None of the oppressive systems of our society felt the prophetic judgment of Paul Johnson more than did militarism. Nurtured in his fundamental personal commitment to pacifism, but supported by his religious, philosophical, and psychological wisdom, his witness both inspired and instructed students and colleagues and contributed to the coming of the day of more rational, sane, and humane international relationships.

Black theology or the theology of the oppressed is instructive of the missionary situation in important ways. Although in its more strident expressions there may have been contributions to the cleavage and polarization in society, it is probably more accurate to observe that this theological perspective has been a candid illumination of and focusing upon the deep separations that exist in society, and the reality of the primal concern of a God who redeems and liberates persons who suffer any form of injustice or oppression, impedimenta, or preventative to the full and free humanity which God intends for all persons.

As critical as liberation is in a society in which oppression and injustice exist, it is also imperative that liberation find its consummation in love and in community. Liberation is a necessary condition for the achievement of just relationships, but justice must find its fullest expression in love if the purposes of God for humanity are to be realized.

Interpersonal perspectives underlie a theology of liberation and love. Liberation suggests a "distancing" required for personal maturation. It implies a new peer relationship. It assumes the assertion of—if not a mutual acknowledgment of—a new dignity and capacity for self-determination and for existence. It suggests the rational appropriation of cultural reality as contrasted to the imposed or subconscious power of culture. It implies more equitable availability of the environing resources needed to sustain and enrich life. It is a requisite for establishing the kind of relationship appropriate to free men.

"Tension in polarity is good and means life" was an observation of a practical churchman. It also suggests the dynamic character of the psychology of interpersonalism. Paul Johnson, with the clarity and sweep of a mind honed by the disciplines of philosophy, often identified the polarities which characterized personal reality. They were not polarities merely of an internal dynamic. They were the polarities implicit in personal existence in the context of the interpersonal relationships in the total context of the living situation. Tension with otherness is basic to religious experience, is characteristic of interpersonal perspectives upon human life, and is at the heart of the missionary dynamic.

The Ministry of Consultation

Berkley C. Hathorne

The mental health consultation method, primarily developed and refined during the past decade as an important dimension of the community mental health movement, provides a significant and practical model for assisting the parish clergyman in his pastoral care and counseling functions and his role as a community change agent. It is obvious that every minister, priest, and rabbi cannot and should not be trained as an expert in pastoral psychology and counseling or in community organization and social system intervention. But it is also becoming equally obvious that the parish clergyman can and should have access to consultants who are so trained to provide specialized and adjunctive assistance to him when needed.

Every parish clergyman has occasions when he is confronted with problems and situations involving his parishioners or community which make him feel uncertain about his role, his knowledge, and his skills. This uncertainty may be at the point of whether he should attempt to counsel with a particular individual, couple, or family, or make a referral; or it may be ambivalence about getting involved or how to handle particular parish or community problems. Often the clergyman ends up attempting to deal with a difficult situation as best he can, with a good deal of personal anxiety, or he makes a referral and then feels that he has rejected someone he perhaps should have been able to assist.

Definitions

Mental health consultation is a process for providing professional expertise to assist another professional person in dealing with a client with emotional problems or in assisting an individual or group concerned with the mental health needs of the community. Mental health consultation is "indirect" in that "the consultant accepts no direct responsibility for implementing remedial action for the client."[1] Usually the client is never seen by the consultant and the consultee's responsibility for the client remains the same as before he sought assistance from the consultant. The issue of responsibility is important in differentiating consultation from clinical supervision.

Ruth Caplan defines mental health consultation as "helping the helpers to help"; with parish clergy this focuses "not on the traditional psychiatric role of diagnosing the mentally disturbed of the parish, and referring them for treatment, but rather, on supporting the minister in his own management of bewildering cases in which mental health issues are blocking his effectiveness."[2]

Although mental health consultation with clergymen is increasingly being provided by clinically trained clergy who function in specialized ministries of pastoral care and counseling, this is still a new dimension for most clinical clergymen. Few of the clergy now involved in providing consultation have been formally trained for that function. In most cases they possessed recognized expertise gained through rigorous academic and clinical preparation coupled with professional experience in appropriate settings and then built upon this foundation, by means of trial and error, their own style of consultation.

1. Gerald Caplan, *The Theory and Practice of Mental Health Consultation* (New York: Basic Books, 1970), p. 19.
2. Ruth B. Caplan in collaboration with David E. Richards and Anson Phelps Stokes, Jr., *Helping the Helpers to Help* (New York: Seabury Press, 1972), preface.

Another developing dimension of the ministry of consultation is consultation with mental health and community organization specialists concerning their work with particular individuals, families, or religious and social groups. Often the clergy-counselor has a knowledge and perspective about the spiritual, emotional, interpersonal, and social aspects of segments of the population that prove invaluable in working with troubled persons or social problems from various parts of the community; and a community mental health center staff and others may tap this expertise by means of consultation.

Experiment and Experience

Quite by necessity I began a program of consultation in 1962. The Washington Pastoral Counseling Service was then in its second year of operation, and although additional trained staff were employed, it soon became apparent because of an overwhelming number of referrals, primarily from parish clergymen, that something had to be done to adequately respond to the need for service. At one point it was not unusual for individuals or couples to be on a waiting list for as long as six months. Two programs were provided to respond to this need: (1) a multileveled training program ranging from one-day intensive specific topic workshops to continuing seminars and clinical internships for qualified clergy; and (2) an announced program of consultation for parish clergy. Rather than accept more referrals and simply add names to the waiting list, the counseling service queried the parish clergymen by telephone to determine whether or not it seemed feasible to offer them consultation so that they might provide the counseling with their parishioners. Originally utilizing either or both regularly scheduled consultations via telephone or personal interviews, these parish clergy frequently became involved in weekly training sessions and group supervisory sessions in addition to the individual consultation.

For example, one parish clergyman had several consultation

sessions concerning his efforts to organize the local clergy and the religious community to respond to the crisis of a tragic commercial airline crash claiming scores of lives in Easton, Maryland. As a result of the consultation a multiphase comprehensive plan was put into operation including such things as (a) providing for the physical, emotional, and religious needs of the many relatives who traveled to Easton to identify the victims; (b) establishing a ministry to the rescue workers and the people who staffed the temporary morgue; (c) the planning of coordinated memorial services; and (d) follow-up services to handle the emotional reactions in the aftermath. The consultant provided an objectivity and expertise concerning disasters and the dynamics of grief that made possible an effective response to both the immediate crisis and the follow-up period with a broad focus on the needs of and the effect on the mourners, the workers, and the community. This particular community had a dearth of mental health resources; therefore the local clergy and physicians coordinated their efforts to respond adequately to the crisis.

During 1970 there were 178 clergy functioning on the staff of the 200 federally funded community mental health centers surveyed by National Institute of Mental Health through the January 1971 Inventory.[3] This included 88 regular staff, 38 full-time and 50 part-time (less than 35 hours per week), and 66 trainees and 24 regularly scheduled volunteers. The clergy trainees worked an average of 14 hours a week and the volunteers an average of 8 hours a week. In relation to total staffing and other staff disciplines (based on reports from 200 centers) there was 0.8 or approximately one clinical clergyman serving 32 hours per week at each community mental health center, while the average total staff was 108.1 persons. For example, each center averaged 0.8

3. Unpublished document, "Preliminary Data on Staffing Patterns in Federally Funded Community Mental Health Centers, January 1971" (Rockville, Md.: Survey and Reports Section, Office of Program Planning and Evaluation, National Institute of Mental Health, 1972).

clergy (clinical), 8.8 psychiatrists, 6.3 psychologists, 11.1 social workers, 12.0 registered nurses, and 11 other categories of employees ranging from attendants and aides, occupational and recreational therapists, to clerical, fiscal, and maintenance personnel, totaling 69.1 persons. Consultation by clinical clergy averaged 6.9 percent of the clergy staff activities, as contrasted to 23.8 percent for training and education (exclusive of in-service staff training), 19.0 percent for outpatient care, 10.2 percent for administration, and 6.8 percent for day care, which indicates that consultation ranks fifth in a distribution of twelve functional staff activities for the clinical clergy staff. Comparing this to other staff disciplines reveals that only two other disciplines devote a higher percentage of their time to consultation—psychologists 10.4 percent, and psychiatrists 7.3 percent. Social workers average 6.4 percent (see Table 1).

In terms of staff activities the clinical clergy in community mental health centers devote approximately the same percentage of their time to consultation as do the psychiatrists and social workers, with only the psychologists devoting slightly more time to consultation. Consultation ranks fifth in frequency of activities for clinical clergy, psychiatrists, and social workers, while it ranks third for psychologists (see Table 2).

Through the recent Membership Information Project of the American Association of Pastoral Counselors, undertaken by Morris Taggart, the patterns of consultation involving AAPC members were surveyed.[4] The patterns of consultation activities suggested by the data, both consultation received and given, may be summarized as follows:

1. The pastoral counselors in the survey consulted most frequently with psychiatrists (50.3 percent) about their own clinical concerns. Consultation with other pastoral counselors ranked second (41.6 percent), followed by social workers

4. "The AAPC Membership Information Project," *The Journal of Pastoral Care,* 26 (1972), 240-44.

Dynamic Interpersonalism for Ministry

Table 1

Comparison of Selected Disciplines and Percentage Distribution of the Five Most Frequent Activities at 142 Federally Funded Community Mental Health Centers, January, 1971

| | *Discipline* | | | |
Staff Activity	*Clergy*	*Psychiatrists*	*Psychologists*	*Social Workers*
Other Training and Education (not in-service staff)	23.8%			
Outpatient Care	19.0%	29.3%	34.4%	41.2%
Inpatient Care	12.9%	20.7%	8.9%	12.7%
General Administration	10.2%	10.1%	13.5%	11.6%
Consultation	6.9%	7.3%	10.4%	6.4%
In-Service Training		7.7%		
Day Care				7.1%
Research and Evaluation			8.7%	

Source: Survey and Reports Section, NIMH

Table 2

Rank Order of First Activities by Selected Disciplines at 142 Federally Funded Community Mental Health Centers, January, 1971

| | *Discipline* | | | |
Staff Activity	*Clergy*	*Psychiatrists*	*Psychologists*	*Social Workers*
Other Training and Education	1			
Outpatient Care	2	1	1	1
Inpatient Care	3	2	4	2
General Administration	4	3	2	3
Consultation	5	5	3	5
In-Service Training		4		
Day Care				4
Research and Evaluation			5	

(21.3 percent), psychologists (19.1 percent) and physicians (not psychiatrists) (15.7 percent). It is of interest to note that the membership level within the AAPC is correlated to the use of professional consultation, with both fellows and diplomates (higher levels of membership) regularly consulting with psychiatrists significantly more than do persons at the member level of AAPC. Taggart makes the point that "it is ironic, though almost always the case, that those who may need high-level consultation the most are least likely to get it." [5] However, the member level pastoral counselors more frequently consult with psychiatrists on a sporadic or need basis. This is not surprising, because generally the member serves in a parish so that his pastoral counseling is not a full-time activity, and sporadic use of psychiatric consultation may be more appropriate to his clinical needs.

However, this is misleading because numbers are being compared when it would be wiser to convert to percentages (see Table 3), because there are twice as many members as diplomates, so percentages eliminate that bias. But more important, when the total percentages of both regular and sporadic use of psychiatrists as consultants are compared, there is no significant difference between members, fellows, and diplomates (see Table 3). Table 4, using numbers, compares members and fellows when regular use and sporadic use are combined and shows that there is no significant difference.

2. Parish clergy (50.9 percent), other pastoral counselors (41.8 percent), and local church lay groups (25.7 percent) are the most frequent consultees of AAPC members on a regular, scheduled basis. This indicates, as Taggart points out, that "what might be called 'in-house' groups get the lion's share of the consultation offered by pastoral counselors." [6]

3. Diplomates are more likely than either members or fellows to be utilized as consultants with both psychiatrists and psychologists, and "very much more likely to be involved in

5. *Ibid.*, p. 242.
6. *Ibid.*, p. 243.

Dynamic Interpersonalism for Ministry

Table 3

Use of Psychiatrists as Consultants and Level of Membership
In AAPC

	Member		Fellow		Diplomate		N
Regular use	56	37.8%	87	56.5%	46	62.2%	189
Sporadic use	76	51.4%	58	37.7%	27	36.5%	161
Seldom/never used	16	10.8%	9	5.8%	1	1.3%	26
	148		154		74		376

Total Percentage of
Regular and Sporadic
Use 89.2%   94.2%   98.7%

Source: Taggart, "The AAPC Membership Information Project."

Table 4

Comparison of Members and Fellows When Regular and
Sporadic Use of Psychiatrists As Consultants Are Combined

	Member	Fellow	
Regular and Sporadic Use	132	145	277
Seldom/Never Used	16	9	25
	148	154	302

$X^2 = 1.81$, df. $= 1$, p$>$ 0.05

giving consultation to other pastoral counselors (and with
parish clergymen) than either Fellows or Members. Since
perceived and felt competence is a potent factor in the possibility of acting as a consultant to others, one would expect
the Diplomate to report more such activity." [7]

7. *Ibid.*, p. 244.

The significant finding in Taggart's study is the fact that there is a great deal of consultation activity by pastoral counselors, and the range of this consultation is very extensive. The data support the expected finding that diplomates both receive and provide consultation more frequently than do fellows or members, and fellows have a somewhat higher rate of consultation activity than members.

Education and Training

Now that clinically trained clergy are being utilized as consultants in a variety of settings, and it is apparent that opportunities for such service will greatly increase over the next decade, it is imperative that formal training in the principles and practice of pastoral consultation be provided. Although most of the present clergy-consultants who gained their expertise the difficult trial-and-error route perform exceptionally well, this type of self-education is too haphazard a method of training, especially in the light of the greater opportunities and the body of knowledge and techniques that have been developed for training consultants of other disciplines.

Three obvious questions to be answered concerning the education and training of the pastoral consultant are: Who should be trained as clinical clergy-consultants? What should such training include? Where should the training be provided? The suggested answer to who should be trained will not be widely accepted at the present time because there is no strongly felt need by either educational and training leaders or by the trainees themselves. This is probably because neither have been involved in consultation and do not anticipate that the clergy trainees will in fact be expected to provide consultation in an increasing number of clinical settings. The suggested answer to who should be trained as pastoral consultants is every clergyman who in any way anticipates that he may be functioning at some time in the future in a church-sponsored counseling service or in a community mental health center.

For example, the clinical staff clergyman at the community mental health center is in no way the traditional chaplain who functions as a surrogate pastor to people who are physically separated from their own clergyman and religious community. Instead, the clinical clergy on the staff of the community mental health center may consult with the local minister, priest, or rabbi concerning the referral of a parishioner to the community mental health center; he may consult with the staff of the community mental health center concerning any special concerns of the individual, the family, or the particular clergyman; he may consult with the clergyman concerning the treatment program and the role in that program of the religious leader in relation to the patient, the family, and the CMHC staff; and then, at the time of discharge or termination, he may consult concerning the after-care and follow-up which the parish clergyman may be able to provide. Throughout this entire process and period of time the clinical staff clergyman at the CMHC may never have personally met or worked with the parishioner-patient, nor did he necessarily need to, although he has been very much involved through his consultation with the local clergyman. The same example can be cited, with only slight change, for the pastoral counselor functioning in a church or community based program.

What the education and training of the clinical clergy consultant should include is open for experiment, experience, and evaluation; however, a few generalizations are in order. There is a rapidly expanding literature[8] on mental health consultation which should be utilized for didactic purposes. The definitive textbook for several years to come will certainly be Gerald Caplan's *The Theory and Practice of Mental Health*

8. Fortune V. Mannino, *Consultation in Mental Health and Related Fields: A Reference Guide.* (U.S. Government Printing Office. Public Health Service Publication No. 1920, National Institute of Mental Health, 1969.) "Selected References" in *The Scope of Community Mental Health Consultation and Education.* (U.S. Government Printing Office, Public Health Service Publication No. 2169, National Institute of Mental Health, 1971), pp. 29-32.

Consultation. This book or the existing literature does not substitute for the need for many specific articles dealing with all aspects of pastoral consultation, but they do provide a foundation and a framework upon which an accepted system for pastoral consultation may be developed.

The question of the appropriate settings for the training of pastoral consultants raises many issues. Ideally the training should be part of an integrated academic and clinical experience, but there are very few programs in the United States where the resources necessary to provide a balanced, comprehensive, and interdigitated didactic *and* supervised clinical experience also provide access to consultation programs. At present most of the pastoral consultation is being done in the larger pastoral counseling centers and community mental health centers, and although there are clinical training programs for clergy in both, and training in consultation can be and is provided, it often lacks the academic rigor that is needed. On the other hand, few of the academic based programs in pastoral care and counseling are related to the clinical settings where consultation is practiced. What is needed is a bridging of the academic and the clinical, in the same way it has been done in clinical pastoral education and pastoral counseling, by relating the advanced degree programs in the departments of pastoral care and counseling of selected theological schools to approved clinical supervisors and clinical centers where consultation is effectively practiced. In some cases such collaboration has already been effected, but in many others there are barriers to cooperation which need to be mutually resolved.

Summary and Recommendations

Consultation has emerged as an important activity for the clinical clergyman and the pastoral counseling specialist, and every indication is that this function will increase in importance over the next several years.

Pastoral consultation offers a viable model for assisting the parish clergyman with his counseling and mental health functions and provides a form of continuing professional education in that the consultee gains knowledge and experience which will increase his care-giving skills in other situations.

Clinical clergy on the staff of community mental health centers devote approximately the same percentage of their time to consultation as do staff psychiatrists and social workers.

Members of the American Association of Pastoral Counselors are involved in a great deal of consultation activity, both receiving and providing consultation, most often with parish clergymen and other pastoral counselors.

There is a dearth of education and training opportunities in pastoral consultation, including continuing education. Training for the ministry of consultation should be made available for all clergymen serving in or preparing for service in clinical ministries of pastoral care and counseling.

The American Association of Pastoral Counselors should develop guidelines for pastoral consultation and in concert with the Association for Clinical Pastoral Education develop clinical training and supervision standards in approved settings.

Community Involvement as Ministry

William E. Ramsden

It is significant that this chapter should be included in this volume. Its presence represents a growing trend to see as a whole things which not long ago were seen as very much apart. The whole pastoral care movement (that part of it which followed Paul Johnson's lead in understanding itself in terms of dynamic interpersonalism and all the other parts of it as well) was seen by many as an alternative style of ministry to community involvement. To the generation of activist young clergy in the sixties, pastoral care was the great "cop out" of clergy to avoid dealing with the pressing realities of social need. It is both ironic and probably historically inevitable that what had been the "cutting edge" of one generation of ministry became the "cop out" of the next.

Obviously, the need for a generation gap had much to do with the activists' perception of the pastoral care movement, but there were reality factors present as well. Concern for community involvement was never a dominant theme in the various writings on pastoral care—including those of Paul Johnson. I remember well a conversation with a few close friends just at the conclusion of the 1965 conference in Miami Beach of the organizations which became the Association for Clinical Pastoral Education. We realized that it was the only gathering of religious leaders any of us had been to that year in which we had never once heard an expression of concern for the church's stance toward racial or economic justice.

Reflection on this incident has suggested that what caused the lack of expression was not an overwhelming absence of personal concern on the part of the individuals present. Rather, it was an implicit acceptance of the myth that pastoral care and community involvement were alternative styles of ministry, along with that conference's explicit professional focus on the latter.

Such a division could only restrict the potential of each concern, and more recently there have been substantial movements toward redressing this problem. The foci of the Association for Clinical Pastoral Education Conferences in Denver in 1969 and in San Francisco in 1971 were both basically on the community and its culture and subcultures. That movement is the underlying significance of this chapter, but its immediate significance is the attempt to take seriously in dynamic interpersonalism the conceptual reflections of those whose experience has deliberately been in both camps.

These reflections are not shared as the views of pioneers, but as those of second- or third-generation actors. All who have studied with Paul Johnson have been aware that the same "Boston personalism" out of which he was moving had given birth also to major efforts, both activist and conceptual, in the area of social action (for our generation of students this was personified in Dean Walter G. Muelder). Those who are fortunate enough to come to know Paul Johnson fairly well will recognize that he never lost touch with the movement of social concern. Both in his intellectural contacts with fellow faculty and in his personal involvement in a variety of community concerns Paul Johnson retained the spirit of social concern that had at the very beginning of his teaching ministry sent him as a missionary to China. While he remained clear that his primary emphasis had to be on developing dynamic interpersonalism within the general context of pastoral care, he was a constant source of encouragement and stimulation for students and colleagues who wanted to place both those concerns within the context of community involvement.

These reflections are the result of a decade and a half of that effort by one whom he had encouraged—as teacher, as colleague, and as friend. There are three major foci to these reflections. One centers on the parallels that have become obvious between pastoral care and community involvement. A second centers on the need to adapt dynamic interpersonalism to thinking about community involvement. The third centers on the attempt to understand community involvement as ministry.

The first and most important parallel between pastoral care and community involvement concerns lies in the basic values providing the goal of ministry. In operational terms those values have to do with enhancing the possibilities of persons' experiencing the full potential of their humanity. Paul Johnson has said it well:

> The group we actually seek, to undergird the individual person, is a community where persons are known and trusted. Here we find each person unique in his own identity, yet seeking to find the meaning and fulfillment of his life in the whole network of his interpersonal relations. [1]

The other area in which a striking parallel became clear could be labeled "technique." Much of the approach recommended by Johnson (and others) for the pastoral care of individuals is amazingly paralleled by the approaches found necessary for effective community involvement.

Like the naïve pastoral counselor parodied in the line, "I'm going to make you well whether you like it or not," the naïve activist clergy went into the community in effect saying, "I'm going to improve your conditions whether you want it or not." The real problem in each approach was not that there was inappropriateness in the energy and insight of a dif-

1. *Person and Counselor*, pp. 54-55.

ferent perspective offered by the clergyman. The basic difficulty was what activist clergy have come to call imperialism. It starts with the assumptions "I know what is best for you; I am the powerful one here," and "of course we will do it my way."

Just as pastoral counselors had to learn to listen first and then help the person to arrive at his own decisions about changing himself, so also the clergyman involving himself in a community had to learn to discover the strengths in the community and help it to clarify its own goals and mobilize its own resources to achieve them. The counselor says, "It is your life. You must make and live with your own decisions." In parallel, the activist clergyman comes to commit himself to the value of "community control."

Again, such an approach in either arena of concern just won't "come off" unless it is based on genuine caring. The give and take required to have people work together will inevitably deteriorate into the traditional imperialism or into an unhelpful permissiveness unless it is founded in genuine caring which is clearly and consistently communicated. In the words I once heard Cesar Chavez use of his efforts to build the Farm Workers Union: "Organization may be triggered by issues and helped by money, but organization is not built on either issues or money. It is built on Trust."

Conceptual Development

Those who have struggled to bring their understanding of dynamic interpersonalism to bear in the battle for community involvement have found they needed to add more sociological concepts to their primarily psychological, intellectual armory. This fact grows out of the inseparability of the interpersonal arena from the surrounding social reality. Paul Johnson, of course, recognized this connection, although he focused on interpersonal manifestations rather than on the societal aspects. As he commented, "The unique person, as I see him, attains significance and reality through his participation with other persons in the interactive relationships of our world." [2] He added, "It is truer to the evidence to see personality as an open system, adjusting ever to the changing character of its social context." [3]

The need to focus on more sociological concepts was enforced upon the ministry of community involvement as it recognized that it would be perpetually "too little too late" if it only tried to help people cope with their conditions. The effort to "help society's downtrodden" made it clear that real help could only be offered in changing the conditions. In short, as community involvement matured from its early posture of social service into one of social change, purely interpersonal concepts were not adequate to help it understand what it had to do.

The resulting change was not simply adding some new ideas, but a basic reshaping of the understanding of the whole interpersonal dynamic. The actions of society, or culture, and its instrumentalities came to be seen as major determinants of both personality and patterns of interpersonal interaction. Three specific concepts illustrate this process.

1. Acculturation. This concept refers to the process by which an individual becomes adapted to the culture in which he lives. We have come to learn that, in fact, it is the culture that supplies the language, the thought forms, and the traditional patterns of relationship which make growing self-understanding possible—and which predetermine the basic shape of that self. We are obviously at the beginnings of a new age in which a pluralist culture exposes its members to various subcultures, sometimes reinforcing and oftentimes competing with one another. We will be even less able to minister sensitively in that cultural environment than we have been in the past if we do not understand acculturation, with

2. "The Trend Toward Dynamic Interpersonalism," *Religion in Life*, 35 (1966), 752.
3. *Ibid.*, pp. 755-56.

259

its great gifts of potentials and its crippling limitations on vision.[4]

2. Racism. Where those whose concepts were personality-oriented concentrated on "prejudice," those who took acculturation seriously came to concentrate on racism. As a "disease" it does not principally infect the individual but the culture or subculture—in such an insidious degree that even the unprejudiced person is caught in racism. The distinction was neatly summarized by one ghetto worker: "Prejudice is the white man swearing that no black will ever be able to marry his daughter; racism is the unconscious and arrogant assumption that any black man would want to." [5] The most virulent form of racism in action, furthermore, has proved to be not bigoted political leaders but institutions with racism embedded in their practices.[6]

3. Institution. This concept deals with the operating instruments of a society that set the actual context within which personal and interpersonal action occurs. It has two foci of meaning. The broader one refers principally to a culture's instrumentalities of acculturation. As such, "marriage," or "family," or "education," or "business" is an institutional arrangement developed by a culture to shape people. The narrower meaning of institution focuses on the large social organization developed in Western society to carry out its "business"—the public school systems, the often giant multiversities of higher learning, the "full-service" banks, the business corporation, and the labor unions. As the business consultant and social philosopher Peter Drucker put it, "Historians two hundred years hence may see as central to the twentieth century what we ourselves have been paying almost no attention to: the emergence of a society of organizations

4. Cf., e.g., Oscar Lewis, *The Children of Sanchez* (New York: Random House, 1961).

5. Paul Johnson has written a moving description of his painful personal discovery of what racism really meant for him. Cf. *Personality and Christian Faith,* pp. 206-10.

6. Cf., e.g., Whitney M. Young, Jr., *Beyond Racism* (New York: McGraw-Hill Book Co., 1969).

in which every single social task of importance is entrusted to a large institution." [7]

Thus, while many parallels with the pastoral care focus become apparent in a ministry of community involvement, it became necessary to broaden the understanding of dynamic interpersonalism to take account of cultural factors. Such changes in understanding come not in order to be different but in order to be effective in ministry.

Community Involvement as Ministry

Human relations are not really complete after all. For every human person is finite and fragmentary, not eternal or ultimate. So his relations are also finite and incomplete. If we are evil we poison all our relationships with evil. If we are fearful we bring the shudder of anxiety into our relations. If we are confused or despairing we infect our relations with chaos and despair. We seek a dimension of spirit that is more sufficient and sustaining than our fragile and faltering existence.[8]

When we add to Paul Johnson's insight into the interpersonal need for ministry an appreciation of the incredibly mixed blessing of acculturation processes, it is very difficult to miss the impulse to ministry if one is at all alive to God's outreaching spirit. That has been, and is, the reason why there is a ministry of community involvement.

Because of this basic reason and because of growing understanding of community dynamics, there has been continual development in the understanding of the ministry of community involvement. One of the major shifts was that from social *service* to social *action*. Another equally major shift seems to be occurring at present—from a clergy-oriented to a lay-oriented view of the ministry of community involvement.

Community involvement has tended in practice to be predominantly the work of the clergy. Some were in special

7. *The Age of Discontinuity* (New York: Harper & Row, 1969), p. 171.

8. "The Trend Toward Dynamic Interpersonalism," pp. 756-57.

positions created for that purpose. Most were parish clergy who used their parish as a springboard into its community. Most of the financial and some emotional support for these efforts came from the laity, although it was often observed that few parishioners objected to his community activism when the pastor "paid the rent"—i.e., provided them with basic pastoral care. Such artificial division of ministry created an equally artificial division between activist pulpit and resistant pew.[9]

Now a shift is occurring in the light of two insights: (1) it is institutions that are now most powerful in determining the opportunities of humanity, and (2) laity are the churchmen who have already "infiltrated" these institutions and who thus are best able to influence them—if they are willing and able. The clergy thus are called to be enablers of this lay ministry of community involvement, both by working directly with "lay ministers" and by their leadership of the congregation (so that it can be an enabling community).

Experience thus far has shown that such enabling has three necessary features. The first is the raising of value-consciousness in specific terms to develop commitment. This process involves helping people to look at their involvement in an institution in terms of the values of their faith—really working out operationally what values they are committed to and where they diverge from those implicit in their institution's operation. The second feature is developing certain basic skills to make it possible to work from their position in the institution to bring about change in it. This process recognizes that genuine commitment is possible only to the extent of capacity to fulfill it, as is implied in Jesus' emphasis on giving his disciples power to fulfill the ministries he gave them.[10] The third feature is interpersonal support, which is needed in three distinct forms. Each effective lay minister needs to work as a part of a task force seeking change in his or her institution.

9. Cf., e.g., Jeffrey Hadden. *The Gathering Storm in the Churches* (Garden City, N.Y.: Doubleday & Co., 1969).

10. Cf., e.g., Mark 6:7-13, and parallels.

He or she needs the general support of a lively congregational life—worship activities, pastoral care. Finally, the lay minister needs a small intentional "support group," probably within the congregation, who can provide the necessary emotional support, value-testing, and problem-solving adi each of its members needs to be effective in his institution.[11]

It is significant to note the essential congruence of this emerging form of the ministry to community involvement with Paul Johnson's stance in regard to pastoral care and counseling. Both are aimed at helping persons to become through relationship, although the one focus is on interpersonal transactions and the other on institutions. Further, the styles of the counselor and of the enabler will have much in common. The counselor works to help persons cope more adequately with life by overcoming the barriers to growth they have internalized. The enabler works to help them become more effective Christians by exercising a positive ministry of social change through institutional change.

Summary

This chapter may be summarized by suggesting: (1) that a ministry of community involvement is a natural and inevitable response of dynamic interpersonalism to the social environment; (2) that to be effective in community involvement, dynamic interpersonalism must incorporate certain changes; (3) that theoretically these changes require an empirical and conceptual effort to deal with the social context, especially as it is internalized within persons; (4) that the ministry of community involvement as it has come to emphasize institutional change is coming to see the primacy of the laity in this effort, with clergy serving as enablers and

11. For a more complete discussion of this lay ministry see the report of a special study task force of the Metropolitan Christian Council of Philadelphia: "Report of the Lay Ministry Task Force of the Metropolitan Christian Council of Philadelphia, 1971" (available through the council.)

leaders of enabling congregations. Finally, one implication that has been running throughout must be lifted up—both dynamic interpersonalism and community involvement are brought closer to the fullness of ministry by their being pursued together.

The Healing Community as Ministry

Virgil V. Brallier

My first act in beginning this chapter is to remind myself to be honest. For the past fourteen years my life and action have been well removed from the academic scene. Yet my first impulse was that I must now begin to sound like a scholar. Well, I am not in the life of scholarship, nor is there any likelihood that I shall return to it. I am involved in a relatively isolated, yet really frontline battle with the dilemmas of human malfunctioning. The demands on my time are such that I am doing a scattered job in keeping track of developments in the counseling field. Most of the reading I do is stolen from hours that might normally be devoted to sleep. Sometimes I complain about the choice I have made, yet I have no intention of abandoning it. So I make no pretense of writing this chapter as a scholar. In the first place, I can't find the time to do it that way. In the second, I would come off as phony if I did.

For the past nine years I have been involved, in one way or another, with Gould Farm, a rehabilitation center in the Berkshires of western Massachusetts. For nearly seven of those years I have also been pastor of the church in Monterey, the same town in which Gould Farm is located. Long since, it would have made both economic and professional sense to stop being pastor of this church. But a part of my self-knowledge includes a persistent tendency to retain certain patterns, even when efficiency would rule otherwise. In this chapter I intend to write primarily about the dynamics of the healing center, Gould Farm.

Let me outline my various relationships to the Farm. About nine years ago the executive director contacted Paul Johnson to see if there might be a graduate student in his department who would spend a summer at the Farm. None was available, but Paul told him there was a graduate of the department who was pastor of the First Congregational Church in North Adams, a town fifty miles north. As a consequence, I made my first acquaintance with Gould Farm. My family and I spent part of my vacation in a cottage on the grounds. The rest of the summer I came there on my weekly day off. At the end of the summer there was an invitation to move to the Farm to serve as pastoral counselor, but I could not win my own consent to leave the pastorate and work solely for the Farm. Two years went by, during which I continued coming down on my day off. Finally, the pulpit in Monterey was vacated; then came the opportunity to consider working for both the church and the Farm. An acceptable plan was devised and lasted for five years. At the end of this time the need for a full-time counselor had become urgent. Either I had to serve full-time or vacate the position so that a full-time counselor could be secured. My decision was to continue as pastor of the church and go into private counseling practice. I maintained my relationship to Gould Farm by becoming consultant to the staff. Within a short time I was elected to the Board of Directors, and immediately afterward became chairman of the board. It is from these various perspectives that I write about the Farm. It will be meaningful to some readers to know that Albert and Jessie Danielsen have long been members of the Board of Directors.

Gould Farm Background

The Farm was founded fifty-eight years ago by Will Gould, a young man with a dream. He was the son of a Congregational minister. He had long been aware of the blights that boys were suffering in the city. His purpose was to establish a place where such youths might become part of a warm, accepting family, be enabled to see themselves as good and useful persons, and thus move on to their rightful place in the larger world.

The family model was the pattern Will Gould believed essential to achieve this restoration of personality. His own family embodied firmness, structure, and stability, yet was at the same time warm and caring. Though Gould believed in the value of beautiful country, fresh air, and wholesome work, it is clear that he saw the healing of persons as coming primarily from their interaction with other persons. Gould suffered more than half-a-dozen failures trying to give his dream concrete fulfillment before Gould Farm came into being. He envisioned it as a boys' facility. It didn't turn out that way. It soon developed into a haven for persons of both sexes, incorporating both youth and age. Today, in its literature, Gould Farm describes itself as:

A non-sectarian recuperation and rehabilitation center offering milieu therapy—rest, care, work, and counseling; and accommodating about forty guests in winter and a few additional in summer. . . . We welcome men and women and young people of all creeds and races who find themselves overwhelmed by our demanding and complex society. One guest may be an adolescent on the verge of breakdown, . . . another be experiencing marital difficulties, . . . still another be an older person having trouble in adjusting to retirement. Some guests are mentally disordered or disorganized . . . . Some simply need a respite from life's cares. We've those who have a moderate problem with drugs or alcohol, while other guests are suffering from emotional shock, and others need to learn how to get along in social contacts.

The Farm has over six hundred acres of forest, field, and stream, including more than a dozen cottages and various farm buildings. Guests come mostly from a 150-mile radius, principally from New York City, the Albany area, and Boston, but a scattering come from the whole of the United States.

Currently there is a paid staff of fourteen, five service workers, and eight retired staff members and volunteers.

The staff is composed largely of lay persons, that is, neither medically nor psychiatrically trained. This is deliberate, stemming from a fear that professional training may interfere with personal qualities. However, since I myself first came to the Farm, there have been other counselors with professional training and background, as well as registered nurses, trained administrators, and so forth. Still, the fact remains that staff members are chosen primarily on the basis of their "feel" for people and their expected capacities for relationship. Other considerations, of course, are capability in a particular field, such as farming, hostessing, cooking, or whatever may be needed. The importance of the lay and personal aspect of the staff character is not something to be noted incidentally. It is deeply rooted in the nature of Gould Farm itself, and will bear upon much that is to follow.

Treating Life as a Whole

Gould Farm attempts to give attention to the broad range of influences and concerns that constitute human life. It seeks to draw into the family persons who are related to the major dimensions of our common life. The person coming to Gould Farm for help finds that work and faith, love and relationship, are elements that continually confront him in the community.

The most obvious confrontation is work. The guest may have come on Monday. On Tuesday morning he is expected to attend the work meeting, at which the community organizes its tasks for the day. This frequently comes as a shock to him if he has come directly from a hospital, where the full responsibility for his well-being was in the hands of others. Now the ability to take more responsibility is assumed. Indeed, it is an economic necessity for each guest to share in the Farm's work to the extent he is able. It is a working farm. There are dairy cows and beef cattle, sheep, pigs, chickens, and a few other assorted animals. In the summer there is a very active truck farming operation. The Farm is able to provide a surprisingly large amount of the food it uses. There is no "make-work." The guests soon recognize that the work they do is basic to the existence of the community. Work, then, becomes more than just economic necessity; it moves into the realm of cooperation with fundamental life processes.

The new guest soon senses the religious atmosphere surrounding him. To be sure, the first impressions may come from formal rituals, such as prayer before meals, a hymn after breakfast, or worship services twice a week. But surely the deepest evidence that he is in a religious community comes from more personal expressions of faith. In many ways the belief that healing may be in what we do is impregnated into the bloodstream of Gould Farm, but there is always an element lying beyond what we can see or control. It is reverence for and cooperation with this healing force that constitutes the most convincing evidence of all.

It is in the domain of the formal expressions of faith that we have the most difficulty in defining ourselves, for we have no official religion. Traditionally, we have remained primarily within the mainstream of Protestantism. Yet staff and guests come from a broad spectrum of religious denominations. Some have no religious affiliation; others describe themselves as agnostics. A recent attempt to identify Gould Farm's religious stance speaks of it as being in the Judeo-Christian tradition. Yet an earlier statement was even broader. It made no reference to any specific religious grouping, but still clearly characterized the Farm as having deep religious commitment.

As a religious community, it reflects the ambiguities of our age and vascillates between trying to sharpen up its religious self-image, on the one hand, and seeking, on the other hand, to be all things to all men. Perhaps this is why the clearest expression of the role religion plays at Gould Farm comes from the life style of the people who are there, rather than from formal religious observances.

In the Gould Farm pattern, love is recognized as fundamental for healing. Yet love is no easier to describe in the life at Gould Farm than it is anywhere else. However, the fact that former guests so frequently refer to the farm as a loving, caring community bears direct witness to the impact its lifestyle has had upon them. New guests arriving at the Farm also comment upon their initial impression of having entered a loving community. Perhaps those who are most guarded in discussing the "love quotient" are those in the midst of their stay at the Farm. Struggles with problems arising in the daily routine and occasionally explosive encounters with other members of the community make these persons more cautious in using the word "love" to describe what they are experiencing. Yet the impressive fact remains that those who have been helped are usually strong in affirming that love has been a central factor in the accomplishment of their healing.

The interpersonal element in Gould Farm's philosophy regarding healing is one of its most dearly held "articles of faith." Indelibly inscribed on much of what we accomplish is the belief that some particular individual or some group of persons may be the most crucial factor in helping a troubled human being find his way back to health. The operating principle of the Farm is to trust that, given a reasonably open setting, those relationships will form that may enable a person to gain leverage on what seems an otherwise insoluble problem. Where will these persons be found? Who is wise enough to plan for bringing them here? This is where faith must operate. Attractions and repulsions come to the fore, as in any other group, yet the effort to consciously cooperate with these processes and use them for enabling the person to know himself is continuously brought into play. The primary relationship a guest forms may be with a staff member, or with another guest, or a combination of both. Since this element of our philosophy is so basic to our life, it will be dealt with at several different points in this chapter.

The following section will deal more specifically with a

number of the elements that are currently employed as part of Gould Farm's attempt to fulfill its role as a healing community.

Shaping Community Direction

The life of an institution must be understood partly in terms of the way its policy is shaped. For the first twelve years Gould Farm policy emerged largely from the charismatic personality of Will Gould. To be sure, other persons associated with him exercised voice and will in the making of decisions. But, clearly, the same dream that had created the Farm was the one that most fully molded its character during those early years.

With the untimely death of Will Gould in 1925, the Farm was legally placed in the hands of his widow, Agnes Gould. Within a few years, the necessity of incorporation presented itself and thus, also, of grappling with the thread of institutionalization. At that time, Gould Farm officially became "The William J. Gould Associates, Inc." The Associates were those persons living there at the time of Will Gould's death who had caught his vision, had allied themselves with the founder, and had identified their destinies with his enterprise. Others continued to be added as the years went on.

In 1934 another step was taken. A Board of Directors was formed. This included many of the Associates, but also a minority of persons from outside the Farm. The balance of power still lay within the Farm family. Nevertheless, an important step had been taken to broaden the base and draw the larger world into the decision-making process. Well-known persons included on this original board were Dr. Richard Cabot, Mrs. Robert Speer, and Dr. John Beebe.

In 1959 a final step toward institutionalization and survival was taken. The nonresident members of the board now, for the first time, outnumbered the residents. It was by no means a step lightly taken, but rather it represented a profound struggle over the issue of the "personal" versus the "institutional." This issue has characterized the Farm's internal debate and concern over the years. We have wrestled against the institution as the enemy of the personal. Even though some aspects of becoming an institution have been necessary in order to relate to the larger world, and thus ensure survival, the battle to remain personal has been a fierce one. The essence of Gould Farm cannot be understood apart from that battle.

No matter how you arrange the official composition of an organization, laying balance of power here or there, the true character emerges from its internal lifestyle. Officially, the Board of Directors is now responsible for the policy of Gould Farm. But its real life springs from the dynamic interplay of persons and forces within its corporate body. I shall now describe some of the ways in which these interpersonal transactions take place.

Community Meetings. The word "meeting" conjures up sighs and groans at the Farm. Meetings of various sorts are in the very lifeblood of the Farm—staff meetings, "family meetings," and ad hoc committee meetings that form and dissolve around events and needs. Within the last few years a new type of meeting has emerged, the community meeting. It has no authority to take action. Its purpose is for members of the community to tell one another the way things are. At first it appeared that it might turn out to be little more than a "gripe session" for guests who were upset over one situation or another. Open the doors to tell what you think of administration or staff and, unless the place is run by angels, a whole torrent of disaffection may pour forth. What to do with this torrent? The first impulse is to tell the guests to shut up, give up their crying towels, and go do something constructive. Yet providing a way for such feelings to be expressed openly has had a healthy effect, both for the humanization of the "institution" and for the strengthening of the persons who frequently think of themselves as powerless.

The community meeting has proved to be a useful instrument for staff, as well as guests, to unburden themselves, and frequently changes subsequently occur in some dimension of the life they are sharing together. Although this meeting represents for some an occasion for dread, to others it has come to signify the most effective way to try out "being somebody." Within the framework of the Farm's intention to emphasize the personal, it stands as a warning not to become careless or complacent, for if we do, someone will be sure to remind us of it in the presence of the entire community.

Group Therapy. The use of psychotherapy comes most clearly into focus at the Farm in the program of group therapy. Currently there are two groups, each meeting twice weekly for two-hour sessions. Group therapy has a peculiar appropriateness within the whole context of the Farm. The recognition that other persons are involved in our welfare comes at us from all sides. We should be striking a strangely contradictory note if in the psychotherapy program we depended primarily on individual counseling.

It would be hard to describe the specific approach the group therapy program takes, for, as in group work everywhere, the character of the sessions is always profoundly influenced by the personal style of the group leader. There are, however, certain observations that apply fairly well across the board, regardless of the leader. The members of the group have come to know each other quite well, not just in the group but in the various activities they share together. They are people who are working, eating, playing, worshiping, and often just visiting together. They share a wide variety of experiences. This all becomes legitimate material to use in the group. Not only do they have many observations drawn from everyday experiences in common, but I believe their intimate acquaintance in so many areas of reality reduces the amount of fantasy material they produce about each other. Therefore, a person's image of himself is corrected by others reflecting back to him what they see in the therapy sessions, as well as what they have seen of him when he was eating, playing, working, and reacting to the whole climate of the Farm. It is this possibility of a more intimate knowing that gives a different tone to the group sessions. It has both the assets and liabilities built into it that accompany the deeper intimacy of the relationship in individual psychotherapy. Naturally, some restraint is exercised in such groups because these same people will soon again be facing each other at meals and working side by side during the day. Yet this more intimate self-knowledge helps guests to press each other harder to give up their illusions about themselves.

One of the peculiar difficulties under which the groups must function is that the usual contract to remain together over a specific period of time is impossible to fulfill. A guest may join a group and then leave the Farm within a month's time. For the kind of deep knowing we hope to achieve, this is disconcerting. The longer-term guests, however, are usually present in sufficient numbers to provide a genuine sense of continuity. On occasion we do have heavy turnover periods. This hinders some facets of group work, but it also provides an opportunity to deal with feelings of loss and mourning.

A variation from the usual group therapy process has sometimes been used with striking results. We occasionally set up something like ad hoc groups. Because a particular problem or issue has arisen, two or three persons may be placed in a special group which will meet more often, and frequently with more intensity, until the issue is resolved. Even though the smaller group obviously changes the character of the relationships within it, still the basic principles of group therapy are used as fully as possible. Difficulties relating to trust and intimacy have been dealt with in this way, and eruptions of emotion in relationships that might otherwise have called for administrative discipline have also been so handled.

It is not difficult to understand that, since group therapy was first introduced at the Farm half-a-dozen years ago, it has become our principal form of psychotherapy. It "belongs." It is uniquely in character with the whole emphasis of the

Farm upon the importance of interpersonal relationships as a basic resource for healing.

Individual Counseling. The one-to-one relationship in counseling is very much in evidence at Gould Farm, yet in terms of actual time, the average guest spends up to four hours a week in group therapy, over against the half-hour of individual time he may receive from the professional counselor. Many guests may receive no individual time at all, except for entrance interviews set up to deal with transitional problems. Other guests requiring particular attention may receive considerably more than the average. There are many variations from one person to another, and even with the same person from one period to another.

The one-to-one relationship gets more emphasis in the daily routine of the Farm from persons other than the professional counselor. This is a long-standing tradition that existed even before there was any dream of having a professional counselor at all. If there is an unwritten article of faith here, I discovered when I first began coming to the Farm, it is in the capacity of people to help people. The faith includes a belief that, given reasonable opportunity and flexibility, the arrangements for this helping will form "under the eye of God."

Much of the counseling that goes on here might be regarded simply as conversation or discussion between persons. As guests frequently find themselves gravitating toward a particular staff member, when they are working with this person, they will often find themselves engaged in continuing coversations. This kind of interchange may be no more significant than "batting the breeze," but much of it turns out to be soul-to-soul searching, questioning, examining. Most of these conversational exchanges would not in the strict sense be considered "counseling," but as evidence of caring, sharing, and the opening of one person to another; it is human discourse of the highest order. For nothing in the world would I trade off this aspect of our own particular style of caring for a doubled amount of professional counseling. It is an

275

ingredient in creating a healing atmosphere that reaches far and deep.

Relationship to Current Movements in Mental Health

Gould Farm did some genuine pioneering in the mental health field, yet for many years its contribution was little recognized. During most of the Farm's existence, the public has been oriented toward the large hospital with a well-trained professional staff, so that expert care could be given. Yet the Farm continued steadfastly on its own course. Now the wisdom of choosing this course is being hailed as the wave of the future in the mental health field.

Phasing Out the Institutional. Massachusetts has a master plan for phasing out all its large mental hospitals, as do several other states. Why? There is widespread agreement that they have betrayed the hope that caused them to be built. The bane of modern man is the institution, with all its unconscious demonic power to depersonalize. The current revolt against the establishment, whether it be found in church, school, business, or government, is not an accident. Men and women are feeling their humanness being stolen away from them, even in the supposedly "normal" institutions of society.

How much more crucially has this been happening in those large institutions set up to deal with mental and emotional disorders! The persons they are caring for learned, even before coming to the hospital, to distrust and deny their own feelings. They were already fighting with one hand tied behind the back. Now, as they try to extricate themselves from the smothering effect of the hospital, they find it hard to separate fantasy and reality. Maybe it's not the hospital that makes them feel "done in"; maybe it's just their own jaundiced perception. So the demonic institutional righteousness makes the vulnerable person who already has a hard time defending his human feelings retreat all the further from believing in his own integrity.

Of course, the above is an oversimplification of what happens to the mental patient. Nevertheless, it happens with sufficient frequency to sound the alarm. It appeared for a good many years that Gould Farm was simply a voice crying in the wilderness. Society was listening to the voice of the large city institution. But merely by holding faithfully to our family style of life and care, we began to provide a model toward which the whole mental health movement is now turning with increasing interest. In fact, we find ourselves receiving more and more inquiries about the nature of our work.

Lay versus Professional. Until recent years the only reasons for settling for less than the most expert professional help were financial ones or the fact of long waiting lists in the large institutions. Now, with this growing recognition in the whole field that persons other than doctors or psychologists have important roles to play in liberating the emotionally disturbed person, increasing attention is being given to the "para-professionals." They are becoming recognized as the persons with whom primary relationships are frequently developed and, because of this, they are involved in some of the fundamental transactions necessary for healing.

It is as if all kinds of new forces had been released into the stream of influences brought to bear on the troubled person. Instead of the once sacrosanct province surrounding doctor and patient, not to be violated by the introduction or even recognition of other persons, it is now not uncommon to find something more nearly resembling a parade. Here come mate, siblings, parents, friends—yes, sometimes even enemies—into the arena. The doctor is learning to be more relaxed with forces other than those he himself initiates or controls. In fact, he is taking the lead in many instances by inviting all kinds and conditions of men into the fray. Why? Because this is the best way to avoid the one-dimensional dilemma. It is harder to move if there is only one handle to grasp—and especially so if that one handle has been tried again and again to no avail.

At the time in which the mental health movement was centering its hope in the "expert," Gould Farm was doing a thoroughly creditable job with no expert anywhere in sight. True, it was not accepting as guests persons who required the intensive care and protection that only a hospital could provide. Yet the ability of persons to move through their depressions, their fears, and their compulsions was a part of our life then, even as it is today. I am well aware that the insight of a professional has enabled many persons to be helped who had never found such help before and has facilitated the treatment of others. I want to make it clear that we at Gould Farm do not underestimate the insight into the dynamics of human behavior that comes with professional training. I am simply noting that, whatever flaws the anti-professional attitude may have, Gould Farm has validated the positive values of the interpersonal element in healing. Most certainly, many of these interpersonal relationships have lacked insight into the dynamic elements occurring, yet help came despite this lack. The helping element evidently came more from skill in sharing human qualities than from theoretical knowledge of human interaction.

The truth is beginning to emerge that life is moved by life. Our faith in the interpersonal at Gould Farm is vindicated far less by our anti-professionalism than by our persistent belief that people are the all-important factor in helping people.

Clues in the Healing Process

When all our researching is done and when we have written about our search, one stubborn fact remains. The healing process for emotional disorders still remains shrouded in paradox. Each person in this field can tell of methods he has used and of the good results that followed. Yet the wise will not rush in to declare, "At last I have uncovered the secret. Just use the method I have described, and success will be assured." Even if I have fine statistics to support a method that has emerged from my own experience, how can I be sure that it is my theory and method that are making a difference? It may simply be some aspect of my character or personality that I have not even taken into account.

So this is where the present state of our knowledge lies. With the paradoxes that stalk us on our way, we must still continue to ask, "What are we able to see? What factors enable the person who is locked into emotional difficulties to loosen the grip of the past and present and move into a new freedom?"

Gould Farm, in a very unobtrusive way, has been deeply involved in the search for answers. As with most searchers, we ourselves have sometimes latched onto a certain element in the healing process and acted as if it were the only answer. But our pride is always being confronted with the need to return again and again to the ranks of the searchers. Two elements do emerge, however, from the Gould Farm experience as having sufficient weight to emphasize their importance.

A Natural Environment. Any attempt to define the "natural" or "normal" for man immediately runs into trouble. Man is an inventor and an artificer. He is always shaping and reshaping his environment. Therefore, any specific attempt to describe a norm is always off the mark and fails to describe what a "natural environment" for man really is. Recognizing these limitations, let us, nevertheless, see what Gould Farm produces in its environment that is so important.

Perhaps "anti-institutionalism" should be taken more as a symbol than anything else. It is not hard for a critic to point out that railing against institutions is of little value if you are at the same time depending on certain institutional principles. Of course, Gould Farm is itself an institution. Yet it may just be that our rather self-conscious struggle against the institutional is a part of our ability to maintain enough of the human and natural to be effective.

We strive after the pattern of the family, yet the critic is right when he points out that a group of seventy-five to one hundred persons doesn't come off behaving exactly like a family. Still the family claim does have its impact. It keeps reminding us that we have need to care for each other. Although we may not feel as if we were in a family with the majority, we do feel so with some, or at least a few. Since this claim prevails throughout the Farm, some semblance of the natural family remains and has a positive influence.

Another part of the "natural environment" is found in the need to cooperate with nature in producing food. We consider ourselves fortunate that our work is centered around a basic necessity of life. Suppose it involved manufacturing. This would not invalidate what we are doing, but I have come to feel that the more one has become alienated from self and others, the more such a basic function as the production of food tends to create a desire for closer contact with reality. At every point, then, where we are able to build upon the "natural" within a person, we feel that the force nudging him toward health has increased by just that much.

The passion for keeping life at the Farm related to the roots of our existence is of profound importance for releasing the healing forces within us. And it is my strong hunch that this may be just as valid in the outside world as it is at Gould Farm.

The Interpersonal Dimension. Our explanations at Gould Farm of how one person influences another as an agent of healing may change with the seasons, but the central fact of meaningful personal involvement has been a constant in our program. The critic may properly object that professionalism in itself is no violation of the personal. Indeed, who is the professional, if not a person? In actual practice the Farm is entirely warm and open to specific professionals. The fear, I believe, stems primarily from the nameless, faceless professional, who represents the threat of a role-ridden individual with technical knowledge and skill, but deficient in human qualities. The fierce search for the personal dimension is the most important fact to stress here. The symbol, the antiprofessional, is far less significant as a description of our way of life than is the continuing cultivation of the interpersonal element.

The most important contribution the Gould Farm enterprise could possibly make to the larger understanding of the healing of persons would be to research and document its long-standing struggle to hold this interpersonal dimension in the forefront of all its efforts.

Part III

General Pastoral Care and the Future of Ministries

William E. Hulme

As is obvious from the preceding chapters, pastoral care has undergone much development since Paul Johnson began his seminary teaching career at Boston University. As in those days, so also now it has fashioned itself largely according to movement in psychotherapy. The phenomenal development of transactional analysis with its thousands of institutes throughout the nation has caught the imagination of the church and its ministry. As pastoral care was highly influenced by the psychoanalytic insights of Sigmund Freud, so also it is now influenced by Eric Berne's attempt to improve on Freudian concepts.

While Freud may be experiencing the natural decline that follows a period of domination, the same is not true with some of his former disciples. Alfred Adler, if anything, is more popular than ever. Adlerian institutes on family life are apparently meeting the needs of many anxious parents, largely through the influence of Adler's disciple Rudolf Dreikurs. I read Adler during my student days at B.U.S.T. under Paul's direction, but my knowledge of Adler did not include any awareness of a local Adlerian movement. The same was true in my study of Carl Jung. I was not aware of any Jungian institutes and workshops that I might attend as my own students are now doing. There may have been such, but their appeal must have been to a selected few rather than to any general interest.

Closely allied to the Adlerian family clinics is the newer

parent-effectiveness training. Founded and directed by Thomas Gordon, these programs are likewise appealing to many pastors and laymen. Congregations are sponsoring these family-centered institutes and incorporating their ideas and terminology into their educational programs. The Bernean terms of parent, adult and child, for example, are almost as familiar in clergy circles as Father, Son, and Holy Ghost.

The increasing number of these parish-oriented pastoral care opportunities stemming from developments in psychology and psychotherapy coincide with a growing emphasis on the group. Group therapy in its various emphases of marriage counseling, family counseling, and groupings around other specific life situations and needs has almost surpassed individual counseling in popular and professional usage.

Along with this increase in pastoral care opportunities for parish life, there has been a similar expansion in the chaplaincy ministries in institutions. During the years since Paul Johnson became a professor of pastoral care, there has been a phenomenal increase in clinical pastoral education centers. The Institute of Pastoral Care, with which Paul was primarily associated, has since joined with the earlier Council for Clinical Training and denominational groups such as the Lutheran Advisory Council to form the Association for Clinical Pastoral Education (ACPE). What was largely a summer opportunity for pastors and theological students is increasingly becoming a fall, winter, and spring opportunity as well. In addition there are part-time programs extending from six to nine months which make it easier for pastors to take clinical pastoral education while remaining in their parishes. Residency programs of a year's duration are being offered by a growing number of centers.

The development has been qualitative as well as quantitative. The practice of supervision, upon which the CPE movement is based, has become increasingly effective. I had what was then called clinical training as part of my graduate study under Paul. When I compare my experience with what students are now receiving in their CPE, the difference is largely in supervision. Again, the group context has come to the fore. Under the leadership of the chaplain supervisor, the students participate together in corporate supervision. In the dynamics of group interaction each attempts to share personally with the other. Through this experience the students and supervisor grow in the awareness of their self-identity. When asked what they value most from CPE, students most often refer to this growth in self-understanding.

There are expanding opportunities also for CPE supervisors. While hospitals and correctional institutions are still the primary places for his skills, community-based programs that specialize in marriage and family counseling, community-oriented ministries to particular subcultures, and parish-oriented programs in community nurture are beginning to develop.[1] One area of neglect, however, has been the care of the aged. To my knowledge there is no CPE program based in an institution for older people or that focuses on older people who are living outside of institutions.[2] Obviously this omission is not due to a lack of need, but rather to a general cultural apathy toward the plight of our elderly citizens.

Another significant development in pastoral care is the emergence of the profession of pastoral counselor. Not only may the pastoral counselor be pastor of a congregation or chaplain of an institution, he may also be on the staff of a growing number of pastoral counseling centers, or even in private practice. The formation of the American Association of Pastoral Counselors was a response to this development. Like its counterpart for clinical pastoral education, the ACPE, the AAPC has concerned itself with establishing standards for the certification and accreditation of pastoral counseling centers and pastoral counselors. Its three ranks of member, fellow and diplomate correspond to the ACPE's ranks of advanced

1. In my own area Lutheran Social service agencies have been responsible for two of those innovations, and a medical clinic the third.
2. Chaplain Supervisor Marlin Stenne of Lutheran Deaconess Hospital, Minneapolis, has been loaned on two occasions to conduct a CPE quarter at the Ebenezer Society Home for the Aged.

student, assistant supervisor, acting supervisor, and supervisor, except that the latter are more transitional steps than hierarchical levels.

In addition to mental health clinics which have occasionally had pastoral counselors on their staffs, some medical clinics are also doing likewise. In my own community a medical clinic placed a pastoral counselor on its staff three years ago. Because of the response, another pastoral counselor was added this year. If this local situation is any indication of popular appeal, we can anticipate an increasing number of such staffings.

In contrast to these expanding opportunities in pastoral care, industrial chaplaincies seem not to have caught on. During World War II a few such chaplaincies were established in defense industries. One might have anticipated this as the beginning of a trend. Yet most communities still do not have any industrial chaplains. At the moment "tent-making ministries" or "worker priest" experiments are more in vogue. With the growing surplus of clergy in many denominations, this form of industrial ministry may increase.

However, another factor may reverse things. Urban congregations are becoming increasingly frustrated in their attempts to minister to the growing number of apartment-house dwellers in their communities. Some feel that many of these apartment-house dwellers are more oriented to the community of persons with whom they work than to the community in which they have a residence. If this is the case, it may be worth the effort again to experiment with business and industrial chaplaincies.

Since Paul initiated his clinically oriented pastoral care program at B. U. S. T. most theological seminaries have added similar programs in their practical departments. I imagine that a good number of the faculty in these departments were educated by Paul. I have modeled my own teaching program after that which I experienced under Paul Johnson at Boston University School of Theology. In conjunction with Paul's classes I ministered to patients at Boston City Hospital under the supervision of John Billinsky, to inmates at Charlestown State Prison under Chaplain Howard Kellett, and to patients at the Boston Dispensary under the supervision of Winfred Rhoades. I, as well as others, have incorporated this model of graduate study into the undergraduate department of pastoral care so that our candidates for ministry from such seminaries have a close approximation to that formerly identified with graduate study in pastoral care. This integration of classroom instruction with a supervised laboratory involvement in ministry is, in my estimation, a basic pedagogical model for any functional discipline.

In conjunction with the expansion of the clinical dimension to pastoral care within theological seminaries, the academic dimension of pastoral care has also expanded in its orientation to psychology, philosophy, and theology. An example in point is Paul's own position of dynamic interpersonalism, as is well illustrated in the first section of this *Festschrift*. Although the essentials of this theory were implicit in my studies with Paul, his major interest academically at that time was the psychology of religion. His book by that title had just been published. I recall the class period when he read and discussed Edward Scribner Ames's review of the book in the *Christian Century,* considered the "Chicago" journal, biased toward the Divinity School of the University of Chicago with its opposing naturalistic philosophy of Henry Nelson Wieman. Paul was pleased that Ames was generally favorable toward his book. So far as pastoral care and counseling were concerned, he seemed content with Carl Rogers' theory and method. *Counseling and Psychotherapy* was jokingly considered our Bible.

What was implicit with our class became explicit with later classes. It was obvious that Paul would approach pastoral care with the perspective of Boston University's philosophy of personalism. However, as a student of the various schools of psychology and psychotherapy, he found the limitation of personality to conscious experience too confining and expanded it to include the dynamic of the unconscious, an input from Freud, and bodily functions as well as mental, an input from Gordon Allport. As a teacher of pastoral care he included the interpersonal relationship as another focus in his theory of personality. Probably as an input from Karen Horney, he recognized also the role of cultural influence upon the person. Being a personalist made it logical for him to place his theory into a religious dimension with God as the absolute person and our relationship with him implied or induced from our relationship with our neighbors.

I personally appreciated the support to my own faith that Paul's position gave me. The ease with which the personalist conception of coherence moved from man to God was an intellectual support when my feelings were positive toward faith. When these feelings were negative, however, the support was not there. The conceptual framework more suitable to my needs was the existential approach of Søren Kierkegaard. Because it is not dependent upon rational coherence, the "leap of faith" is particularly adapted to the "emotional" doubter. The Kierkegaardian position, of course, was not in vogue at B.U.S.T. It was only shortly thereafter that Paul's colleague, Harold DeWolf, wrote his attack on this approach entitled *The Religious Revolt Against Reason*. What was in vogue, however, was the concern for an academic base for pastoral care. Due in no small degree to this concern, my own major interest as a teacher has been in the development of a theological motif for pastoral care. The task of spelling out the theological dimensions for the growing accumulation of psychological insights is still a creative challenge.

In contrast to the efforts that have been made toward an academic orientation to pastoral care, psychologically, philosophically, and theologically, there has been little if any progress in the direction of parapsychology. This area was an interest of Paul's when I was his student. Intrigued by the scientific efforts of J. B. Rhine at the parapsychological laboratory at Duke University, he suggested that I consider this field for my thesis. Attracted to the suggestion, I was supported throughout the endeavor by his enthusiasm.

Parapsychology offered a new area to pastoral care. It is still a new area. I realized this recently when I functioned as advisor to a student writing his thesis on religion and parapsychology. In spite of its thorough research, the thesis could have been written when I wrote mine. One reason for this is that parapsychology as a science has not advanced to any appreciable degree. There is, however, a revival of interest in the esoteric and the occult, including extrasensory perception. An instance of this interest is Spiritual Frontiers Fellowship, an organization formed to relate psychic phenomena to the traditional churches. It may yet capture the pastoral imagination. The program for its 1972 annual conference lists the topic "Psychic Experience and Pastoral Care."

Professional Identity of the Pastor

My purpose in this chapter is not only to summarize the current situation in pastoral care, but also to look into the future. The confidence I need to do this has come through futurist Alvin Toffler. The future can be predicted with some degree of assurance, says Toffler, by noting present trends. The trends inherent to the foregoing summary of the present development of pastoral care, then, will serve as our base for anticipating the future.

I believe the present concern for the professional identity of the pastor will increase. This professionalism is in relationship to other professionals in the helping professions, and not in relationship to the laity of the church. In this latter relationship I anticipate an increasing concern for the pastoral functioning of the layman. While the emphasis will continue that the pastor's task is to equip the layman for his ministry to others rather than to substitute for him, I believe we will see more emphasis on the layman's potential for equipping the pastor. Not only does the layman function pastorally in his various involvements, he is also the "consumer" in terms of the professional ministry. In both capacities he has much to offer to the pastor's continuing education.

Evolving in its present forms through association with the fields of psychiatry and psychotherapy, pastoral care's emerging sense of professionalism is largely in relationship to these areas. As a logical concomitant to this professionalism, we can anticipate a continued diminishing of a previous adulation of the psychiatrist and the psychologist. This would imply that fewer specialists in pastoral care would be leaving their profession for the more coveted vocation of "secular" psychotherapy. The increased respect for the professional identity of the pastor would include an appreciation for the theological and ecclesiastical traditions that contribute to the uniqueness of his training.

The American Association of Pastoral Counselors will continue to play a vital role in this trend. Its concern for professional standards fosters professional pride. In opening its ranks to the parish pastor as well as to the professional pastoral counselor, it has reinforced the growing awareness of the congregation as a strategic milieu for pastoral care. The AAPC itself is more oriented to its own profession than it was in its beginning. Previously the psychiatrist played a major role in the supervision of the candidate for certification. Current standards place more emphasis on the pastoral counselor himself for this supervision. As pastors show more respect for their own profession, they can anticipate an increase also in the respect accorded to them by other professions.

The older Association for Clinical Pastoral Educators should also continue to play its role toward professional identity. The membership involvement of theological seminaries in addition to clinical pastoral education centers ought to continue to enhance the theological dimensions of CPE and the clinical dimensions of the seminary classroom. Specifically, I anticipate an expansion in the process of theological reflection in CPE. Implicit to such reflection is the recognition of the pastor as a theologian and of pastoral care as a functional development of pastoral theology.

In so anticipating I am quite aware that we still have a long way to go in this direction. The practice of theological reflection is not of uniform significance among CPE programs. In addition there is the tendency in certain areas of CPE to divorce the pastoral profession from its ecclesiastical identification. Those who favor this divorce contend that a relationship with the institutional church is a hindrance to their pastoral ministry within more secularly oriented institutions. Rather than opting to become psychotherapists, however, they see themselves as a new profession. They are pastoral counselors—ministers—but dissociated from the institutional church. As with most CPE supervisors, they also may utilize theological reflection in the format for the verbatim visitation reports of their students. One can be theologically oriented and still dissociate himself from the institutional church. The only question is—for how long? Theology in its Christian context is the church's theology. The Word and Sacrament belong to a worshiping community. While this community is not confined to the institutional church, the institutional church is its tangible focus. Institutionalization is inevitable if any movement is to have continuum as a social entity. Divorced from its institutional context, theological reflection may be as short-lived as a cut flower—and for the same reason.

As members of their own regional ACPE organizations theological seminaries can exercise their influence to encourage theological reflection at centers where it may be lacking. In my own region some CPE supervisors invite theological professors to join in their programs as participants and as theological resources. By the same token, CPE centers can exercise their influence with their regional seminaries to the extent that all departments of theological education be concerned about the practice of ministry, and in particular its clinical dimensions. Here, too, we have a long way to go.

I brought an interest in theology and its significance for ministry with me to Boston University School of Theology and, through the academic and clinical dimensions of Paul's program, enlarged my perceptions in this area. Paul is a religious person, deeply meditative, and devoted to prayer. He assisted us through his person to reflect theologically upon a religious motif for our clinical experience. His dynamic interpersonalism as a psychological theory of personality is more akin to philosophy or philosophical theology than it is to my own background in confessional theology. The "Thou" implicit in the "I" and the divine relationship implicit in the human are supportive but not basic to Christian theology. Theological reflection upon pastoral care needs to go beyond the religious implications of dynamic interpersonalism—and it has. Paul himself has done so in *Person and Counselor.* So also has Daniel Day Williams in his conceptualization of the relationship between theology and clinical experience.[3] So also have Edward Thornton, Thomas Oden, Eduard Thurneysen, Don Browning, Albert Outler, David Roberts, Seward Hiltner, Wayne Oates, Carroll Wise, David Belgum, myself, and others. I anticipate a continuing creative challenge in this endeavor to integrate pastoral care in its clinical relationship to the behavioral sciences with the theological traditions of the Christian ministry.

Need for a Sociological Base

There is a growing awareness of a need for a sociological control to pastoral care to balance its heavy dependency upon psychology. As pastoral care has become increasingly focused upon marriage and the family, this lack of a sociological context was bound to become a problem. With the resurgence of the prophetic ministry and its concern for our corporate structures, the sociological deficiency in pastoral care was even more obvious.

Although oriented to psychology, dynamic interpersonalism is open in the direction of a sociological balance. Its emphasis is on the person-in-relationship, not only to his unconscious and to God, but also to his neighbor and to his environing culture. Although the latter relationships were not developed sociologically, the opportunity to do so is inherent in the

3. *The Minister and the Care of Souls* (New York: Harper & Brothers, 1961).

theory. When in recognition of his contribution to pastoral care Paul was given an award by the AAPC, his reception address was a critique of Rogers' concept of self-actualization. Believing that Rogers had limited his concept of the person too much to the person's own psyche, Paul contended that self-actualization is the self in relationship to other selves. Dynamic interpersonalism conceives of self-actualization in terms of the dynamic of relationships.

Dynamic interpersonalism is particularly open to the exchange theory of social organization.[4] According to this theory people enter into relationship with each other when they are satisfied with the anticipated exchange in giving and receiving. In the light of this theory, dynamic interpersonalism would depend on this mutual satisfaction in any kind of meaningful relationship. The more mutuality in giving and receiving, the better the exchange and the more secure the relationship, providing the exchange is based also on a mutuality in personal worth and dignity. It is precisely the lack of this latter mutuality in many of our societally institutionalized exchanges that has led to the dissension in society which has initiated changes in our social structures.

With this dissent has come the reassertion of the prophetic dimension of ministry. Somewhat dormant during previous decades when conformity rather than dissent was the more dominant social trend, the prophetic emphasis is having its effect today in all areas of the ministry. As might be anticipated, the prophetic tone is highly critical. An example is Robert Hudnut's description of the church as *The Sleeping Giant*.[5] In this book Hudnut takes the church to task for being infatuated with psychology and neglecting sociology. While he does not specifically attack the ministry of pastoral care, it is this ministry that is more vulnerable to the charge.

The realization of this imbalance has led to a new conception of training programs for ministry called action training

4. Developed in specific emphases by Peter Blau, George Homans, John Thibaut, Harold Kelley, and others.
5. (New York: Harper & Row, 1971).

and to the formation of the Action Training Coalition, which has established standards for the accreditation of action training programs. The action training movement has at various times and places been critical of clinical pastoral education. In fact some have seen the imbalance of CPE and in pastoral care as a whole toward psychology and the ministry to the individual, as a motivation for initiating the action training movement. This dissension between ministerial training programs is another evidence of the unfortunate separation of psychology from sociology. It implies that psychology and sociology—pastoral counseling and social action—are inherently incompatible. The falsity of this implication is as harmful to pastoral care as any factional feud.

Paul's vision and guidance have proved helpful in anticipating the prophetic challenge. As my advisor he suggested I take social psychology under Wayland Vaughn and a sourse in social agencies taught by Emory Bucke. As the liberal editor of *Zions Herald*, Bucke had the prophet's concern for social issues. Boston University School of Theology's involvement in the social scene was also a challenging milieu within which to study pastoral care. Seminarians were as committed to taking part in a picket line of a strike as they are today in regard to anti-war demonstrations. The former dean of Boston University School of Theology, Dr. Walter G. Muelder, was proudly proclaimed as a specialist in the cause of organized labor. Paul's own social concern was expressed largely through the Fellowship of Reconciliation. He was committed to the prevention of war. Yet as a person Paul was more priestly than prophetic by nature.

My background and training have thus made it natural to consider clinical pastoral education and action training as necessary complements in a balanced approach to pastoral care. This balance is structured into my own graduate program in pastoral care. Called Ministry in Social Change, it has a prerequisite of a quarter of CPE. Students are assigned to congregations, to community-based action programs, and to clinically oriented counseling programs. Input seminars are taught by persons representing the various areas of concern to a balanced concept of pastoral care. These include counselors of various specialties, action training specialists, parish pastors, community organizers, city and state legislators, union officials, corporation executives, and people involved in movements for human rights and societal change. Although it is an offering of the department of pastoral care, the program is accredited by the Action Training Coalition. My purpose is to maintain a constructive tension between the pastoral emphasis on individual needs and the social concern for the structures of political and economic power.

A balanced pastoral ministry is concerned not only with counseling with individuals in their problems, but also with the social conditions that are contributing to those problems. A pastor calling on a patient in a nursing home, for example, may empathize with the patient's will to die; in the same circumstances he might feel likewise. Obviously the patient needs his ministry to her as an individual. But she and the millions like her also need his ministry to these "circumstances" that contribute to her desolation. The cultural values and social structures that undermine the dignity of the aged and their purpose for living are an obvious focus for a pastoral ministry. The recent formation of the "Grey Panthers" to challenge a society that "makes scrap piles of the elderly," is an example of the kind of action that may be needed. Perhaps it is not coincidental that the founders are all retired professional church workers.

An authority in pastoral care stated during a recent conference that pastoral care is not primarily social action. In making this assertion he was showing that he is still hung up on an arbitrary division. His qualifying word "primarily," which he thought protected his position, actually revealed its inadequacy. Ministry to the individual, the marriage, the family, and ministry to the social structures are of necessity of equal importance. This duality of focus corresponds to the ministerial scope of a congregation which is a maturing, curing community and at the same time a prophetic community. Its concern is for individuals, marriages, and families in their needs and for justice in the structures of the environing community. These are mutually related and simultaneous ministries. Congregations, of course, may deemphasize one or the other, but when they do, this very imbalance initiates the reaction that moves us from one imbalance to another.

The individual person, marriage, and family are concerns for pastoral care. So also are the social structures within which they must function. Both are related to the same purpose for ministry. I anticipate that pastoral care in the future will be increasingly influenced by this beginning awareness of the necessity of balance.

A More Aggressive Counseling Methodology

The aggressive nature of the prophetic ministry as manifested in social action has its counterpart in current methodologies in pastoral counseling. Again the stimulus has come from the field of psychotherapy, principally from reality therapy pioneered by William Glasser. The trend is toward a greater emphasis upon confrontation. The change has been difficult for some of the earlier leaders in pastoral care to accept. One, for example, has disparaged confrontation as a military term whose use denotes a coercive trend in counseling.

The use of a more aggressive methodology was needed to cope with the rising sociopathic influence in our society. The earlier counseling approach was based on psychoanalytical insights. The techniques derived from this orientation have not been adequate for sociopathy. Since Freud's patients were largely neurotics, he developed his theories on the basis of neurotic characteristics. Glasser counsels largely with sociopaths in juvenile correctional institutions: a different personality disturbance calls for a different treatment. In counseling with persons with sociopathic tendencies, the counselor needs to focus continually upon the reality of the situation and the counselee's responsibility.

This change in emphasis has accompanied the current criticism of Freud and psychoanalysis. One of these critics, O. Hobart Mowrer, contends that the Freudian "cure" for neurotics may well turn them into sociopaths. Since these personality disturbances are opposites in almost every respect, Mowrer's charge might seem to be warranted. However, a neurotic by virtue of the fact that he already has too much internalization of his societal mores can scarcely become a sociopath who by definition is deficient in such internalization. But the desire to escape from the neurotic results of such conformity to cultural mores can lead to an imitation of sociopathy. This is precisely what we as a culture are now experiencing. In fact the phenomenon of imitation sociopathy is actually changing some of our cultural norms.[6] The new breed of counterculture people are not genuine sociopaths, but they desire the apparent freedom from conformity and responsibility that characterizes the sociopath. The trend is undoubtedly a reaction to the distortions and pressures inherent in the cultural conformity described by David Riesman as other-directedness.

There are several ways in which pastoral care may be extended to persons caught up in this trend. Since genuine freedom is not realized by avoiding reality or personal responsibility, the shift to a more confrontive approach in counseling is helpful. So also is the current trend in contemporary worship services which are free from the traditional forms of the past. The spirit of openness that characterizes the small group ministry assists such persons to assert their own understanding of values. Through the increase in the prophetic ministry, churches themselves are questioning previously assumed values.

In these and other ways churches are becoming prepared to minister to people influenced by the new freedoms. How-

6. See Alan Harrington, "The Coming of the Psychopath," *Playboy* (Dec., 1971).

ever, we have just begun to move in this direction. As social institutions, churches are slow to adjust to change. But we have changed enough to catch a glimpse of the possibilities for change. We can perceive the direction that the pastoral ministry must take. Models for such ministries are obviously locally oriented. Their use in other localities must be determined by an analysis of the specific needs and resources of that locality. Many experimental projects also have not met with the observable response needed for continuance. Yet the churches in their pastoral care have rounded the corner, and I believe we can anticipate more effectiveness in ministering to people whose needs in various ways are characterized by a day of change.

From the Past to the Future

It is a long way from the Rogers I studied under Paul to Glasser or even to transactional analysis. The method of the early Rogers was an extremely nondirective psychotherapy, as the eight verbatim interviews with "Herbert Bryan" in *Counseling and Psychotherapy* indicate. Even then I recall being bothered about this approach. It was difficult to adapt it to the church and its ministry, in which there were structures of a moral and religious dimension. Although these structures are capable of undergoing change and have done so, they cannot be completely identified with the feelings of each individual "Herbert Bryan" in determining what is "right for me." Yet the larger issue for that day—the concern of Paul and other pioneers in pastoral care—was that the Rogerian approach addressed itself to attitudes toward moral and religious values that were creating obstacles to counseling. The clergy had more than its share of this rigidity. Each day brings its own concerns and consequently leads to its own emphases.

Yet in one current emphasis there is a marked similarity to emphasis of that day. Rogers was concerned about making the therapist role available to the nonspecialist. So also is

Eric Berne. Rogers stressed the simplicity of his method in contrast to the more complicated techniques of the psychoanalysts. As Paul used to say, with Rogers you could do no harm. Berne's categories and labels are oriented to the common man. The popularized version by Thomas Harris, *I'm OK, You're OK*, has put Bernean terms into the vernacular of many people. The present popularity of transactional analysis is an example of the continued stress on equipping the nonspecialist to be a counselor.

The group orientation of the transactional model is also an indication of the growing emphasis on group counseling. Rogers himself is an indicator of this trend. He now confines himself almost exclusively to groups rather than the one-to-one counseling mode of his client-centered therapy.

Although group counseling was used in the treatment of servicemen in World War II, it was not a part of B. U. S. T.'s pastoral care program in the immediate postwar years. In 1953 Clinton and Clifton Kew published *You Can Be Healed*, a poor title for a pioneer book in pastoral group counseling in congregations. The brothers, one a psychologist and the other a pastor, "discovered" their method when two married couples arrived at the same hour by mistake and the counselor decided to take them together. The results were so satisfactory that the practice was continued, and the book was the result. Group counseling may have begun in other congregations for similarly unsophisticated reasons. Normally the press of time makes the group counseling method appealing. Also the potential of each person in the group to be both counselor and counselee allows the leader to share his authority.

Since these early days in group counseling the Gestalt encounter groups, T-groups, interpersonal (IP) groups, and sensitivity groups have all become popular. Although they have differences in methodology, they each stress group interaction and communication. The group in a sense develops family-like relationships. For the original family, the Adlerian movement under the leadership of Dreikurs has established family counseling centers in which the entire family of parents and children is counseled together. Virginia Satir's *Conjoint Family Therapy* is based on a similar model. There is also the mushrooming of transactional analysis (TA) groups in society as a whole as well as in churches and CPE programs.

Institutional ministries are also becoming group-oriented. In our local treatment center for delinquent boys, for example, the exclusive treatment model is "guided group interaction." One-to-one counseling is virtually eliminated. Instead, the chaplains and other professionals have organized the boys into their own counseling groups of peers. Delinquents are frequently deficient in the "parent ego state" and lack inner direction. They are also basically hostile to the parent-adult world. Guided group interaction is an attempt to utilize peer group support for the development of individual identity and direction.

Rather than a continued increase in group-oriented counseling, I anticipate a leveling off of these ministries and a subsequent decrease. We live in an age characterized by a quick and intense response to innovations. The new catches on with phenomenal speed and little restraint. It is followed, however, by an equally quick drop in interest. Aware of this pattern, merchandisers no longer plan on lasting products but rather for those of short-lived appeal. According to Toffler, all of us can better anticipate the future if we reckon with the transitory nature of what is currently satisfying.

Therefore as we hear our day described as post-Freudian or post-nondirective or post-client-centered, so we can anticipate tomorrow as a post-TA or post-Gestalt era. The "in" thing —the sophisticated approach—will then be to criticize Berne, to parody *I'm OK, You're OK*, to object to the limits of here and now, and to question the value of groups. Those who are "with it" will then not wish to be identified with any of these current movements.

It is pleasant to think that maybe we shall also have leaders who wish to retain the group model along with any renewal of interest in the one-to-one relationship or whatever new arrangement may then be in vogue. It is to the advantage of the parish ministry with its structure in a fellowship of believers to retain functionally the current emphasis on group interaction.

Dynamic interpersonalism is not bound to a methodology in group or individual psychotherapy and counseling as are some other schools of thought. It is a psychological interpretation of human functioning and development with philosophical and theological implications. I anticipate its continuing value as a viable option in our attempts to formulate meaning in human behavior. I no longer see it in contrast to the dialectic approach. Because of its built-in openness, dynamic interpersonalism is not in opposition to other theories, but only to the restrictive nature of those theories. Nor do I any longer see in the Kierkegaardian leap of faith a panacea for the frustrated intellect. The secularization of our culture has made *any* assumption of the transcendent a leap in faith.

For dynamic interpersonalism, as for Paul personally, God is known in immediate encounter. Despite all our emphases on means for achieving this encounter, it is the encounter itself that provides the assurance, for it is "the Spirit bearing witness with our spirit that we are the children of God." Pastoral care is mediatory toward this end in the parish and in all other forms of ministry.

Biographical Sketches

David Belgum is Professor in the School of Religion at the University of Iowa, Associate Professor in the College of Medicine of the same university, and the Coordinator of the Clinical Pastoral Education Program of the University of Iowa Medical Center. He received his B.A. from the University of Minnesota, his B.D. from Northwestern Lutheran Theological Seminary, and his Ph.D. from Boston University. He has published widely, his most recent books including *Religion and Medicine* (Iowa State University Press, 1967) and *Why Marry?* (Augsburg Publishing House, 1972).

Peter A. Bertocci is the Borden P. Bowne Professor of Philosophy at Boston University. He received his A.B. from Boston University, his M.A. from Harvard University, and his Ph.D. from Boston University. Before coming to Boston University, he was Professor of Psychology and Philosophy at Bates College. His most recent books include *Sex, Love, and the Person* (Sheed & Ward, 1967), *Personality and the Good* (MacKay, 1963), and *The Person God Is* (Humanities, 1970).

Virgil V. Brallier is Minister of the Monterey United Church of Christ in Monterey, Massachusetts, and Chairman of the Board of Directors of Gould Farm, located in the same community. He received his A.B. from McPherson College, his B.D. from Bethany Theological Seminary, and his Ph.D. from Boston University. Besides his pastoral responsibilities in the local church and his administrative responsibilities at Gould Farm, he is in private practice in pastoral counseling.

James H. Burns is Career Counselor of the American Baptist Center for the Ministry in Oakland, California. He received his B.S. from the University of Missouri, his B.D. from Andover Newton Theological School, and his S.T.M. from Boston University School of Theology. At one time he was the Protestant Chaplain at the Massachusetts General Hospital. An accredited Chaplain Supervisor of the Association for Clinical Pastoral Education, he has written several articles and chapters for pastoral care journals and books.

James E. Doty is President of Baker University in Baldwin, Kansas. He received his A.B. from Mount Union College, his S.T.B. and Ph.D. from Boston University. He holds honorary degrees from Mount Union and DePauw. The founder of twelve counseling centers, he is a Fellow in the American Association of Pastoral Counselors. He has written widely for denominational and educational magazines, and his most recent books include *Authentic Man Encounters God's World* (Baker University Press, 1967) and *Students Search for Meaning* (Lowell Press, 1971).

Berkley C. Hathorne is Staff Assistant for International Activities, Office of the Director, the National Institute of Mental Health. He received his A.B., S.T.B., and Th.D. from Boston University. Before assuming his present position, he was the Assistant Chief of Suicide Prevention in the National Institute of Mental Health. He has served as a consultant to several Annual Conferences and agencies of The United Methodist Church, the Department of Ministry of the National Council of Churches, the World Council of Churches Family Life Project, and the National Institute of Mental Health. He has written for *Pastoral Psychology* and has a chapter in Howard Clinebell's *Community Mental Health: The Role of Church and Temple* (Abingdon Press, 1970).

Judson D. Howard is Associate Professor of Pastoral Psychology at Boston University. He received his A.B. from William Jewell College, his B.D. from Andover Newton Theological School, and his M.A. and Ph.D. from Boston University. Before joining the Boston University faculty, he was Chaplain at Boston State Hospital.

William E. Hulme is Professor of Pastoral Care at the Luther Theological Seminary in St. Paul, Minnesota. He received his B.S. from Capital University, B.D. from Evangelical Lutheran Theological Seminary, and his Ph.D. from Boston University. He has published extensively, two of his most recent books being *Pastoral Care Come of Age* (Abingdon Press, 1970), and *I Hate to Bother You, But* (Concordia, 1970).

John W. Johannaber is the Executive Secretary of the Office of Missionary Personnel, Board of Global Ministries, The United Methodist Church. He received his A.B. from the University of Omaha, his S.T.B. and Ph.D. from Boston University.

Robert C. Leslie is Professor of Pastoral Psychology and Counseling at Pacific School of Religion and the Graduate Theological Union in Berkeley, California. He received his A.B. from DePauw University, his S.T.B. and Ph.D. from Boston University. His most recent books include *Jesus and Logotherapy* (Abingdon Press, 1965), *Professional Growth for Clergymen* (with Emily H. Mudd) (Abingdon Press, 1970), and *Sharing Groups in the Church* (Abingdon Press, 1971).

Walter G. Muelder is Dean Emeritus and Professor of Social Ethics Emeritus of Boston University. When he wrote the Foreword to this volume he was serving as Visiting Professor at Berea College. He received his B.S. from Knox College and his S.T.B. and Ph.D. from Boston University. He holds honorary degrees from Claflin College, Colby College, Boston

College, Knox College, and West Virginia Wesleyan College. His writings include *Foundations of the Responsibility Society* (Abingdon Press, 1960) and *Moral Law in Christian Social Ethics* (John Knox Press, 1966). A *Festschrift* in his honor was recently released entitled *Toward a Discipline of Social Ethics,* edited by Paul Deats (Boston University Press, 1972).

William E. Ramsden is the Executive Director of Training Ecumenically to Advance Mission (TEAM) of Philadelphia. He received his B.A. from the University of Buffalo, his S.T.B. and Ph.D. from Boston University. He has written for the *Christian Advocate* and *Pastoral Psychology.*

S. Paul Schilling is Visiting Professor of Philosophical Theology at Wesley Theological Seminary in Washington, D.C. He received his B.S. from St. John's College, his A.M., S.T.B., and Ph.D. from Boston University. Before joining the Wesley faculty he was Professor of Systematic Theology at Boston University. His books include *God in an Age of Atheism* (Abingdon Press, 1969) and *Contemporary Continental Theologians* (Abingdon Press, 1966).

Charles W. Stewart is Professor of Pastoral Theology at Wesley Theological Seminary in Washington, D.C. He received his B.A. from Mount Union College, his B.D. from Drew Theological Seminary, and his Ph.D. from Boston University. On the Editorial Board of *The Journal of Pastoral Care,* he edits and writes for it, as well as for other publications. His most recent books include *Adolescent Religion* (Abingdon Press, 1967) and *Minister as Marriage Counselor* (Abingdon Press, 1970).

Vernon L. Strempke is Professor of Pastoral Theology at the Pacific Lutheran Theological Seminary and Professor of Religion and Personality Sciences in the Graduate Theological Union, Berkeley, California. He received his A.B. from Wartburg College, his B.D. from Wartburg Seminary, his A.M.

from the University of Wisconsin, and his Ph.D. from Boston University. He is a Supervisor-Consultant for Clinical Pastoral Education of the Lutheran Council, U.S.A., and an Editorial Board member of *The Journal of Pastoral Care.*

Orlo Strunk, Jr. is Professor of Psychology of Religion at Boston University School of Theology and in the Division of Theological and Religious Studies of the Graduate School. He received his A.B. from West Virginia Wesleyan College and his S.T.B. and Ph.D. from Boston University. He has edited and written numerous articles and books, his most recent books including *The Choice Called Atheism* (Abingdon Press, 1968) and *The Psychology of Religion: Historical and Interpretive Readings* (Abingdon Press, 1971).

Foster J. Williams is the Area Counselor of the Indiana Area of The United Methodist Church and the National Chairman of the Finance Committee of the American Association of Pastoral Counselors, Inc. He received his A.B. from Syracuse University and his S.T.B. and Ph.D. from Boston University. A Diplomate of the American Association of Pastoral Counselors, he lectures at the Christian Theological Seminary in Indianapolis.

Index

Index